Awakening the Dreamer

Awakening the Dreamer

Clinical Journeys

Philip M. Bromberg

Routledge
Taylor & Francis Group
New York London

Routledge
Taylor & Francis Group
711 Third Avenue
New York, NY 10017

Routledge
Taylor & Francis Group
27 Church Road
Hove, East Sussex BN3 2FA

International Standard Book Number: 978-0-415-88808-0 (Paperback)

Visit the Taylor & Francis Web site at
http://www.taylorandfrancis.com

and the Routledge Web site at
http://www.routledgementalhealth.com

For Lee Caligor and Steve Mitchell

CONTENTS

Acknowledgments

I am deeply grateful to my patients for their willingness to let me into their minds and to enter into mine. From each relationship I've learned in a unique way that when self-growth takes place in a patient it also takes place in me. I especially want to thank those patients, necessarily disguised, who have not only shared with me their lives and their most private experience, but have trusted me still further by allowing me to draw upon aspects of their treatment for illustrative use in my writing.

Lee Caligor and Steve Mitchell, two dear friends and colleagues to whom this book is dedicated, passed away before I could thank them in person.

Lee Caligor died in 2004 when he and his wife Judith were tragically killed in an accident. In an introduction to Lee's obituary in the Division 39 Newsletter, Lew Aron expressed what I can only echo here: that although 82 at the time of his death, Lee was struck down in the prime of his life. I well knew the truth of this. He, with Jim Meltzer and myself, were a threesome whose synergy never diminished, and it was Lee's loving soul that most provided our bond with its enduring vitality.

Steve Mitchell, who died in 2000, is probably the person I would have most wanted as a brother when I was growing up. He was a trusted friend who could perceive what I saw but also could see beyond it; someone who could respect and use what I had to offer but who could help me grow beyond it. He was a man who was his own person and a man who believed in his dream. Steve, though he was chronologically my junior, gave me the opportunity to rekindle a flame I wasn't sure was still burning, and I wish he had lived to witness the birth of this book.

To John Kerr, my editor and comrade, whose sensitivity to the body and soul of my contribution–the pragmatic as well as the nuanced–enabled me to transmute a group of individual essays into a book with a coherent thesis and unity. I am indebted to John in more ways than I can ever repay.

Three friends, Les Havens, Karol Marshall, and Jim Meltzer, have been part of my personal/professional life in ongoing dialogues that have been sustained over many years—sometimes weekly, sometimes monthly, each time an unanticipated source of excitement, nurturance, and inspiration. I owe each of them more than it is possible for me to express here, and will say simply, Thank you, my dear pals.

There are many others toward whom my gratitude is keenly felt. Certain people were invaluable collaborators on panels at which early versions of some of the chapters in this book first saw the light of day; others have contributed to creating the affectively rich and intellectually fertile climate that inspired my thinking; still others seemed always to know when I most needed encouragement and were there for me without being asked; and lastly there are those who, simply by their ongoing connection to my life, nourished my desire to publish this book. I wish I could properly thank each and every person by name but I cannot do so here. So, with both appreciation and apology to those whose names I have omitted, I want here to acknowledge my debt to the friends and colleagues whose wisdom and supportive presence in making this book possible has been particularly apparent to me over many years: Neil Altman, Fran Anderson, Lew Aron, Graham Bass, Tony Bass, Jessica Benjamin, Debbie Birnbaum, Joerg Bose, Robbie Bosnak, Lou Breger, Larry Brown, Wilma Bucci, Velleda Ceccoli, Rich Chefetz, Mary Ann Coates, Peggy Crastnopol, Jody Davies, Peter Fonagy, Hettie Frank, Larry Friedman, Melinda Gellman, Mannie Ghent, Jason Gold, Jay Greenberg, Adrienne Harris, Anita Herron, Linda Hill, Elizabeth Howell, Marcel Hudon, Hazel Ipp, Nancy Kahn, Alan Kintzer, Sharon Kofman, Bob Langan, Beth Lawrence, Holly Levenkron, David Mark, Stephanie Noland, Camille Norvell, Craig Piers, Therese Ragen, Susan Robertson, Dan Rothenberg, Debbie Rothschild, Robin Schindler, Kirsten Schwanke, Harry Smith, Don Stern, Nina Thomas, Luz Towns-Miranda, Mark Ulrich, Sondra Wilk, Polly Young-Eisendrath, and Larry Zelnick.

I have been privileged once again to have a book published by The Analytic Press and to have worked with a staff of professionals who made the process of its publication a pleasurable collaboration. I especially want to thank Paul Stepansky, Lenni Kobrin, Nancy Liguori, Joan Riegel, Kristopher Spring, and Nadine Simms for their invaluable help.

By far the most profound influence on my writing, and indeed on my life, has come from my wife Margo to whom my loving gratitude continues undiminished.

1

Introduction
When Reality Blinks

Are you going to tell me
none of the stars are really there? Well some are there but
some burned out
ten thousand years ago.
I don't believe that.
How can you not believe it, it's a known fact. But I see
them. You see memories.
Have we had this conversation before?

—Anne Carson, *Autobiography of Red*[1]

In 1893, Freud published a memorial essay on Charcot, in which he recalled a verbal duel between them that Charcot won with a good-humored piece of repartee—a "one-liner." It was an incident that Freud held in his memory with seemingly great fondness even though Charcot had the last word. Freud cited it frequently throughout his career:

> Charcot . . . never tired of defending the rights of purely clinical work, which consists in seeing and ordering things, against the encroachments of theoretical medicine. On one occasion there was a small group of us, all students from abroad, who, brought

[1]Excerpted from Carson's glorious verse novel that speaks to the searing pain of being "other": Carson, A. (1999), *Autobiography of Red.* New York: Alfred A. Knopf, p. 65. Thank you, Karol Marshall, for telling me about this book.

> up on German academic physiology, were trying his patience with our doubts about his clinical innovations. "But that can't be true," one of us [in fact, Freud himself] objected; "it contradicts the Young-Helmholtz theory." Charcot did not reply by saying "So much the worse for the theory, clinical facts come first" or words to that effect; but he did say something which made a great impression on us: "*Theory is good; but it doesn't prevent things from existing*" [p. 13].

During the two decades from 1978 to 1998, my writing, culminating in *Standing in the Spaces* (Bromberg, 1998c), might not unreasonably be seen as my emulating Charcot by arguing that "theory is good; but it doesn't prevent things from existing." That is to say, I have been trying to convince Freud (or at least his ghost) that even after 100 years of attempting to exclude the phenomenon of dissociation from his theory of mental functioning, it remains more alive than ever. In my view, if psychoanalysis is to remain a theory relevant to understanding the mind, and a therapeutic process relevant to healing the mind, certain concepts, such as unconscious conflict, interpretation of resistance, and unconscious fantasy, need to be rethought in light of our current understanding of self-states and dissociation.

This book continues my journey into the phenomenology of self-states that was begun with *Standing in the Spaces.* To reprise: Self-states are what the mind comprises. Dissociation is what the mind does. The relationship between self-states and dissociation is what the mind is. It is the stability of that relationship that enables a person to experience continuity as "I." A flexible relationship among self-states through the use of ordinary dissociation is what allows a human being to engage the ever-shifting requirements of life's complexities with creativity and spontaneity. It is what gives a person the remarkable capacity to negotiate character and change simultaneously—to stay the same while changing. And it is this relationship that determines what is meant when we speak of conscious and unconscious.

Lancelot Law Whyte (1960) observed more than 40 years ago that the "antithesis conscious/unconscious may have exhausted its utility" (p. 174). The trouble, he noted, was "not that we do not yet know the right definitions to use, the meanings of which would throw most light on the structure of mental processes. What we need is not merely words with definitions using other words, but insight into the changing structure of mental processes" (p. 15). It may be wrong, Whyte added,

> to think of two *realms* which interact, called the conscious and the unconscious, or even of two contrasted kinds of mental *process,* conscious and unconscious, each causally self-contained until it hands over to the other. There may exist, as I believe, a single realm of mental processes . . . of which only certain transitory aspects or phases are accessible to immediate conscious attention [p. 15].

To underscore his argument, Whyte quoted Hippolyte Taine, the 19th-century French philosopher and literary historian who also questioned the idea of separating conscious and unconscious into different realms. In imagery that I find breathtakingly comparable to current thinking about the structure of the mind, Taine wrote,

> One can . . . compare the mind of a man to a theatre of indefinite depth whose apron is very narrow but whose stage becomes larger away from the apron. On this lighted apron there is room for one actor only. He enters, gestures for a moment, and leaves; another arrives, then another, and so on. . . . Among the scenery and on the far-off backstage there are multitudes of obscure forms whom a summons can bring onto the stage . . . and unknown evolutions take place incessantly among this crowd of actors [Taine, 1871, cited in Whyte, 1960, pp. 166–167].

My own accounting of human mental processes (Bromberg, 1998c) is highly compatible with Whyte's suggestion of a "single realm of mental processes . . . of which only certain transitory aspects or phases are accessible to immediate conscious attention" (p. 15). When considered together with Taine's vision of the mind as a stage with a lighted apron on which "there is room for one actor only" and a further recess in which evolutions take place incessantly among a crowd of actors, Whyte's imagery is in harmony with my view of mental life as a nonlinear, self-organizing repatterning of self-state configurations that produce shifting representations of "me."

From this vantage point, *normal* dissociation, a mind–brain mechanism that is intrinsic to everyday mental functioning, attempts to assure that the mind selects from the "multitudes of obscure forms whom a summons can bring onto the stage" of selfhood, that self-state configuration which is most immediately adaptive within the constraints of affective safety. I see this process as an ongoing system, an evolutionarily derived psychodynamic that is mediated at the brain level by processes not yet understood, and at the level of selfhood by the need to maintain self-continuity in the context of moment-to-moment changes in the environment. There is increasing support for this view of the mind, provided not only by clinicians, but by contemporary neuroscience research. Johnson (2004), for instance, discusses the shifting dialectic of the mind in these terms. Johnson takes his neuroscientific cue from Gerald Edelman's (1989, 1992, 2004) theory that the internal mechanisms of both the brain and the immune system run miniversions of natural selection:

> Think of those modules in your brain as species competing for precious resources—in some cases they're competing for control of the entire organism; in others, they're competing for your attention. Instead of struggling to pass their genes on to the next generation, they're struggling to pass their message on to other groups of neurons, including groups that shape your conscious sense of self. Picture yourself walking down a crowded urban street. As you walk, your brain is filled with internal voices all competing for your attention. At any given moment, a few of them are selected, while most go unheeded [Johnson, 2004, p. 199].

Through the creative use of dissociation, the mind selects whichever self-state configuration is most adaptive at a given moment without compromising affective safety. The need to preserve affective safety organizes the mind's responsiveness to novelty. The heart of mental functioning is a complex interface between what is experienced as safe enough and what is potentially traumatic. The felt boundary between surprise and trauma is thus particularly sensitive. It is the relative permeability of this boundary that underlies normal personality development, its pathology, and an optimal psychotherapeutic relationship that is "safe but not too safe."

When the normal function of dissociation is enlisted as a defense against trauma, the brain uses dissociation to inhibit potentially discrepant views of reality held by different self-states, which, if "on stage" at the same time, would be more than the mind could contain without destabilizing. But this aspect of the mind's ability to use dissociation in the service of psychological survival is in another respect a Faustian bargain: survival is offered at an extraordinarily high price to be collected later. Psychological self-continuity plays a role that is as central for the survival of a member of the human species as biological self-continuity is for lower forms of animal life.

When self-continuity seems threatened, the mind adaptationally extends its reach beyond the moment by turning the future into a version of past danger. That is, the mind not only functions to preserve self-continuity in the face of immediate threat, but also underwrites a temporal sleight of mind, sometimes termed "retrospective falsification" (see Terr, 1984), whereby future self-continuity is proactively guaranteed by the creation of a dissociative mental structure—an early warning system, if you will. The linear experience of time is collapsed into itself as a protective device, producing relative amnesia for perceptual memory of past trauma but leaving bodily and affective memory intact, often horrifyingly intact. This time condensation supports the early warning system by freezing the person's image of the future and of the present into relived replicas of the past. Instead of being able to deal with "what happened to me," the person enters therapy to deal with what he is sure *will* happen to him and what is happening to him *now*.

What was formerly a fluid and creative dialectic between self-states through the normal process of dissociation is slowly replaced by a rigid Balkanization of the various aspects of self. The process of dissociation has now become enslaved to a dissociative *structure* that takes as its highest priority the preservation of self-continuity through turning the act of living into an ongoing reminder that trauma is always waiting around the next corner and that it will be more than the mind can handle. Self-states that were formerly parts of an overarching configuration able to alter its own patterning of "me-ness" spontaneously, while simultaneously preserving overall coherence (through each state's potential for communication with the others), become sequestered islands of "truth." Each island vigilantly protects itself from potentially disjunctive input of the others by the dissociative "gap" surrounding it. Self-continuity is now preserved within each state, but the overarching coherence among states is sacrificed. Past trauma is not allowed to enter narrative memory as an authentic part of the past; it is transmuted into affective and body memories in the form of experiences that are beyond relational self-regulation and that shape the present and the future in a way that plunders life of both genuine safety and of spontaneity.

This structure works. But it does so at a cost: the experience of intrapsychic conflict becomes highly difficult to maintain. Indeed, for some people, such experience is unachievable altogether because the capacity to experience intrapsychic conflict is dependent on the mind's ability to access and tolerate two or more discrepant self-states at the same time. Thus, a consequence of trauma as it becomes embedded in structural dissociation is to limit and often foreclose the possibility of conflictual experience.

Developmental Trauma and Enactment

Clinically, the phenomenon of dissociation as a defense against self-destabilization is observable at many points in every treatment, but it has its greatest relevance during enactments, a mode of clinical engagement that requires an analyst's closest attunement to the unacknowledged affective shifts in his own and his patient's self-states. Through the joint cognitive processing of enactments played out between the "not-me" experiences of patient and analyst, a patient's sequestered self-states come alive as a "remembered present" (Edelman, 1989). These moments allow the patient, affectively and cognitively, to construct, with the analyst, an authentically remembered past. Because the ability to experience conflict safely is then increased, the potential for resolution of conflict is in turn facilitated for all patients.

To reiterate, dissociation is not only a mental process but also a mental structure that exists in everyone—for some people more extensively than for others—a structure that hypnoidally sequesters certain self-states and limits their communication with one another as a proactive defense against the repetition of what has already happened. This proactive defense operates when massive trauma has occurred but operates equally and in some ways even more extensively when early "developmental trauma" has created areas of dissociative mental structure *with or without subsequent massive trauma.* The reason that developmental trauma (also termed relational trauma) is of such significance is that it shapes the attachment patterns that establish what is to become a stable or unstable core self.

A child's core self becomes internally bonded to the early parental objects through interactions that reinforce who the parent perceives the child to be and who the parent denies the child to be. The main source of power that parents have over children comes not so much out of what they tell the child to do as from "showing" him who he *is.* That is, by relating to the child as though he is "such and such" and ignoring other aspects of him as if they do not exist, the parents "disconfirm" (Laing,1962) the relational existence of those aspects of the child's self that they ignore. This disconfirmation, because it is relationally nonnegotiable, is traumatic by definition and is intrinsic to the existence of developmental (relational) trauma. Such trauma is typically cumulative. If the child's sense of self is to remain intact as he matures, he has to preserve the early attachment patterns on which his core self rests by continuing to exist in the mind of each new significant other that comes along as the same "self" that was "his parents' child." As he does so he continues to dissociate those aspects of self that originally were too disjunctive with the core attachment to be contained as "me."

This is a major reason why it is so difficult for many people to change in treatment. An unreflective attachment to the early disconfirming object means having to be whoever the other person seems to see you as (in order for you to prevent self-destabilization), not simply having to do what the other person seems to want you to *do*. Thus, a central goal of any treatment is that the therapist enable the patient to move from experiencing his enacted patterns of behavior as the person he *is*, to experiencing these patterns as something that he *does*, and thereby facilitate the development of self-reflection. Again, for many patients characterologically, and for all patients in some areas of their personality, the development of self-reflection must precede any attempt at investigating conflict. In the areas where development has been thwarted, the analyst attempts to help a patient change what is classically called ego syntonic to what is classically called ego alien. Thus the enacted ways of being are no longer "who I am" but are gradually replaced by the cognitive perspective of "what I do." As this change takes place, a person is more able to hold, reflect on, and potentially resolve disjunctive self-experiences as states of conflict without the effort's being automatically short-circuited by dissociative processes designed to protect self-continuity.

Dissociation is a defense unlike any other. It protects the stability of the self by controlling unsymbolized traumatic affect that it cannot regulate. It is not simply a different term for the concept of repression. Repression defines a process that is designed to avoid disavowed mental content that may lead to unpleasant intrapsychic conflict. Dissociation shows its signature not by disavowing aspects of mental *contents* per se, but through the patient's alienation from aspects of *self* that are inconsistent with his experience of "me" at a given moment. It functions because conflict is *unbearable* to the mind, not because it is *unpleasant*.

In those (sometimes pervasive) areas of personality in which dissociation has significantly organized the development of mental structure, not only has the capacity to bear internal conflict suffered; the capacity for intersubjectivity is likewise impaired or even foreclosed. The person is largely unable to see himself through the eyes of an other. When intersubjectivity is absent, there is a collision of realities without a channel of communication that uses the ongoing subjectivity of the other to reshape the "truth" that exists in one's own mind, a situation that makes interpersonal negotiation difficult or impossible. An interpretive stance by the analyst not only is thereby useless during an enactment, but also escalates the enactment and rigidifies the use of dissociation. During an enactment, the patient's response to interpretation is very different from his response when repression is operating. When dissociation is operating, there is bewilderment, consternation, and a sense of having been misunderstood totally. The patient either overtly or covertly experiences the other as misrepresenting him, mistaking him for someone else, or attacking him. Sometimes, the person feels that he was *never* understood and that he was naive to think he had been.

In general, one could say that a response is triggered in the patient that, in one form or another, is a denouncement of the other's perception—the patient reacts with, "That's not who I *am*." This reaction is any human being's reaction to being seen as someone he has painstakingly relegated to not-me. Not-me, I might add, is the hallmark of dissociation. Basically, dissociation mediates the dynamic of enactment through a subsymbolic form of interpersonal engagement that results in one's not-me self-states being experienced as existing in the other, as existing *only* in the other, and sometimes as defining the total *truth* about the other. For such a patient the other becomes an object to be managed and lacks a separate center of subjectivity. Thus, one of the central aspects of therapeutic action is the joint cognitive processing of such enactments as they are played out in the not-me experiences of patient and analyst that continue to communicate, as long as necessary during the course of treatment, through their own channel of affective reality. As the relationship evolves, the processing of not-me evolves with it because both parties become more conversant with the fact that what they bring to the table includes what they are trying to hide underneath it.

"There *Are* Gaps"

There is something entailed in the foregoing discussion, an issue that informs the essays throughout this book, that I think is particularly salient in the way I work as a clinician: because I imagine the mind as comprising relationally interlocking stage sets, I pay special attention to the dissociative gaps in subjective reality that are created because of unannounced changes in cast. By cast I refer to the self–other configurations that constitute the world of mental representation that defines for each person in the analytic dyad the subjective reality of what is taking place between them in the here and now.

The very moment of change, the moment when the "switch" in cast takes place, is the moment when a dissociative gap is created. This is the moment when "reality blinks" and the moment of the blink is not available to reflective thought. Indeed, the moment itself normally goes unobserved by the person in whom it is taking place, although it is potentially recognizable by another person who is prepared to see it. It is only *after* this moment that something new can take place, and for me it usually begins by discerning that something is "off"—an experience that is apparent more by being felt than thought. Whatever relational experience existed before the creation of the dissociative gap seems to have vanished; the analyst's experience of the patient now feels somehow unreal, inauthentic, and impersonal. The experience is that something is "missing"—a sense of absence rather than something else is present. Little by little the sense of absence is replaced by a conscious awareness of what Bion (1970, pp. 19–20; 1978, p. 3) called the "presence of an absence," the presence of a "no-thing" whose thingness, even in its no-ness, permits thought. Through this aperture to consciousness an analyst has the chance to enter the dissociative gap creatively. The gap is no longer an empty space without access to thought but is now a space in which something new and thinkable has happened and is continuing to happen—a space that patient and analyst have already been shaping but that now can be shaped *therapeutically* because self-reflectiveness and symbolic processes have an opportunity to participate.

In the earlier years of psychoanalysis, such subtle "countertransferential" moments were typically noted only with regard to highly dissociated patients—they were reported because they were especially unusual. Slowly, therapists began paying more attention to this phenomenon clinically even though it did not significantly influence classical theory. Usually, it had to be pretty *dramatic* stuff for analysts to pay attention, for example, "I'm going along, and suddenly I feel like stabbing this guy." Eventually, a literature developed on the concept of "enactment," and once that happened the classical frame no longer fit. For me, the moments do not have to be dramatic. *They are always there.*

Given that I pay such attention to these moments in my office, it ought not surprise you that I look for them in other places as well. I am pleased to report that they are easy to find. The notion of "spaces" as the presence of an absence is a phenomenon acknowledged by artists and writers in almost every creative discipline. The jazz critic Ben Ratliff (2005), for example, in a review of Thelonious Monk's musical legacy as translated by Ben Riley's septet, writes that Riley's arrangements

> deal upfront with a unifying characteristic of Monk's music: the sudden silences, and the way they work as rhythm. . . . always trying to retain the surprise negative spaces in Monk's improvising and composing. The little holes left room for Mr. Riley's light, elegant drumming to shine through [p. B17].

As I read Ratliff's piece I recalled having been captured at other times by the same theme appearing in reviews of art and literature, and a search of my files led me to a number of quotations from other sources that I had squirreled away without fully recognizing at the time why I had done so. I have selected a few of these to help you enter the following chapters in a state of mind that is organized affectively as well as cognitively, and I ask tolerance for what might be an excessive number of journalistic quotations taken from my file cabinet.

The painter Francesco Clemente (1999), in an exhibition of his work, commented, "Because fragmentation is an inevitable part of the creative process there are gaps between the fragments, and in these gaps something happens. I believe in those spaces in between. The main question is how to make room." Less than a year later, in a review of the Chardin show at the Metropolitan Museum of Art in New York City, *The New York Times* art critic Michael Kimmelman (2000) stood in the gaps to which Clemente referred and proposed that making room for those spaces, the creative process of allowing something to happen in them, entails an aesthetic engagement between artist and viewer as an actively forged event.

> Chardin somehow makes brief instants seem to stretch toward infinity, assuming sudden gravity. In the process, he conveys both the sensation of glimpsing something unremarkable and the effect of having that glimpse impressed on the mind as a memory. This memory, because it is vivid, mysteriously takes a place in the imagination out of proportion to its significance, like a smell or some notes of music or a breeze that triggers the

> recollection of a childhood game or a trip or a lost relative. It stays there, waiting. . . . A tiny observation, but like many simple facts of life, strangely marvelous when it turns out to be a key to some greater truth. Chardin's work is a compilation of these little facts that together make as true a record of the value of seeing as exists in the history of art [pp. E33, E35].

Here let me digress for a moment to talk about perception. I believe it might be similarly said about the value of perception in psychoanalytic work that psychoanalysis is a compilation of tiny observations that become strangely marvelous when they turn out to be a key to some greater truth. In this way, unconscious experience, I suggest, becomes part of self-narrative through a compilation of all the tiny and "insignificant" relational moments when language slowly takes on new meaning through the here-and-now perceptual contexts of those moments. It is in this sense that I believe the leverage of therapeutic action is in the relational transformation of dissociative moments into nonlinear events, and that the awesome power of what we call transference resides in its ability to facilitate this transformation as a *perceptual* phenomenon.

Why do I emphasize "perceptual?" Relationally, words in themselves do not exist in time or space. Only the speaker's meaning exists in time and space; and the speaker's meaning is constructed from a perception of his words framed by the immediacy of the context in which they are spoken. In psychoanalysis, "speaking" is therefore a relational act that shapes the content of what is spoken about. This is a particularly critical issue when the patient carries a sense of internal isolation as his natural state, but for every patient there are areas of the personality in which words are felt to be futile and the act of trying to convey *this* feeling in words is itself experienced as an exercise in futility. Because a patient is expected to speak, both partners have to go through a "mess" together unless there is a collusion to avoid it. If the mess is not avoided indefinitely, a communicative route can potentially be constructed through a relationship in which pain is an inevitable but reparable part.

When the analyst finally gives up his attempts to "understand" his patient and allows himself to know his patient through the ongoing intersubjective field they are sharing at that moment, an act of recognition (not understanding) takes place in which words and thoughts come to symbolize experience instead of substitute for it. Through this act of recognition, something new can occur—something that emerges out of what patient and analyst do in an unanticipated way. I have called these unanticipated relational events "safe surprises," because it is only through surprise that a new reality is coconstructed and infused with an energy of its own. When the patient–analyst relationship reaches this place—through enactments that invite symbolization of their individual subjective experiences—the distinction between what is me and what is not-me becomes, in turn, more and more permeable. The phenomenon of standing in the spaces between me and not-me is often communicated most evocatively in literature, so I want to share another excerpt from my file cabinet, a creative tour de force written by the contemporary poet and essayist Albert Goldbarth (2003)[2]

> You know *Our Mutual Friend?*—Dickens? . . . There's that scene where a man who was drowned in the Thames is revived. It's *so* fucking powerful. . . . I remember thinking: *Wow!* A man who'd been in two worlds as completely unattached as Life and Death! It seemed so ideal to me. I don't mean I was suicidal, far from it. I felt more alive than ever. Sort of as if . . . in *admitting* these gaps we all of us stumble through . . . if you *truly admit* them, you carry a charge across the gaps! Sometimes, in those days, I was very depressed; but other times I tingled all over, I had this special vision of things. My power: *I was aware of the gaps* [pp. 27–28].

Goldbarth adds in a footnote, "There are strange, incomprehensible lacunae. Reality blinks: we don't know *what* takes place in those betweens. We shirk from acknowledging this, we shrink from its inhuman implications. But there *are* gaps; not that we're meant to stare at them long, any more than at sunspots" (p. 133). I have used Goldbarth's evocative phrase "reality blinks" as part of the title for this introduction, but the phenomenon that the metaphor is attempting to capture is, in fact, the foundation of the book as a whole.

The image of blinking was chosen also by Malcolm Gladwell (2005) for the title of his book, *Blink: The Power of Thinking Without Thinking.* Gladwell writes (shades of Taine) that there is a mighty "backstage" process in our brains. He illustrates this phenomenon by a series of compelling vignettes, one of which I think merits our attention here: Two Dutch researchers asked groups of students questions from the

[2] I want to thank Dr. Lawrence Brown for first making Goldbarth's writing known to me.

board game of *Trivial Pursuit*. One group was asked to think beforehand about what it would be like to be a professor, and the other group was asked to think about what it would be like to be a soccer hooligan. Those in the "professorial" state did much better than those whose self-state was that of "hooligan" (p. 56). Gladwell's other examples demonstrate, similarly, how one's actual capacities in a given situation can be reshaped in the blink of an eye when the state of mind organizing one's self-perception shifts.

The same argument was offered in a different venue, with perhaps more widespread impact, by Oscar Hammerstein II. I am thinking here of his lyric to "I Whistle a Happy Tune" from the show *The King and I* (Rogers and Hammerstein, 1984). Hammerstein's lyric is persuasive because almost everyone who hears it knows the phenomenon personally; they do not need scientific evidence to support it.

Whenever I feel afraid
I hold my head erect
And whistle a happy tune
So no one will suspect
I'm afraid.

While shivering in my shoes
I strike a careless pose
And whistle a happy tune
And no one ever knows
I'm afraid.

The result of this deception
Is very strange to tell
For when I fool the people
I fear I fool myself as well!

I whistle a happy tune
And ev'ry single time
The happiness in the tune
Convinces me that I'm not afraid.

Make believe you're brave
And the trick will take you far.
You may be as brave
As you make believe you are.

Is it really possible that "You may be as brave as you make believe you are"? Is it really possible to do better on a task that tests brainpower if you first make believe you are a college professor? The answer seems to be, mysteriously, yes. The mystery lies in what is meant by "making believe" and in what takes place in the mind and brain between the end of "pretending to be" and the start of really being.

Consider, for example, those dissociative patients who in the midst of telling you what they feel happened to them suddenly start to feel that they are pretending, that they are making the whole thing up, and who sometimes experience internal voices telling them that they are lying. And then there are those people who perform beyond their capacities in an emergency and when the emergency is over talk about the experience with a strange sense of distance from it. If they are pressed for details, they look as if they are being modest, but from another vantage point they look as if they truly do not know what you are talking about when you describe them as brave. Such individuals, of course, include war heroes who disclaim that they did anything special and who are assumed to be simply modest when they say so—modesty being a renowned virtue of heroes. In both these examples it is possible to feel how tenuous the distinction is between what we pretend and what we are.

To put the question another way, when you *become* brave are you still "making believe?" I think not. Somehow, you have achieved the ability really to be brave even though the bravery starts as pretense. This phenomenon has captured my interest. Whistling a happy tune in a state of fear makes the mind blink, and during the blink, dissociation facilitates a self-state switch in the direction provided by the "careless pose" of Hammerstein's lyric. You now are brave because the self you have become is organized by bravery. Similarly, I suggest that the phenomenon of dissociative self-state shifts is what takes place during the blink to which Gladwell (2005) refers in his title, the phenomenon that led to his belief in the "power of thinking without thinking."

It can begin with "pretense" (whistling a happy tune). Then, the "happiness in the tune" becomes *your* happy tune because it is you whistling it. (The same point is developed in chapter 3 with regard to the relationship between reader and author, whereby the permeability of boundaries between self-states can allow an author to become *your* author.) When it is no longer *a* happy tune you are whistling, but *your* happy tune, you are no longer pretending not to be afraid; your self-state has become one in which you are genuinely no longer afraid. It has become organized around a new affect, a new dominant affect that has become the core of a discrete self-state that is adaptively dissociated from the other, frightened self. The important point is that when any self-state switches to a new one, *all* the variables constituting the former self-state are changed in the new self-state. Putnam (1988) emphasizes that mental states are

> self-organizing and self-stabilizing structures of behavior. When a transition (switch) from one state of consciousness to another state of consciousness occurs, the new state acts to impose a quantitatively and qualitatively different structure on the variables that define the state of consciousness. The new structure acts to reorganize behavior and resist changes to other states.... [S]witches between states are manifest by non-linear changes in a number of variables. These variables include: 1) affect; 2) access to memory, i.e., state-dependent memory; 3) attention and cognition; 4) regulatory physiology; and 5) sense of self [p. 25].

The person becomes, in effect, a new self, and the qualities that organize that new self are consistent with a new dominant affect. Keep in mind that all this is taking place through a normal dissociative process. That is to say, because each new self configuration is sequestered from the others, the person is not likely to be aware of an inconsistency that has any personal relevance, nor is it likely that self-reflection on the switch itself will occur.

In the example of whistling a happy tune, the affect that organizes the new self is not simply happiness per se. It is part of a self-state that is better able to counter the intrusion of fear in the face of danger or adversity. It is a special kind of happiness that embodies a sense of purpose as a central feature. The person is aware of the danger but is now ready to face it. The danger is now a trigger for action that others define as courage. I am not saying that I disagree with those who so define it. Willingness to face danger has become the context for a new self-state to exist with authenticity. The person is not pretending to be unafraid. He is no longer *trying* to be brave. He is, in fact, not trying to "be" anything; he is now just "himself." But because that self-state is dissociated, it functions without input from other parts of the self that could potentially interfere with his ability to take on the difficult task at hand.

All well and good, but if the new self-state *remains* dissociatively preeminent, a problem can arise. That is, if the "unafraid me" that has emerged as a substitute for potentially unadaptive fear holds center stage too long, the person will be denied access to parts of his self that *can* feel fear, and he may eventually place himself in danger because courage without the capacity for reflectiveness can easily become foolhardiness. In most cases, however, the person does eventually allow the dissociated "unafraid self" to return to what Taine (cited in Whyte, 1960) called the "far-off backstage" when the emergency is over. The "happy tune" has served its necessary adaptive function, and, when the danger passes, interestingly enough, the unafraid self tends to become relegated to *not-me,* because it no longer feels personally like him. This is where the "modesty" of heroes begins.

Katy

There is another aspect of my work that informs the chapters of this book that I would like to draw attention to in this introduction: I talk about myself–about my own experience while I am with a patient, about what I am experiencing in our relationship, and especially about what I feel is taking place off stage while we are engaged in something else. A person cannot transcend his dissociation without the presence of another who recognizes his own. I share mine in the belief that if I share it, it is as close to the relational unconscious as it is possible to get. If the interaction goes relatively well, new meaning will gradually emerge through the joint linguistic symbolization of what is shared and through which, as Adrienne Harris (2005) has expressively stated, "analyst and analysand can come upon the uncanny sense that an experience is both clear and opaque, known and unknown, foreign and familiar" (p. 78).

By talking about my own experience I hope to provide a relational invitation that will make alternative self-states feel welcome. My further hope is that if this invitation is accepted, the patient and I will be able jointly to process what emerges. That is, we will be able to "stand in the spaces." Sometimes the boundary between self-protective dissociation and the growing capacity to stand in the spaces is hard to discern, as illustrated in the following clinical vignette from my own work. I think the vignette shows vividly how dissociation is both an intrapsychic and an interpersonal process. The vignette illustrates, too, the role dissociation plays in the processing of enactments in a treatment relationship, including when one is working with dreams.

Katy was nearing what we both understood to be the final phase of her analysis, and we had, I thought, done a pretty good job of processing what each of us was feeling about both our experience of the analytic relationship and the approach of its ending. In this session she had just reported a dream in which she was water-skiing in back of a boat driven by her mother and saw a fin following her in the water. She was an expert water-skier, having overcome a fear of drowning that she had since a child but that she was dreadfully afraid might return. In the dream she started to panic because she did not know whether it was a shark or a dolphin that was following her.

As I listened to her dream, I found myself experiencing, simultaneously, two states that seemed to be pulling me in opposing directions. One was a sense of urgency to interpret her dream all on my own, but not *simply* to interpret it. I realized that I was *aching* to interpret it as a revelation that she was not yet ready to terminate because she had not dealt fully enough with a core dissociative gap in her feelings about me that led her to doubt if she could survive in the world without me. Happily, I was simultaneously in touch with another, less urgent part of me that felt oddly calm despite the manifest anxiety she was feeling in the dream. I say *oddly* calm because, unlike my other state, it was the calmness that here felt extreme—so extreme that I felt myself relaxed to the point that I lost my focus on the dream itself and in a different way lost my direct experience of Katy.

I found my calmness slowly transforming into a kind of reverie state in which my sense of time and space also shifted. An image from my own past popped into my mind and held my attention, for how long I am not sure. The image was strangely vivid and immediate. There I am, teaching my daughter to ride her first two-wheeler. Standing behind the bike, I am holding the back of the seat on which she is perched precariously. She is very nervous about falling and makes me promise again and again that I won't let go until she says I can. I see myself running along behind her as she pedals. One moment I am gently stabilizing her in her upright position; another moment I am firmly holding her upright as she teeters from side to side; another moment, pushing her along as she seems to stop pedaling on her own; another moment, being pulled along by her as she picks up speed with a steadiness that is clearly coming from her. Amazingly, I can feel each separate experience as well as see it; I feel it with a physicality that links past and present.

When is the moment I am not needed to stabilize her and she takes off on her own? I had no memory of my daughter saying, "Okay, *now!*" But I clearly *felt* my memory of the moment when I let go and watched her zoom down the street—I felt the pride, the exhilaration, and then the anxiety: Does this mean she doesn't need me anymore?

As I thought about this experience, I wondered to myself, Did she ever really say *now?* Or did I just feel the *now!* between us? Is such a moment even knowable? If it does exist, maybe it is only after the fact. Even if she did say it, maybe the reason I didn't remember it was that the moment that stayed with me was really the moment *before* she said it—the moment when we were communicating without words and we could each feel that she could be on her own even if it couldn't be said yet.

At that point I left the twosome of my daughter and me and returned more concretely to the twosome of Katy and me, without any sense of how long I had been away. In retrospect, I still wonder about it. One could call where I had been a daydream, but I think that to do so obscures more than it clarifies. As I returned to Katy, I asked myself, What made me switch self-states? Am I afraid of losing her and can't deal with it? Do I want to hold on to her longer by heightening my sense that she still needs me to stabilize her? Neither possibility seemed right. It seemed more as if I had entered a new way of being with her that I did not yet have language to describe.

I shared my experience with Katy. She took it in with great interest, but, even more compelling, at least to me, was that, contrary to what might have been anticipated, she did not focus on *me* but went more deeply into the dream space than she had been. Without needing encouragement she entered into to a reverie state of her own that was physical as well as mental. She could see and feel herself on the water skis and described what she experienced in detail, including the "fin" following her. She could now see it clearly. The first thing she uttered was an anxious, "I don't know if it's a shark fin or a doll-fin." I use the term doll-fin here because that was exactly what it sounded like to me. I asked if she could let herself get closer to it without its being too scary. She agreed and, as she closed in on it, began to laugh, "It's not either! It's just a regular fish; it could be a tuna."

As we explored her associations to "doll-fin" she remembered that her mother used to talk about what a "doll" she was and how it was a life-or-death matter never to let her mother see how hateful she also felt about having to be "mommy's little girl." Little by little we engaged the shame-ridden residue of this "life-or-death matter" that was now surfacing around the issue of termination, including its relation to my own waking dream of my daughter and the bicycle. One could say that, as the dreamer, Katy was entering the environment of her still partly dissociated fear that our attachment bond would not endure her being genuinely ready to "ride on her own."

Not surprisingly, the benign reputation of the so-called termination phase in analysis—a phase when it is supposedly "safe to go back in the water"—was once again revealed as pure fantasy. I was being recruited for a final performance as "mommy" in Katy's internal drama and found myself drawn into a new enactment, which, to my astonishment, included the involuntary activation of an inner drama of my own. Would Katy be able to emerge from this complex event with greater self-coherence than when she entered it? Would she be able to terminate analysis with a sense of self that allowed loving attachment and assertive self-expression to coexist, or would her enacted self-states of "doll" and "shark" remain dissociated from one another to assure that her core identity would survive our separation? The answers to these questions depended on whether, in this final stage of treatment, a relational context of new shared meaning could be created (or more accurately, *cocreated*) from what was being enacted around the termination itself. Once again we each needed to engage the linguistically sharable raw experience of the other in order to emerge, *intersubjectively,* from the dissociative cocoon in which we were trapped as subjective isolates.

Despite her dissociated fear, Katy's longing to be more fully recognized by me before she left had grown stronger as the date of termination approached, but I had been unable to feel it *personally*—the only way that such recognition can occur. I had been dissociating the part of myself that might have engaged her longing until, without warning, "reality blinked." Katy-as-dreamer had triggered within me an affective encounter with my dissociated state that took the form of a vivid waking dream—a relived memory that bridged past and present, and because of this bridge, connected me with Katy's longing by connecting me with my own. My dissociative processes, until then in collusion with Katy's, became able to surrender their protective function enough to allow this highly personal waking dream into my conscious awareness. Katy had brought to the session not simply her dream but also her dreamer. It could be said that her dreamer had awakened my own, and that my "awakening" allowed Katy's enacted, shame-ridden, "life-or-death matter" to enter the termination phase as a manifest part of our relationship that could now be processed between us. Although it is not likely that phenomena such as waking dreams are frequent analytic occurrences, I believe that my experience exemplifies an intrinsic aspect of working with enactments; namely, that the boundary between "personal" and "professional" becomes dramatically permeable during enactments, and *must* become so, for the deepest and most enduring self-growth to take place. In this case, the sharing of our formerly dissociated and enacted self-state experiences enabled Katy to *be* the selves that until then could only be "supposed" to exist. As the dissociative gap between our respective not-me states became more and more bridged by shared meaning, Katy's not-me personae, "doll" and "shark," became increasingly amenable to self-reflection and more able to *coexist* as a coherent expression of "me" within our relationship and in her relationships with others.

This vignette illustrates a postclassical psychoanalytic view of the analyst's self-revelation as part of a process that leads to the coconstruction of an intersubjective reality that incorporates the experience of each partner. When patient and analyst can each access and openly share the dissociated thoughts and feelings that are "too dangerous" to their relationship to be thought, then the externalization of the patient's relationship with his own internal objects becomes available to intersubjective negotiation, self-reflection, and conflict resolution. How much self-revelation is enough and how much is too much cannot be known in advance, and it is the ongoing and often painful effort to relationally negotiate its usefulness that leads to growth. The process of negotiation inherently involves communication between many different self-states of analyst and patient, a process that relies on the fact that at any given moment subjective consciousness ("I") adheres to whatever self-configuration is present because the natural hypnoid capacity of the mind functions to keep dissociated any other self-states that would feel too disjunctive with the present configuration.

Here is perhaps the place to talk a little about the title of this book. "Awakening the Dreamer" is a metaphor for what I see as central to a clinical process informed by the phenomena of self-states and dissociation. The "dreamer" refers to a self-state with which people are most familiar during sleep when it emerges as part of the dissociative phenomena we call dreams. However, because the dissociative gap between a sleep state and a waking state is as permeable as the space between any two states, I have found that the dreamer can enter that gap and participate in the cocreation of new relational meaning. This phenomenon resonates conceptually with Bion's (1962a) use of the word dream as a shared reverie state that unites mother and infant. It also resonates with Bucci's (1997a, p. 220) cognitive research that has elucidated how a shared referential space is created when one person's internal representations become linked to another's through a multilevel connection between subsymbolic and symbolic channels of inner experience.

In the same relational context that "shared reverie space" and "shared referential space" are relevant to the title of this book, I would be remiss if I did not mention here the rapidly growing interest among neuroscientists in what are termed "mirror neurons." In the 1990s, three neuroscientists at the University of Parma in Italy (Giacomo Rizzolati, Leonardo Fogassi, and Vittorio Gallese) stumbled across a curious cluster of cells in the motor area of the brain of a macaque monkey. The cells fired not only when the monkey performed an action, but likewise when the monkey saw the same action performed by someone else. Because the cells reflected the actions that the monkey observed in others, the neuroscientists named them "mirror neurons." Later experiments confirmed the existence of mirror neurons in humans and revealed that in addition to mirroring *actions,* the cell firing mirrored sensations, emotions, intentions, and even motives. The firing of these cells is an involuntary and automatic response to what another person is doing, feeling, or intending, without requiring thought or verbal language; we seem simply to "know," relationally, in the same sense that Lyons-Ruth (1998) uses the phrase "implicit relational knowing."

Since their discovery, mirror neurons have been implicated in a wide range of mental and social phenomena associated with what we think of as "empathy," such as understanding how a child develops a "theory of mind" and the capacity to "mentalize"–the ability to reflectively experience another mind experiencing his own (Fonagy et al., 2002). In a seminal research report, Gallese and Goldman (1998) argued that this latter developmental achievement (what they call "mind-reading") is best accounted for by a "simulation theory" of mirror neuron functioning, which I see, in essence, as a neuroscience version of a relational theory of *psychological* functioning based on a self-state model of the mind. In a breathtakingly interpersonal statement about how they view the evolutionary function of mirror neurons, Gallese and Goldman propose that "one possible function is to enable an organism to detect certain mental states of observed conspecifics [members of the same species]. This function might be part of, or a precursor to, a more general mind-reading ability" (p. 493). A more general mind-reading ability! Is this not a way of saying that, neurologically, we are *natural* mind readers? To my knowledge, this is about as close as neuroscience has come to claiming that, not just the mind, but *the brain itself, is intrinsically relational.*

"Mind-reading," Gallese and Goldman write, "is the activity of representing specific mental states of others, for example, their perceptions, goals, beliefs, expectations, and the like" (p. 495), and that "*according to simulation theory, other people's mental states are represented by adopting their perspective; by tracking or matching their states with resonant states of one's own*" (p. 493, italics added). In other words, these authors contend that when we interact with someone, our brains do more than just observe the other person's behavior. They believe we create internal representations of their sensations, emotions, and motives within our own brains, as if we are the ones that are sensing, feeling, and intending.

In this light, it may not be unreasonable to suggest that when Katy brought into our termination process not only her dream but also her dreamer, the mirror neurons in our brains began firing away. That is to say, the sudden appearance in my mind of a waking dream in which I had to struggle with letting my daughter ride away, could have been responsive to my mirror neurons having created internal representations of the emotions, sensations, and motives of Katy-as-dreamer—representations that became "known" first to *my own dreamer* in a half-waking state. And once my dreamer "knew," then Katy-as-patient and Bromberg-as-analyst were off and running.

I hope it is now clear that, although I have tended to describe the "dreamer" in the context of the *patient's* mind, I am not suggesting that when this self-state is accessed during the analytic work, it is located only in the patient. By "awakening the dreamer" I refer to a multitude of processes whereby shifting self-states in the patient, and in the analyst, come forward onto the stage of intersubjective dialogue, generating greater self-state coherence in both parties. It is through the felt immediacy and increased intimacy of this mutual awakening that therapeutic change takes place. Clearly, the treatment is for the benefit of the patient, and the analyst works under this responsibility throughout, but, if the analysis is to be successful, the analyst will find his own "dreamer" awakening in synchrony with the patient's, as I did with Katy in the foregoing vignette. It is this complex dialogic process engaged in for the patient's benefit that prompts my title.

A Preview

I would like to take a minute or two to preview for you the contents of this book and also to explain briefly some of the more general clinical and theoretical issues I see as informing it. If there is a single overall argument uniting these essays, it is that the concepts of self-states and dissociation provide the clearest basis for ordering clinical observation.

These concepts also provide the greatest leverage for fostering therapeutic change as well as offering the most useful point of contact between clinical findings and the findings of contemporary research in neuropsychology, human development, and other relevant disciplines.

Some issues that are given special attention in the chapters that follow are the centrality of affect tolerance and affect regulation; annihilation anxiety and the experience of an "abyss"; the phenomenon of surprise as the royal road to the unconscious; "*safe* surprises" as the transition between trauma and spontaneity; "developmental trauma" and "massive trauma"; the ubiquity of shame; the role of dissociation in symptom disorders and personality disorders; the relevance of self-states and dissociation to current research in child development and attachment as well as neuroscience and cognitive studies; and, of special interest to me, the role of the analyst's self-disclosure as not simply permissible, but a *necessary* source of therapeutic action.

I have divided the book into three parts. The three chapters of part I, "On Self-States," have in common an emphasis on what might be thought of as the normal multiplicity of self-states that, at least in health, we all live with day to day. I am interested in this multiplicity chiefly as it pertains to what happens in the office. But the multiplicity is there to be experienced in all regions of life—in dreams, in literature, and in childhood—not only in the aftermath of trauma.

Part I also has to do with the transitional nature of what is entailed in "awakening the dreamer." Inasmuch as I have written regularly about self-states as potentially constituting separate realities, I am sometimes asked whether I believe in objective reality at all. Marcia Cavell (2000), in her review of *Standing in the Spaces* (Bromberg, 1998c), noted that although "points of view are multiple . . . *reality is one and the same for all of us*" (p. 525). My reply to this assertion was that, although I felt that this was a useful point when made by a philosopher, it was highly problematic if offered by a clinician because a clinician is always working within a complex field where such a distinction more often than not inhibits rather than facilitates personality growth (Bromberg, 2000). Indeed, I believe now, as I did then, that the concept of objective reality has validity. I do not believe that a person's every subjective experience constitutes a different reality, nor that there are as many different realities as there are perceptions. Such a view would be unsound not only philosophically but clinically. My perspective is derived from a self-state view of the mind, from which vantage point reality is shaped by the self-organizing configuration of each self-state. The reality thus experienced will be consistent or inconsistent with the realities of other self-states to the degree that a dissociative protection against future trauma is present as a defensive mental structure.

From this vantage point, a patient's movement from the use of dissociation to the capacity for holding and resolving intrapsychic conflict depends on the negotiated coconstruction of a transitional space in which the question of what is objective and what is subjective is not to be formulated. "Reality" in this space is *not* one and the same for all of us. As Winnicott (1951) stated, whether it is objective reality or subjectively conceived reality is not only a question that must not be asked, but also a question to which no answer is expected (p. 12).

The three chapters of part II, "Collisions and Negotiations," take us to the limits of transitional space and beyond. What I mean by beyond addresses once again the ineffable nature of reality: trying to navigate therapeutically in areas of trauma and dissociation leads to interpersonal collisions between analyst and patient that are intrinsic to the process of enactment. Such collisions reflect self-state differences in what is experienced as reality, and there is no way to avoid these clashes of subjectivity without stifling the emergence, in both patient and analyst, of dissociated self-states that need to find a voice.

Because these collisions reduce the level of interpersonal harmony, they also disrupt the felt context that organizes safety. But the analyst's ability to provide a safe environment is not in itself the source of therapeutic action. While the analyst must indeed try not to go beyond the patient's capacity to feel safe in the room, it is inevitably impossible for him to succeed, and it is because of this impossibility that therapeutic change can take place. The line between empathy and otherness is a thin one, and it is partly in the eye of the beholder as to how far that line has been crossed. The analyst is always to some extent experienced as "going too far," and it is that certainty that allows him the chance to recognize firsthand what "going too far" means, subjectively, to his patient. The relational process through which that recognition takes place is what *negotiating collisions* is all about, and, in each chapter of part II, I emphasize different aspects of this process, most importantly the therapeutic use of the analyst's own dissociative reactions and the powerful role of shame.

Shame as a clinical phenomenon is a therapeutic issue of immense significance. The role played by shame is initially conceptualized in chapter 4, but the details of its ubiquitous presence in the clinical process become most vivid in the chapters constituting part II and part III. More than any other issue, shame is the conceptual thread that humanizes our understanding that the process of collision and negotiation is not a sign of faulty technique even though it may sometimes feel interminable.

Rather, it is a sign that, in the enacted reliving of early trauma, certain of the patient's dissociated self-states have not been sufficiently acknowledged by the therapist and that the thwarted desire for such acknowledgment is accompanied by shame. As she did in her original trauma, the patient hungers shamefully for recognition of her pain—shamefully, because the person from whom she needs acknowledgment is the person least likely to offer it because he also is the person causing it, however inadvertently in this case.

The nature of the enactment creates an interpersonal dynamic in which shame is felt by both patient and analyst, an experience that is destabilizing to each person because it is linked to a need for something from the other that, because it is not forthcoming, supports the reality of their needs' being illegitimate. Those self-states that experience the need and those that hold the shame are dissociated, thus shutting down intersubjective communication at least temporarily. My argument, which I hope to demonstrate many times over in part II and part III, is that accessing shame has to precede accessing need. That is to say, the task that is most important, and simultaneously most difficult for the analyst, is to watch for signs of dissociated shame both in himself and in his patient—shame that is being evoked by the therapeutic process itself in ways that the analyst would just as soon not have to face. Bringing this here-and-now shame into the open is inherently a "messy" process. It is not easy on an analyst's professional stability, but if analyst and patient are able to live with it and stay authentically engaged through the many repetitions of the same mess, and the analyst does not try to restabilize himself by invoking the concept of "intractable transference resistance," something can indeed be done.

The two chapters of part III, "Safe but Not Too Safe," take us to another issue that I feel is not given enough discussion in the literature; namely, what do we conceptualize is taking place inside the patient as treatment progresses? How we answer this question will reflect our view of what constitutes wholeness and optimal mental functioning. And that answer will, in turn, inform how we believe healing takes place. It is worth noting here that to truly enjoy being a therapist it helps to have a feel for what might be called the "aesthetics of incompletion." Pat Barker (1991) is well aware of this aesthetic when she asserts through the voice of her protagonist, psychiatrist William Rivers,[3] that the process of

---

[3]Dr. Rivers appears again in chapter 3, more prominently and more simply human.

change mimics deterioration: "Cut a chrysalis open, and you will find a rotting caterpillar. What you will never find is that mythical creature, half caterpillar, half butterfly, a fit emblem of the human soul, for those whose cast of mind leads them to seek such emblems" (p. 184).

My own version of Barker's perspective, which I have stated many times and return to again in the two chapters of part III, is that we should not think of change as linear or of wholeness as progressive development toward oneness. Translating this assertion into Barker's language, I would say that, when a therapist enters a "cast of mind" that leads him to experience his patient's change as partly "completed"—half caterpillar, half butterfly—he should try to be aware that his experience may be emblematic more of a *wish* than of a perception. Such a wish is not in itself a mistake, but an inevitable consequence of participating in a therapeutic context that is defined by an aesthetic of incompletion—an everlasting process of shifting self-state patterns. As a therapeutic context, this aesthetic inherently denies a therapist the hope of eventually achieving a "finished" treatment, such as might be imagined were the outcome indeed organized by linear cause and effect. In other words, when we are working with dissociation, my caveat is to be wary of thinking of the therapeutic process as if it were a progressive integration of many into one. Rather, I contend that optimal mental functioning consists in our being able to access disparate self-states and that treatment ought to provide a context for facilitating internal communication between these states as a nonlinear, repetitive process.

My intent in part III is to alert you to how difficult this repetitive process can be for the therapist and the patient as they necessarily explore the darker not-me recesses of their own personalities. This journey, never easy, need not be burdened further by a faulty conception of what therapy can offer or what psychic wholeness means.

In an extraordinary novel about multiplicity and human relatedness, Matt Ruff (2003) illuminates the dissociative personalities of his two main characters as their respective self-states interact with each other internally and externally. His book is both enthralling as a story and so clinically perceptive as to seem somewhat eerie. Ruff writes that unity and multiplicity are inseparable, and that in therapy the important thing is "to eliminate the confusion that resulted from uncontrolled switching. . . . Whether you end up with one soul, or ten, or a hundred—that [is] a side issue" (p. 109). Comparing the aftermath of trauma to a rosebush torn apart by a storm, he makes the concept of reintegration a flawed idea therapeutically because

> the branches get scattered all over the garden, but they don't just lie there; they take root again, and try to grow, which isn't as easy now that they are competing with one another for space and light. Still, they manage—most of them manage—and what you end up with, ten or twenty years after the storm, is not one rosebush but a multitude of rosebushes; some of them are badly stunted; maybe all of them are smaller than they would have been if they each had a garden of their own. But they are more, much more, than a simple collection of puzzle pieces [p. 107].

Regardless of the extent of dissociation, when the therapist is able to relate to each aspect of the patient's self in terms of its own subjectivity, each part becomes increasingly able to coexist with the rest and in that sense is more subjectively linked to the others. This linking of self-states necessarily increases a person's sense of wholeness, but the active ingredient in treatment that makes this possible is human relatedness. Self-unity, the mysterious force that holds selfhood together and permits the coexistence of self-continuity and self-coherence across self-states is made possible by what happens between people.

Ultimately, self-unity is a shorthand term for the experience of being fully in life—life being our connection with the rest of humanity. And in therapy the patient's connectedness with humanity is lived by being fully in the relational experience with the therapist, and vice versa.

PART I

ON SELF-STATES

2

Bringing in the Dreamer[1]

I'm the gap between what I am and am not,
between what I dream and what life makes of me.
—Fernando Pessoa, *The Book of Disquietude*

Sometimes a patient begins a session with, "I don't have anything to talk about today; I wish I had a dream." Most analysts are familiar with this kind of remark and would agree that its meaning can be fully grasped only as an event that is unique to the analysis in which it occurred. The meanings that emerge most frequently, however, are organized around the concept of resistance, as if the patient were simply saying, "If I had a dream, I would be spared having to think about why I have nothing to say today."

There is another version of that opening remark that occurs seemingly less often, but captures my attention more than the first when it appears in my own work. The patient about whom I speak in more detail in this chapter put it this way, "I *feel* like I want to tell you a dream, but I don't *have* a dream." As the session progressed, the patient's felt need to tell a dream was more and more clearly understood as expressing the same thing that the dream itself would have expressed had he indeed arrived with one. A voice from a dissociated part of the patient's self was ready to be heard, but the patient was not quite ready to acknowledge it as "me." There are different variations of this opening

[1]This chapter revises and expands the original publication of the essay in *Contemporary Psychoanalysis,* 2000, 36:685–705, and includes material adapted from "On Being One's Dream: Some Reflections on Robert Bosnak's (2003) 'Embodied Imagination.'" Adapted by permission.

remark, and I have discovered that, if such a comment is not seen routinely as "resistance," it will more often than not be conveying the message, "I don't have anything to talk about today, but maybe someone else inside does."

If the continually shifting configuration of mental states that we call selfhood is to function optimally, it must be at once fluid and robust. That is, a person's transitions between self-states must permit spontaneity and novelty without threatening the stability of self-continuity, self-cohesiveness, and secure attachment to others, thereby allowing the person to lead his life creatively, relatively safe from the traumatic specter of self-invalidation or, in its most extreme form, self-annihilation. My approach to working with dreams is a reflection of my overarching self-state perspective on the human mind and represents my belief that, no matter what one's theoretical persuasion or loyalty, a clinical stance derived from this perspective optimally facilitates enduring personality growth within a psychoanalytic relationship.

The developmental achievement of a sense of self that is simultaneously fluid and robust depends on how well the capacity for affect regulation and affective competency has been achieved. Interpersonal transactions between infant and caregiver mediate the earliest development of self and shape the subsequent capacity for relational affect regulation and, in turn, the security or insecurity of human relatedness.[2] When these early patterns of interpersonal interaction are relatively successful, they create a stable foundation for relational affect regulation that is internalized as nonverbal and unconscious. Thus, further successful negotiation of interpersonal transactions at increasingly higher levels of self-development and interpersonal maturity is made possible. If one believes that the concept of a core self is useful, this would be it.

---

[2]Particularly relevant to this understanding are the contributions of attachment theory (see Goldberg, Muir, and Kerr, 1995). Mitchell (2000) made note of Main's (1995) observation about the "recent 'relational turn' by attachment theorists . . . [and that] this development within the attachment tradition, together with the turn toward relationality in the psychoanalytic tradition, makes this a particularly appropriate time to explore the convergence between these quasi-independent lines of theory making" (p. 83). "At this point in the evolution of psychoanalytic ideas," Mitchell wrote, "attachment theory and psychoanalytic theory, rather than offering alternative pathways, offer the exciting possibility of a convergence that is mutually enriching" (p. 102).

These early interaction patterns have profound implications for the ease or difficulty a person will experience in attempting to utilize a psychotherapeutic relationship. I believe that part of the work in any analytic treatment involves the patient's effort to negotiate unfinished business in those areas of selfhood where, because of one degree or another of traumatic experience, affect regulation was not successful enough to allow further self-development at the level of symbolic processing, thought, and language. In this light, a significant aspect of the therapeutic process, whereby words can come to symbolize what has been nonverbal, is an increased competency in regulating affective states without fear of retraumatization.

Psychological trauma can be looked at in different ways. I see it as the precipitous disruption of self-continuity through the invalidation of the patterns of meaning that define the experience of "who one is" (Bromberg, 1996a, p. 273). It occurs in situations (explicitly or implicitly interpersonal) in which self-invalidation cannot be prevented or escaped and from which there is no hope of protection, relief, or soothing. If the experience is prolonged or assaultively violent, or if self-development is weak or immature and the only significant "others" available behave as though the experience does not exist as a reality, then the level of affective destabilization becomes too great for the event to be experienced self-reflectively and integrated into ongoing self-meaning through cognitive processing.

Physiologically what takes place is an autonomic hyperarousal of affect that cannot be cognitively schematized and managed by thought. In its extreme form, the experience is that of a chaotic and terrifying flooding of affect that can threaten to overwhelm sanity and imperil psychological survival. The mind's normal capacity for dissociation is typically enlisted as the primary defense. To the degree that this defense is successful, the process of dissociation itself will then, for some people more than for others, become a central organizing structure in mental functioning. It will ensure that what has already happened is unlikely ever to be repeated in the same way. But the price for this protection is to plunder future personality development of its resiliency and render it into a fiercely protected constellation of relatively unbridgeable self-states, each rigidly holding its own truth and its own reality "on call," ready to come "on stage" as needed, but immune to the potentially valuable input from other aspects of self.

Viewed in this way, the meaning of the struggle between patient and analyst that we call enactment entails an externalization of the war within the patient's internal object world. The actual battlefield of this war, within the patient, is not reached by addressing the intrapsychic *associative content* that is organized by enactment. Rather, it is the interpersonal *dissociative context* through which enactment takes place that is the location of the action. The more powerful the dissociative forces that are preventing the linking of the various islands of selfhood in the patient's mind, the more his capacity to relate is compromised because of the *objectification* of self and other that is built into his mental organization—and the more powerful is the enactment. (By objectification, I mean seeing the other as more or less wholly outside the self and thus unavailable for intersubjective dialogue. Also entailed in objectification is seeing an unwanted aspect of the self in an other who refuses dialogic intimacy.) With regard to the overarching relational dynamic of enactment, one could say that the analyst is immersed, at least for a time, in a dissociative process of his own that is linked with the patient's and is objectifying his patient no less than his patient is objectifying *him*. It is because of the relative absence of intersubjectivity during enactment that an analyst will often concretize the event as something taking place within the patient.

It could thus be argued that the reason the same dynamic is enacted again and again during the course of an analysis is that, within a given analytic relationship, what seems to be a patient's repetition compulsion is not, in fact, a real repetition. But it can *seem* like a real repetition and often does. Actually, however, time is moving along, and each so-called repetition potentially changes the relationship in the same sense that the Greek philosopher Heraclitus said that "one cannot step into the same river twice." The point at which the analyst usefully becomes aware that it is a different river is the point at which he stops believing that what is going on is simply a return of material from the patient's past. At that moment he "wakes up" and *feels* that something is going on between himself and his patient (a here-and-now experience), rather than continuing to *believe* that the phenomenon is located solely in his patient, who is "doing the same thing again." The therapeutic leverage then shifts to increasing the potential for negotiation between the patient's and the therapist's perceived realities. The analytic goal is that the experience of the struggle in the here and now will feel increasingly safer to the patient over time, and that safer feeling will, we hope, lead to a gradually more enduring capacity for holding as a symbolized state of internal conflict that which was formerly a collision of realities between dissociated self-states. The increasing symbolization of what is enacted is dyadically constructed bit by bit through the creation of a transitional reality. As this process progresses, the collisions between subjectivities that take place during enactments are no longer seen as inevitably irreparable and beyond the pale of mental struggle, because they are no longer beyond what Donald Nathanson (1992) calls hope of surcease or solace. Let me offer an example.

Ernest

Ernest entered treatment with a history of "failed" sexual conquests. Women who initially seemed interested in him romantically very shortly (usually on the first date) found an excuse to not see him again. Ernest was a man whose capacity for dissociation was so extreme that his inertia was sometimes almost unbearable. He could literally not allow a here-and-now experience of aliveness with another human being to exist for more than a few moments. Intersubjective give-and-take was seemingly unknowable to him.

I can recall the first time I felt a moment of authentic contact between the two of us as real people. He was recounting another of his dissociated ventures into dating and said, in his usual robotlike delivery, "Every time I ask a woman to go to sleep with me, she turns me down." Something at that moment, perhaps my need to avoid recognizing my own hypnoid trance (sometimes called boredom), made me attend to Ernest's use of language more carefully than I might have otherwise.

"Your choice of words just struck me," I intoned. "You described what you do as asking a woman to '*go to sleep* with you.' I think, though I'm not completely certain, that the typical way of putting it is 'asking a woman *to sleep* with you.' I wonder if that difference might be important. When you ask someone to 'go to sleep with you,' it usually means what it literally sounds like it means—going to sleep. When you ask someone to 'sleep with you,' it is usually understood to mean an invitation to engage in sex. I have a feeling that your use of language may involve more than just a lack of familiarity with the right words."

"What do you mean?" asked Ernest, speaking as from a cave below ground. As I was about to "explain" what I meant with another torrent of words, the boring quality of my own voice made me "wake up." I chose instead to respond with what I was experiencing at that moment: I was flooding him with words and could well understand if he could not get what I was talking about. I then wondered aloud (probably a bit wordily) whether my nonstop wordiness might be my way, unconsciously, of trying to deal with something I was not letting myself recognize happening between us: we were talking to each other as if we were on separate islands, each alone in his own space with no way to connect personally to each other. He asked again what I meant. This time I felt more connected. I replied that I might have been trying to overcome my feeling of being all by myself by substituting words—a lot of words—for the personal contact I really wanted and could feel some of right now, but had kind of given up hope of having without realizing it. I wondered if this made any sense to him in terms of his own experience of what had just happened between us.

He allowed that my explanation actually was very close to what he felt but that he was not really aware that he felt it until I said it. He continued, hesitantly, saying that my using the word personal scared him and made him feel that he was not understanding me again. But he knew that what I was saying was true, and he, too, felt hopeless about it ever being different because that was just who he is. I asked if what I had said to him about wanting to get closer to him may have felt like more than he could handle at that moment. I wondered aloud if perhaps his wish not to "understand" me was a wish to lower the volume of his feelings by moving himself to a safer place—a safe island inside his own head where he could talk without having to risk being flooded by more than his mind could deal with. I said that I knew I might be scaring him by just asking this, but that I wanted to try anyway. Ernest then revealed, for the first time, that he lived in a state of terror and that everything he did in his life was a way of appearing as if he were like everyone else while knowing that he was just pretending. He always hoped I would show him how to do the right way what others seemed to do so easily. He said that he was scared at that moment but that he was glad that he could at least say this much.

Suffice to say that it was a long analysis. Was this enactment a turning point? I don't know. Perhaps the "real" turning point had already happened and this was just the fallout. I guess I really do believe that change precedes insight. Yes, he did then start to think about the fact that, in the act of trying to relate to another human being, whether a date or an analyst, he usually shifts to a self-state that is so deadened to the immediacy of here-and-now aliveness that he literally forces the other person either to "go to sleep with him" or to retreat into an equally boring and impersonal exchange of words.

Self-States, Enactment, and Bringing In the Dreamer

Any analyst is inclined to be most welcoming to certain parts of his patients' selves because, no matter how unpleasant or frustrating those aspects may be at times, as a steady diet they feel sturdier, less vulnerable to collapse, and more able to "hang in." With regard to some *other* parts, the therapist, sometimes feeling bored, hopeless, confused, or frightened, will often wish to get as far away from them as possible. It is when these feelings are operating dissociatively within the self-state aesthetics of unconscious communication that the process of enactment moves to center stage. The process of enactment does not stop just because the therapist chooses to call a later phase of treatment working through. Enactment goes on. And if at any point the analyst tries to turn it into something more palatable by dissociating the problematic aspects of his own experience, that is where the therapy will run into trouble and the enactment will get "louder." As Smith (1995) felicitously put it, "to speak of *a* blind spot, as to speak of *an* enactment, implies . . . that these are unusual, discrete phenomena, thus obscuring the fact that analysts and patients are always immersed to one degree or another in mutually conceived states of relative blindness or clarity of vision" (p. 75).

When the therapist for too long dissociates his awareness of those parts of the patient's self that he would just as soon not deal with, the patient will hear the analyst's lack of recognition as if it were a voice saying, "I don't need *you* here; *you* are only getting in the way. I only need the one who is able to reflect on things without having to react as though everything were an emotional crisis."

There is an old joke that in its imagery captures the concept of "unconscious favoritism" better than can be conveyed by language. It's about two brothers, Jake and Harry, who were lifelong fishing companions despite the fact that Harry could never catch any fish and Jake always had incredible success. They were out together in their rowboat one day with the usual results: Jake was pulling in one after another while Harry couldn't get a single bite no matter what lure he used or how close to Jake he cast. Finally, Harry did something he had never done before: he asked Jake if he could borrow his rod to help change his luck. Jake said, "Sure." So Harry, using Jake's rod, casts Jake's lure and immediately feels a tug on the line. Elated, he reels it in, but when he gets the lure to the boat there is no fish on it. What he finds is a note on the hook that says, "Where's Jake?"

The analyst, like the fish in the story, wants Jake. He wants the patient's self that he can work most comfortably with. And God forbid Harry should drop a line. The implications of this joke for clinical psychoanalysis are particularly well illustrated in the context of working with dreams. Let me ease my way into this topic by making reference to a book by Edward Tauber and Maurice Green (1959), two of the William Alanson White Institute's most creative researchers and interpersonal analysts. The book remains today a landmark in psychoanalytic thinking about the mind, self-states, dissociative processes, and dreaming; it pointed the way, predictively, toward much of the work being currently done in brain research.

> [S]ubthreshold perception is an ongoing process covering a broad spectrum of different states of consciousness. The subthreshold processes are, so to speak, busily engaged in picking up huge packets of sensory input and in sorting, filing, and organizing this input in ways that defy understanding. Scientific discovery and verification of this important aspect of man's inherent equipment open up new and promising possibilities for extending our understanding of essentially, nonverbal, dissociative aspects of human functioning [p. 83].

I contend that contemporary scientific exploration and contemporary clinical experience have borne out the promise of investigating these subthreshold processes. But what I would like to draw attention to here is that these processes also can be accessed through dreams and that, as Tauber and Green write, "some of the subthreshold perceptions of the self [emerge in] dream content. And, possibly, such amorphous forms may be the stuff out of which presentational experience of the self can be created in awareness" (p. 91). I believe that these authors were more on target than they could ever have known, especially in regard to how this understanding translates clinically in working with dreams. Here I can summarize my own clinical position in one sentence: *When a patient brings in a dream, the analytic task is to enable him to bring in the dreamer.*

If one holds the view, as do I, that a dream is the most familiar special case of the more general phenomenon of dissociation, the normal self-hypnotic capacity of the human mind, then dreaming might be considered among the most routine day-to-day dissociative activities of the mind–its nocturnal function being an adaptational effort to cope with minimal levels of affectively disruptive not-me experience without interfering with the waking illusion of central consciousness. One of its manifestations in psychoanalysis is to contain and hold, as a separate reality, unprocessed affective experience that is not safely containable at that moment within the "I" that defines the analytic relationship for the patient. In other words, the use of a dream in analysis might, at one level, be thought of as a transitional experience that allows the potential linking of self-states that are hypnoidally disconnected and permits the voices of other self-states to be heard and to find access to the dynamic structure that the patient defines as "me." The process through which all this takes place is one that I feel is not adequately described by the phrase "dream interpretation" (see also Caligor, 1996).

I would depict the process as a gradual development of dialogue between the waking self-state of the patient-as-patient and the sleeping self-state of the patient-as-dreamer, a dialogue that is shaped by the creative use of the projective and introjective process that takes place between patient and therapist as part of every analytic relationship. The analyst, by engaging all of a patient's self-states in relationships that are affectively responsive to each in its own terms, finds out in detail *all* the patient's realities, thus allowing the patient to experience "who he is" with a sense of clarity and personal authenticity. And for the therapist, it is not necessary to work so hard to figure out what things mean and how they are connected to the past. A similar sentiment has been expressed by Cecily de Monchaux (1978) in a clinically illuminating paper on the nature of dreams, which she calls "night thinking." Describing her work with a patient who "began to feel like . . . someone who had swallowed their twin" (p. 449), she writes that "dissociation with no access to consciousness, as in the numbing or freezing stages of the primary stress response, gives way to dissociation with partial access to consciousness via night thinking, and this provides a trial ground, a way station on the road to integration" (p. 448).

As to how the foregoing shapes, concretely, my clinical approach to dreams, I start from the fact that a dream, in its essence, is a nonlinear reality and must be related to as such—not as a kind of story or a kind of movie, but as a real space in which the patient has been. If we accept that the dreamer is inside his dream (inside a separate psychic reality), then not only is our way of approaching dreams in psychoanalysis changed, but also everything that takes place between ourselves and our patients is experienced differently, including how we perceive and use the transference and countertransference field.

Infrequently observed is that, in chapter 1 of *The Interpretation of Dreams,* Freud (1900) suggested that waking and sleeping realities may not be as experientially unbridgeable as one typically believes them to be when awakening from a dream. He wrote, "The unsophisticated waking judgment of someone who has just woken from sleep assumes that his dreams, even if they themselves did not come from another world, had at all events, carried him off into another world" (p. 7). Freud elaborated further, "Thus the dream experience appears as something alien inserted between two sections of life which are perfectly continuous and consistent with each other" (p. 10). Freud's wording carries the clear implication that dreaming and waking reality are not wholly separate. But he did not pursue that implication with respect to the analytic process itself.

Historically, most analysts have tended not to see a patient as potentially able to "reenter" in a session what Freud called "another world" and thereby access the sleeping self-state of dreamer without losing the waking one of patient. To be sure, Erich Fromm (1951) commented on how certain dreams are disturbing because "they do not fit the person we are sure we are during daytime" (p. 8), a theme that was developed further by Charles Rycroft (1979), who stated that "dreams are messages from *parts of the self* of which the waking self is unaware" (p. 106, italics added). By and large, however, analysts have tended to collude with their patients' waking experience of a dream as something experientially alien that can be known only indirectly, through associations to the *remembered* dream. Yet I have found that most people, particularly in the presence of an appropriately involved other, hold *the capacity to reenter their own dream space while simultaneously retaining their waking reality* and that, in treatment, some people can do it easily and naturally. I am convinced from my own work and that of others, especially the writing of the Jungian analyst Robert Bosnak (1989, 1996, 2003), that what we call the therapeutic use of potential space in psychoanalysis (Winnicott, 1967, 1971) is effective because patient and analyst are simultaneously using this capacity in the interest of a shared goal. In potential space, *each party allows himself to experience the other's waking reality as if it were his own "dream."*

What do I mean? If one views the normal process of human personality functioning (including that of patient and analyst), as a shifting configuration of multiple self-states (what Freud, 1908, called part-egos), it is then not too difficult to conceive of the analytic process as a relationship involving an interconnection between the multiple realities of both persons. So far so good! The next step is to accept that our "dreaming" reality is simply a different state of consciousness and that its taking place during sleep does not make it more unbridgeable to waking reality than *any* two dissociated self-states are to each other. This is to say that it is possible to be awake and dreaming at the same time. A familiar example is the unusual phenomenon that we refer to as *pavor nocturnus,* or "night terrors"[3]—those cataclysmic eruptions of somatized anxiety into terrifying dreams that continue to be felt as real even after one is fully awake and that the mind and body cannot shake off for a long while. The main point is that the patient is not just relating to the analyst through a unitary, waking state of consciousness, even though we might want to believe so, but through many different self-states, one of which, at least potentially, is that of the dreamer. In other words, the patient's subjectivity, although it cannot be directly known except by its author, is, in fact, experientially accessible as if it were the analyst's own dream, and vice versa, opening a space in which the waking realities of patient and analyst make room for potential dreamers.

This way of working with dreams, in part because of the dissociative nature of dreams themselves, makes use of the mind's capacity to enter hypnogogic states. I think that most analysts, regardless of theoretical persuasion, would probably acknowledge that the same could be said of psychoanalysis itself. If this were not true, the phenomenon of transference would be unexplainable in its extraordinary power to bridge psyche and soma, affect and thought, and self-states that have been defensively isolated from one another through dissociation, interpersonally as well as intrapsychically. That is, the full potency of transference is realized when and if the analytic relationship facilitates a patient's intrinsic capacity to enter a light trance state. I am not talking here about the use of a hard-edged hypnotic trance induction but an invitation to the patient-as-patient to "bring in the dreamer"—an *invitation* that, because it is itself subject to intersubjective negotiation, enhances rather than intrudes into the natural flow of the relational analytic process.

---

[3]Night terrors are unique among dreams because technically (as shown by EEG studies) they are not really dreams but a stage IV sleep phenomenon—an alternate state of waking consciousness (see Broughton, 1968; Fisher et al., 1970, 1974; Stern, 1988). Another example, less familiar, is that of *lucid dreaming* (see Tart, 1969; LaBerge, 1985), the phenomenon of being "awake in your dreams"; that is to say, "dreaming while being fully conscious that you are dreaming" (LaBerge, 1985, pp. 2–3).

In this same vein, I feel drawn to Marianne Goldberger's (2000) way of using *daydreams,* and I can easily translate how she works into a version of my own approach. She repudiates the idea, as do I, that just because night dreams occur when asleep, a different state of consciousness, they provide a more "royal" access to the unconscious. She makes a strong argument for the sometimes superior access provided by daydreams because they at times have more immediacy and allow patients to make playful use of their imaginations. One could argue that, in my own way of working, I attempt to turn night dreams into daydreams.

I hearken back to Count Alfred Korzybski's (1954) frequently cited admonition that one should not mistake the map for the territory. In this same sense, one should not mistake the reported dream (the map) for the subjective dream (the territory).[4] If, as Reik (1936) once asserted, the royal road to the unconscious is created by the experience of surprise rather than discovered by the "interpretation" of dreams, then what is it that links dreams and surprise? My answer is *affect.* Take nightmares, for example: they are unique among dreams because they are so bodily powerful and vivid that the affect sometimes spills over into waking reality. I am here defining the essence of "nightmare," not by its being frightening but rather by its being affectively embodied and immediate.

The analytic work, as I see it, is to make every dream as somatically real as a nightmare without turning the analytic experience itself into a nightmare. The general principle is to see a dream as part of a session rather than as a "thing" brought into a session from the outside. It is not a narrative to be understood but a reality to be experienced in as much detail as if it were taking place now. That is, to return to Count Korzybski, I try to help a patient return to the dream *experience* and feel into it as the physical "territory" rather than tell it as if it were "only" a story. So, I try to ask for details in a way that most helps a patient enter the dream as a here-and-now bodily experience. It is a version of what Edgar Levenson (1988), expanding on Sullivan's (1954) concept of the "detailed inquiry," called the "pursuit of the particular." But I am using

[4]What I am calling the territory of the dream (the subjective dream reality), as opposed to the map (the dream text), is organized by the affective experience while dreaming. And this is true even if there is no affect, because the "presence of an absence," to use Bion's (1970, 1978) language, is still the most personal substrate of the dream reality as experienced subjectively by the dreamer.

a *dream* as if it were no different from a reported event that took place in what we call the "waking world." For example, "What is it like as you are seeing that man in the corner? Not, "What *was* it like?" "Where *are* you standing in the room? Look around you and describe what you see." "Look up. How high *is* the ceiling? Where is the light coming from?" "You say you are feeling somehow close to this man. Does he seem to be aware of your presence? In what way *do* you feel close?" And so on. The idea is to enable the patient to get further and further into the dream *space* and not simply remain in the dream *text*.[5]

What happens clinically varies among patients. Some can go freely into the dream space while others cannot. But for those who can lend themselves to the journey even minimally, the affective experience of being *in* the dream becomes increasingly vivid and real, and here is where my main point becomes clearer. The patient's associations to the dream, as they arise, will tend to do so spontaneously because they will emerge affectively rather than conceptually. Equally important, the patient–analyst relationship is now drawn into the construction of the "royal road" to the patient's unconscious. As I stated earlier, I believe that the road to the patient's unconscious is always created nonlinearly by the analyst's own unconscious participation in its construction while he is consciously engaged in one way or another with a different part of the patient's self. Thus, while the analyst is leading the patient deeper and deeper into the affect and physical experience of the dream, the self-state of the "dreamer" is being invited to enter the session, and this takes place mainly through enactment. Consider, in this light, Knoblauch's (2000) observation that "affects are not in the person. An affective field is continuously constructed and shifting between persons who affect each other" (p. 158).

In one way this process is no different from what takes place when you are helping patients talk about real-life traumatic events from their past. What begins as a story being "told" becomes an event that is relived at first subjectively and then drawn into a relational enactment. Similarly, when a *dream* is being told and gradually relived subjectively, those aspects that represent unprocessed real-life experience

---

[5]I am especially indebted to Robert Bosnak, whose 1996 book *Tracks in the Wilderness of Dreaming* provides many of the illustrative questions selected here as examples. I also recommend to those interested in learning more about the detailed application of Bosnak's approach a highly informative volume based on his work, *Dreamwork for Actors* (Sonenberg, 2003).

(frequently, unsymbolized experiences of the analysis itself) will, like all unprocessed experience with high affective significance, be enacted in the patient–analyst relationship. In other words, the analyst is not simply a guide accompanying his patient on a journey down the royal road; he is a participant in the road's construction and, we hope, in the paving of its potholes.

The following clinical vignette is about dreams and "surprise." But it is not about surprise in any dramatic sense, and that is why I chose it. There was no burst of something that emerged in a wondrously transformational moment. What happened was a surprise in a different way. My patient, Daniel, surprised me by being in a place, developmentally, that I had no idea he had reached, and also by his knowing what was most important to him even when I did not. At the same time, I surprised him by responding to his unanticipated confrontation of me in a way he did not expect. Each of us had to deal with something unconscious in ourselves and in the other that was being enacted in our relationship—something dissociated of which we were each a part and that neither of us was able to grasp fully and process alone, even though each of us was experiencing some part of it personally. Either we escaped the dissociative cocoon *together,* or we both remained trapped in it. This was an example of the kind of moment a patient tends to remember as meaningful years after the analysis has ended, but he cannot really say why. It is a "surprise" moment when the personal and professional are unexpectedly bridged, and the bridge becomes an affective marker in personality growth that does not fade.

Daniel

Daniel was a man in his early 30s whom I had been seeing in three-times-a-week analysis, on the couch, for six years. He had been sent to me for analysis by his internist, who had thrown up his hands trying to diagnose Daniel's mysterious leg pains, a condition Daniel had apparently suffered from since adolescence. I say apparently because, for Daniel, there were no such things as facts, including historical data. He was concrete to a fault. Mental representation of his past, as something on which he could reflect, did not seem to be possible. Everything was like a "snapshot" on film that had important parts slightly blurry. If he could not see it as if it were a sensory image in front of him, happening now, "maybe I am just imagining it," Daniel would say.

I can still remember our initial interview, when I sat, trying to record the usual developmental stuff I ask about when I first meet someone; each time I wrote down something he said I had to cross it out. I ended up with three pages of scribbles that looked as though they had been scrawled by a dyslexic second grader. It is difficult to describe the sensation of being told that such and such happened at such and such a time during someone's life and having it disappear like the Cheshire Cat in *Alice in Wonderland,* fading a piece at a time, until all that is left is the grin. You are probably thinking at this point, "Yeah, poor guy. I know what it's like treating a world-class obsessional," but Daniel wasn't really *that.* It was not that he simply "undid" what he had said; it was also that he was able to put me into a state that frequently made me not sure he had even said what I thought he had said in the way I thought he had said it. Nothing was connected to anything else. He possessed "snapshots" of his life in abundance, it is true, but they were snapshots that had never even been put into an album; it was not difficult to discern that he had more than a few issues relating to trauma, dissociation, and hypnoid states. We worked together for six years in what I believed to be a pretty good analysis, and even his leg pains had disappeared, or so I thought. In any case, his internist was happy with me.

However, it was not an easy analysis. Working in the here and now with transference–countertransference enactment to access dissociated self-states played a big part in it. But despite our seeming success I always felt as if there were "someone else" in the room who was more angry at me than was ever expressed to me and that this part of Daniel had never been allowed to have a voice. The following session took place after we had decided to start talking about termination.

Without fanfare, he had cancelled the previous session because of pains in his legs. In the past, he had cancelled other sessions for this reason, but it had not happened for a long, long time. I thought we had come to grips with that symptom and that we were finished with it. So I found myself a bit grouchy when he came in for his next session. I was determined to get to the bottom of the transferential meaning of his leg pains "once and for all," even in spite of knowing full well that the return of symptoms during a termination is more or less expectable. He arrived in an upbeat mood and with a dream.

> I'm running a race on a concrete and asphalt surface with someone else who is running behind me. In the dream I'm a novice; he's a pro, and I'm always thinking he'll catch up but he never does. I just keep running my race but with an eye on him.

> There's a bend in the road and he thinks I'm going to make a wide turn because I'm a novice, but I don't. I effectively cut him off from passing me. I even get stronger toward the finish line and I end up winning. But it's my first race and I'm not sure which line is the finish line, so I keep running just to make sure.

I, with my own agenda, went immediately to the fact that many of his earlier dreams had been about running races. I said, "Running seems to play a prominent part in your dream life." He growled, "Hmm. I don't think so! I don't see that. It feels like you are switching the subject." Then he went on,

> I just remembered another dream I had last night. I was in a room talking to you. I was sitting up and you were facing me. You were telling me things that weren't fitting. You were sounding very intelligent but you were wrong. Then, somehow, we were near each other. I'm not sure if we were on the same couch. But Carol was sitting at the other point on the triangle. Carol was talking and I was thinking that she would be a perfect match for you. I was pissed at you. The reason I was dreaming of Carol is that she's always weaving irrelevant theories. She has to be right. She can't admit she's wrong. When she talks to someone, she talks with an exclamation point.

I said, "It does sound like me. I do often talk to you with an exclamation point. In fact, I think I fit very well with that guy who keeps trying to get ahead of you. Actually, I was all ready to do it again today. I wanted to figure out why your leg pains had come back, as though it were a personal defeat if I couldn't."

"You don't give me enough credit," he replied. "I'm very bright. I know when things are right or wrong. In fact, I even have a quote from Harry Stack Sullivan, who said, 'In the present state of our society, the patient is right and you are wrong.'"

I was unfamiliar with that quotation and was not at that moment delighted to have it brought to my attention; but in an unexpected way I found myself more interested in where he was going with it than whether it was leading me to where *I* wanted to go.

"You compare me with an 'average' patient," he said angrily. "So you make 'average' interpretations. I'm not average. I'm me. Behind my vagueness is a sharp brain—and you don't give me enough credit."

There was a long pause and I was feeling kind of stunned at his directness. He now had a pained look on his face that came and went, and came and went. I could sense his vacillation between a wish to dissociate "just in case" the presence of shame began to feel too great, and his simultaneous struggle to stay alive with me in the moment. I said, "I can feel how terribly hard it is for you right now to hang in with me, after having just said what you did, and I'm thinking that maybe it's because a part of you might be scared that it's too much for our relationship to bear. Does that feel right, or am I off base?"

"Yeah, it's hard to believe you are willing to hear this," he replied. "It's hard to believe I haven't hurt you badly and that you're secretly hating me. I never said anything like this to you before. Actually, I don't think I felt it this clearly before.

"But I'm not finished with you yet. There's more. It's strange, though. Now that I said that, I also feel like I want to tell you that I appreciate your saying what you just said about how hard it was to hang in. You didn't have to say it, but you somehow knew I needed it. It wasn't just empty words, and it wasn't false sympathy. I *was* starting to get fuzzy. I was trying not to. I was fighting to keep myself from disappearing, and maybe I would have stayed here anyway, but your knowing about my shame—even though you didn't use the word—made me feel like it was worth staying here. You could have just let me be 'grown-up' all by myself, and I might have done it, but another part of me would have continued to hate you. I can still feel that other part now—the part that hates you—but it doesn't really feel like a different part of me. I feel like I know something about you that I wasn't clear about before, and it's okay to know it."

I then asked him if he would go back to the running scene and try to let himself feel into it physically. We had done this before, so he was already familiar with what I meant. When he indicated that he was there, I asked him to look around and focus on visual images, sounds, physical sensations, and even smells.

After a few moments he said, "It's funny. I can feel what a hot day it is. There's steam coming off the concrete."

I asked what it was like to be running a race on such a hot day. He paused and then said that he felt great. "The heat's not getting to me, but I can see the face of the guy behind me, and *he's* feeling the heat. He looks like he's pushing too hard—wanting to pass me—and I'm seeing everything he's doing, and I'm getting stronger as we get to the finish line."

I asked what it is like to see him so clearly, and Daniel replied that it feels great, "especially when I cut him off." I then asked him to move closer to the guy, so he could see his face very clearly as the guy was trying to pass him. When Daniel indicated he had done that, I asked what the guy's face looks like. He began to fidget and said that right now he feels like *I'm* pushing too hard. "I don't want to look at his face any more. I think you want to lead me somewhere." I said, "Like I want to be ahead of you?" He replied, "Yeah, exactly." And then he got the point and grinned. "Yeah . . . I see it now. It's weird. Suddenly I don't feel threatened by your leading me someplace. All right. I want to get back into the dream now and look at his face." There was a long pause. "I can't figure it out, but he looks happy. He doesn't look angry that I'm going to cross the finish line and leave him behind. I feel a little sad now, and I don't know why."

I asked him to feel into this guy from the inside and let himself experience what it is like to *be* him so that he can see himself through this guy's eyes. (This, also, is something he had done with me before when working with other dreams.) After a minute or so, tears began to run down his cheeks. "He likes me. He's feeling good for me, even though he lost the race. He's surprised at how strong I am at the finish line. He didn't know I had it in me because he saw me as a novice—but he's really happy for me that I ran my own race." I then asked, pushing it a little more, "What's it like to know he's feeling that way toward you?" He replied, "I want to come out of the dream now. I can feel what the dream is about and I want to talk about that.

"I know why you keep trying to get ahead of me. Carol has a friend who looks like she is made up of feathers. She floats around, but underneath she's summa cum laude. I told Carol about being angry at you, and she didn't say anything. First I felt hurt and then I felt freer because she didn't jump in right away with something that was supposed to make me feel better. I began to feel like I could do something else besides feel helpless. It was weird! I could actually feel the pains in my legs start to go away in a way that they hadn't really gone away before. I liked it but I didn't like it. It didn't feel like 'me.' I guess I don't know who I really am without my leg pains.

"As a kid, with pains in my legs I was powerless to run my own life and that felt like 'me.' I couldn't have been athletic if I had wanted to. If I stop analysis, part of me feels like I'll be letting you win—maybe like you will win the race. You won't have to keep on following me, trying to keep up. You will get to your goal. But where will *I* be? All alone? So I guess I keep a race going—but you keep it going too, in your own way. You keep trying to 'one-up' me; to get me to buy your ideas. And I always feel like it's my fault that you're needing to be right. But I'm not feeling that now. And it doesn't feel as alone as I thought it would. I sort of feel like I can give myself some of what you were giving me."

During the next six months his associations led to his recognition that, even as he was getting ready to leave analysis and go off on his own, he was more and more aware that he was being shadowed, as if by another part of himself. Running, at this point, had become his metaphor for his newly found love of living life for its own sake, for being in the immediate experience but trying to get somewhere also. The guy behind him was, in this sense, the self-image he had always been burdened with, the self who was filling the emptiness of his being by compulsively pushing to get to some future goal, the self who was proving he was not a failure, proving he was good for something. The shadow runner in this dream was a version of the self-image that he used to have in earlier dreams of being in races in which he tricked his competitors in some manner and magically won the race but felt empty once he did. Now he could also see this figure as representing all the ways he had tried to control life rather than live it by compulsively pushing himself, the ways, in other words, he had tried to infuse vitality into a self deadened by dissociative isolation from full participation in the world.

As he approached the final months of treatment, his main insight into the dream was that this part of him *remained* important, even as he was terminating; that he must never be "cured" of being that self or he will lose the creative energy that connects him to his own past. What is behind him he can now own as a genuine past rather than enact as a substitute for the present. Because he is no longer as possessed by that self, he more and more feels its presence as an essential part of him that will "keep him moving"—a source of forward energy. But he knows he cannot afford to let it get ahead of him, let it get ahead of his desire to live life by being in it. He knows he must still keep an eye on his own capacity to "let it win" and also on his propensity to "trick" it through magical means or he will lose his relatedness to the immediacy of life itself and will go back to his old feeling that life has not yet begun.

Some aspect of what is unconscious in the patient and unconscious in the analyst is always present in what we call enactment. It is the enacted piece of each partner's impact on the other that makes the royal road a bumpy road and makes it evident that the raw material from which the road is constructed is drawn from the unconscious not only of the patient but also of the analyst. The clinical use of dreams is no exception. I believe that working with dreams is, exactly as Freud (1900) said, an indispensable aspect of the process I have just described, even if it is not literally a "road" in the way he perceived it, and that Freud was correct in his view that dreams provide something unique.

3

Playing with Boundaries[1]

In this chapter, I revisit my central contention in the last chapter from a different angle. There I argued specifically with reference to dreams that working clinically is most powerfully enhanced if one takes advantage of the natural self-state organization of the mind, that is, the ability to shift between different self-states without losing self-continuity. It is because the mind is fundamentally organized this way, I contend, that it becomes possible for patient and analyst alike to use the other person's momentary self-state as part of his own. This process of mutual borrowing entails a permeability of boundaries, both between self and other and between self-states within each party. In this chapter I give some sense of the essential familiarity of this phenomenon by examining it as it manifests itself within and between reader and author in works of literature.

Eva Hoffman, in her 1989 book with the wonderful title, *Lost in Translation,* writes,

> I love words insofar as they correspond to the world, insofar as they give it to me in heightened form. The more words I have, the more distinct, precise my perceptions become—and such lucidity is a form of joy. Sometimes, when I find a new expression, I roll it on the tongue, as if shaping it in my mouth gave birth to a new shape in the world. Nothing fully exists until it is articulated. "She grimaced ironically," someone says, and an ironic grimace is now delineated in my mind with a sharpness it never had before. I've grasped a new piece of experience; it is mine [pp. 28–29].

---

[1]An earlier version of this chapter was published in *Contemporary Psychoanalysis,* 1999, 35:54–66. Adapted by permission.

When it comes to words about one's "self," however—and this is a big however—especially when the words are coming out of the mouth of one's analyst, "loving" them is a more complicated piece of business. It is not as simple as taking them in, rolling them on your tongue, and grasping a new piece of self-experience. The feeling "it is mine" that Hoffman so poignantly describes does not translate neatly into "it is me."

For the new words about one's self to be pleasurable, they have to be acceptable to a self for whom the old words are still defining reality. The new words are often initially received from an adversarial perspective by at least one part of the self, sometimes with grave misgivings, sometimes with outright antagonism, and sometimes even with rage. The old words, and the self-meaning of those old words, may crucially constitute one's internal self-narrative. To use Eva Hoffman's language again, if the new words are to give "birth to a new shape" of selfhood, and not remain just empty words, they must bridge the discontinuity with whatever words already define self-narrative as it then exists. Until then, the new words are not pleasurable. New words about the self can be "rolled on the tongue" and tasted pleasurably only in the safety of a relational context (whether real or imagined) that enables present self-experience and the old words that give it symbolic meaning to be preserved with a sense of security and continuity.

But I see that my position has been anticipated and put even more felicitously by Virginia Woolf (1928). With characteristically understated perceptiveness, she casually observed that

> these selves of which we are built up, one on top of another, as plates are piled on a waiter's hand, have . . . little constitutions and rights of their own. . . . One will only come if it is raining, another [will emerge only] in a room with green curtains, another when Mrs. Jones is not there, another if you can promise it a glass of wine—and so on. . . . [E]verybody can multiply from his own experience the different terms which his different selves have made with him—and some are too wildly ridiculous to be mentioned in print at all [pp. 308–309].

Rarely has the wondrous nature of the self been portrayed with such matter-of-fact honesty and simplicity. Woolf's evocative description is easily embraced by the reader with feelings of pleasurable recognition, and even her use of the phrase "different selves" has a felt rightness to it that is accepted without resistance. Perhaps her language, so personal and down to earth, allows her such a warmly congenial relationship with the reader that it helps to overcome the potential for discontent that sometimes can be evoked by the notion that we each comprise different selves. That idea is not always welcome; sometimes the dominant self-state wants to know nothing about any other self-states. As Popeye put it, flexing his muscles belligerently, "I yam what I yam and that's all that I yam," and any idea that suggests otherwise, whether offered by an analyst to a patient or by a writer to a reader, seems "right" only if presented in a manner that simultaneously supports one's basic experience of self-continuity. (It is when an analyst fails to provide such support that he is most apt to experience his patient as "difficult.")

To repeat, new words about the self can be tasted pleasurably only in the safety of a relational context that provides a sense of security and continuity. The kind of relational context to which I am alluding is, I think, captured well in the idea that "every patient enters psychoanalysis with the same 'illogical' wish–the wish to stay the same while changing" (Bromberg, 1993, p. 170)–and that a primary task of the analyst's therapeutic role is to contribute to preserving this illusion. To the extent he is able to do this, he is not just an analyst; he is *your* analyst. Similarly, an author stops being just an author; he becomes *your* author. He becomes yours when the "otherness" of his words does not obtrude, when the interplay among his self-states allows you to imagine yourself into them. Then he writes for *you,* and you become *his* reader. This same sensibility has been echoed by Langdon Hammer (2005) in his review of Helen Vendler's book, *Invisible Listeners,* an exploration of how poets forge bonds with readers. Hammer, addressing the relationship between the self-states of a reader and those of a poet, writes,

> [T]he "tones of voice" by which a speaker is created imply a relationship between the speaker and a listener or reader . . . [creating] an uncanny intimacy, inviting us into a space outside ordinary time. . . . Often, this means overhearing the poet talking not so much to himself as to someone who is not there. . . . Poetry of this kind begins in the poet's craving for a listener, a desire so keen it calls the object into being [p. 8].

One might thus say that a reader who "plays with the boundaries" between his own internal dialogue and the author's, is the reader an author wants: writing for such readers is what the author strives for.

Let us consider now the *different ways* an author's states of mind are embodied in his words, and how they shape and shift the states of mind of a given reader so as to evoke not simply the world in heightened form, but simultaneously, a heightened and expanded experience of selfhood. Let us play with the notion that the reader must be able to enter and engage the author's words in the way that Hoffman (1989) describes, so that while we are living in the book, the difference between "it is mine" and "it is me" can be safely surrendered. The reader must be able to "live the words" in order to live in states of mind that otherwise might be difficult to attain in real life. Through this complex relationship with an other who is inaudible to the ears and invisible to the eyes, but not to the mind, the reader is able to grasp a "new piece of experience"—a "new shape in the world"—that becomes his and, if he is lucky, becomes *him,* at least for a while. I think it is not unreasonable even to suggest that this relationship is actually a form of (not a substitute for) a "real" human relationship and holds the potential for being carried playfully into the "real world," as long as the reader does not live in the author's world indefinitely or exclusively and become "lost in translation."

William S. Baring Gould (1967), in his introduction to *The Annotated Sherlock Holmes,* quotes the following remark by Sir Arthur Conan Doyle: "It has always seemed to me that so long as you produce your dramatic effect, accuracy of detail matters little. I have never striven for it and have made some bad mistakes in consequence. What matter if I hold my readers?" (p. 4). "And hold his readers he did," writes Baring-Gould. Much has been written about this remarkable phenomenon of Conan Doyle's storytelling that transcended its genre, detective fiction, and evoked a "real" relationship between the character of Holmes and the reader that has continued to enchant generations of readers, worldwide, in a way that seems to defy explanation. Although I have been one of these Holmes nuts since childhood, even for a while a member of the club—some would say cult—that calls itself the "Baker Street Irregulars," I have only the most tentative explanation of my own to offer. Baring-Gould suggests a "psychological basis to account for our devotion" that amounts to an uncomplicated identification between reader and protagonist:

> It is not Sherlock Holmes who sits in Baker Street, comfortable, competent and self-assured; it is ourselves who are there, full of a tremendous capacity for wisdom, complacent in the presence of our humble Watson, conscious of a warm well-being and a timeless imperishable content. The easy chair in the room is drawn up to the hearthstone of our very hearts—it is *our* tobacco in the Persian slipper, and *our* violin lying so carelessly across the

> knees—it is *we* who hear the pounding on the stairs and the knock upon the door. The swirling fog without and the acrid smoke within bite deep indeed, for we taste them even now [p. 104].

As an analyst as well as a Baker Street Irregular, I would like to point out that the stories themselves are not told by Holmes but by Watson. I also note that Conan Doyle's experience of the character of Holmes was so ambivalent that he wished to be rid of him and, finally, in one story even killed him off, later resurrecting him in response to reader pressure. Behind the magic of our identification, in other words, lies the literary equivalent of shifting self-states. It seems that the reciprocal process of active involvement with the states of mind of the other allows a person's here-and-now perception of self to transcend the immediate "reality" that defines its own boundaries.

A still more complicated example is that of Dostoevsky, whose personality was far more entangled in his writing than would be true if he simply assumed the role of storyteller. As Louis Breger (1989) has written, when Dostoevsky was in crisis, he was prone to living out one or another of his dissociated self-states, and it was this trait that gave a singular stamp to his literary sensibility.

> Dostoevsky had the unique ability—as a person and a writer—to give himself over to one or another of his self–other scenarios; he would let one of his inner selves play itself out in his life. This is the living version of what Bakhtin (1929, p. 6), referring to the novels, calls "polyphony" and "dialogue": The creation of "free people, capable of standing alongside their creator." He would bring his inner actors on the stage of his life as he fell into one of his extreme situations. Once there, with emotions aroused and the scenario exposed to view, the writer-self could come on the scene and begin to control things by transforming the experience into literature [p. 11].

Again, oddly, it is the polyphony of multiple self-states in the author that facilitates the immediacy of the reader's experience.

Self-States and Otherness

It is sometimes not clear who is the patient and who the therapist. Who is the healer and who the sufferer? When a *writer* makes us feel this way, it might be asked, who is author and who is reader? An author who is able to find language to embody in a piece of writing his own internal dialectic between normally incompatible self-states—such as, for example, horror and humor—evokes in the reader a corresponding self-state disjunction, sometimes disturbing but sometimes not.

Let us start with an example from Gilbert and Sullivan's (1885) *Mikado* in which the Lord High Executioner, Ko-Ko, and two of his coconspirators, in turn, describe to the emperor the cold-blooded details of a beheading that never, in fact, took place, but must sound so believable that their own heads will be spared. For the song to work aesthetically, the state of mind of the reader or listener to the performance needs to be equivalent to the state of mind of the lyricist—playful. The reader must be able to feel the goriness but contain it as humor, as the three narrators, though their heads are on the line, cannot resist turning the story of the execution into a wildly irrelevant—and irreverent—showcase for themselves. And this containment of goriness is indeed what happens. Even though I have truncated (as it were) the chorus from the lyric, you should have little trouble feeling yourself into the state of mind evoked by the description, as sung in turn by each of the three: first Ko-Ko, the earnest "Lord High Executioner"; then Pitti-Sing, one of the deliciously conceited "Three Little Maids from School"; and finally Pooh-Bah, the pompous "Lord High Everything Else."

> [Ko-Ko]
> The criminal cried as he dropped him down,
> in a state of wild alarm—
> With a frightful, frantic, fearful frown,
> I bared my big right arm.
> I seized him by his little pig-tail,
> And on his knees fell he,
> As he squirmed and struggled,
> And gurgled and guggled,
> I drew my snickersnee!
> Oh, never shall I
> Forget the cry,
> Or the shriek that shrieked he,
> As I gnashed my teeth,
> As from its sheath
> I drew my snickersnee.

[Pitti-Sing]
He shivered and shook as he gave the sign
For the stroke he didn't deserve;
When all of a sudden his eyes met mine,
And it seemed to brace his nerve;
For he nodded his head and kissed his hand,
And he whistled an air, did he,
As the sabre true
Cut cleanly through His cervical vertebrae!
When a man's afraid, A beautiful maid
Is a cheering sight to see;
And it's oh, I'm glad
That moment sad
Was soothed by the sight of me!

[Pooh-Bah]
Now though you'd have said that head was dead
(For its owner dead was he),
It stood on its neck, with a smile well bred,
And bowed three times to me!
It was none of your impudent off-hand nods,
but as humble as could be;
For it clearly knew
The deference due to a man of pedigree!
And it's oh, I vow,
This deathly bow
Was a touching sight to see;
Though trunkless, yet
It couldn't forget
The deference due to me!

[pp. 385–387]

There is horror here no doubt. But the horror has been contained several times over: by the characters' smug self-love, by their accounts' being fabricated in the first place, by the song's being sung, and by the whole being very funny. The horror does not reach the characters emotionally, and, though we can feel it, we are not terrified. The magical result is that we are able to attend an execution and not be traumatized.

Now let us look at an author's ability to evoke in the reader an experience of horror so personal that the *need* for humor—the wish to "see it as a joke"—is overwhelming; the horror is so intractable that one cannot rid oneself of it despite one's best lighthearted effort, in the words of W. S. Gilbert, to "whistle an air" (or, in Oscar Hammerstein's lyric, to "whistle a happy tune").[2] Therapists working with trauma know this sort of experience all too well.

Consider in this light a passage from Pat Barker's (1991) novel, *Regeneration,* the first volume of her powerful antiwar trilogy set in a British military hospital during World War I. William Rivers, a talented and dedicated army psychiatrist, has been charged with the inhuman task of restoring the battered minds of soldiers who were traumatized in combat so that these men can be returned to the front lines as quickly as possible. But the inescapable humanity of each treatment relationship has led Rivers closer and closer to the thin boundary between self and other and into the "not-me" aspects of himself. He is forced to question the validity of his own personal identity:

> Rivers had become adept at finding bearable aspects to unbearable experiences, but Burns defeated him. What had happened to him was so vile, so disgusting, that Rivers could find no redeeming feature. He'd been thrown into the air by the explosion of a shell and had landed, headfirst, on a German corpse, whose gas-filled belly had ruptured on impact. Before Burns lost consciousness, he'd had time to realize that what filled his nose and mouth was decomposing human flesh. Now, whenever he tried to eat, that taste and smell recurred. Nightly, he relived the experience, and from every nightmare he awoke vomiting. Burns on his knees, as Rivers had often seen him, retching up the last ounce of bile, hardly looked like a human being at all. His body seemed to have become merely the skin-and-bone casing for a tormented alimentary canal. His suffering was without purpose or dignity, and yes, Rivers knew *exactly* what Burns meant when he said it was a joke [p. 19].

Freud (1908), in "Creative Writers and Daydreaming," spoke to the "inclination of the modern writer to split up his ego, by self-observation,

---

[2]From the 1984 Rogers and Hammerstein musical show, *The King and I.* In chapter 1 the concept of "whistling a happy tune" as a way of overcoming fear is explored more fully to illustrate the mind's self-state organization and use of dissociation as intrinsic to its normal functioning.

into many part-egos" (p. 150). He went on to state that when a creative writer "tells us what we are inclined to take to be his personal daydreams, . . . the essential poetic art lies in the technique of overcoming the feeling of repulsion in us which is undoubtedly connected with the barriers that arise between each single ego and the others" (p. 153). Although Freud was most manifestly speaking about the barriers between the ego of the writer and that of the reader, in his statement that a "piece of creative writing, like a daydream, is a continuation of . . . what was once the play of childhood" (p. 152), it is difficult to miss his undeveloped implication of the need for a "play space" to negotiate boundaries, not simply between writer and reader, but between what he calls part-egos.

Here let me refer briefly to something I discussed in the last chapter, namely, that in the play space of analysis, it is possible to make room for a part-ego that I called the dreamer. By encouraging a patient to reenter his dream while he is still simultaneously present in the analytic relationship (following Bosnak, 1989, 1996, 2003), the analyst potentially fosters a fruitful "polyphony." And, as I have been contending here with regard to literature, this polyphony is not fragmenting but possesses a self-coherent immediacy and vitality.

The Adventure of the Oval Room

If one views the normal process of human personality functioning as a shifting configuration of multiple self-states (what Freud termed part-egos), a correspondence emerges between the psychodynamics of two seemingly distinct relationships, reader–author and patient–analyst, each involving an ongoing dialectic between the multiple realities of both people. Optimally, this dialectic entails an ability to tolerate and even enjoy, as in a good read, the shifts between one's *own* different self-states. As I have discovered personally, this remarkable permeability of the boundaries between one's own states of consciousness can sometimes be an unexpectedly liberating and even exhilarating experience. An example, to borrow the language of Dr. Watson, is what I have come to call my "Adventure of the Oval Room," an event that took place during a hot August vacation in Rome.

It is midafternoon. The art world, mercifully, has finally shut its doors, not to open them again for three hours. Back in my hotel room. Blessed relief. Lying on the bed, windows opened wide, the oval room fills with a breeze. From where? Definitely not from where I have just been! It did not exist out there, only in here, in my oval room. Let me tell you about this room. Being oval, it lacks corners, and, lacking corners, it creates for me an unusual physical state of being—a feeling of being part of a spaciousness that goes beyond the actual size of the room. It evokes a heady sense of being held in limitless space and imparts a bodily and psychological sense of wholeness and well-being. The personality of the room is not defined by the usual hard-edged physical boundaries that say, "This is as far as you can go." My oval room is different, somehow; it gives no sense of being an other with its own requirements as to how far I can exist in any direction. I am in it and of it at the same time.

Being a corner room, it provides separate vistas through the windows, but, because there is an unexpected absence of corners *in* the room, looking out of a window is also different from anything I have ever experienced. The room has three windows, each looking out on a different view of the city. But, because no window is located on a boundaried wall, when I look through any one window I can feel the uncanny presence of the other vistas even if I cannot visually see them. Although each piece of the world out there has its own boundaries, my personal space is not defined simply by these external limitations. I feel at one with the oval sweep of the room that holds me, and the outside feels as much created by my internal reality as by city planning. Unconstrained by normal barriers, I can "play" with boundaries and with reality.

Freud (1907) put it that the "frontier between states of mind described as normal and pathological is in part a conventional one and in part so fluctuating that each of us probably crosses it many times in the course of a day" (p. 43). Freud's image sounds relatively benign, but the crossing is not always exhilarating and certainly not always as painless as it was for me that day in my oval room. With this thought in mind, let me conclude with short passages from works by two different authors who uncannily draw on an identical metaphor—the image of "falling snow"—to convey not only the permeability but also the vulnerability in crossing what Freud called the "frontier between states of mind." The author in one case uses the pain of the crossing as part of, in Ghent's (1990) terminology, a creatively healthy "surrender" to the inevitability of loss, and in the other case, "submits" to it as part of a descent into madness. Each author, through the metaphor of falling snow, evokes a dramatically different state of consciousness in the reader.

The first passage is from an extraordinary little book by C. S. Lewis (1961), *A Grief Observed.* It was written following the death of his wife, Joy Davidman (whom he refers to as "H"), an American poet with whom he fell deeply in love and then lost to cancer. Despite its having been rendered into a story, told years later through the film *Shadowlands,* it was not created as a narrative but was handwritten as a journal, in notebooks, during the long nights of Lewis's anguish. Alone in his room, he doubted and questioned everything he had ever felt was real and meaningful. The kaleidoscopic shifting of his states of mind possesses the reader with an uncanny immediacy that transcends the reality of whether the reader has or has not himself actually lost a beloved. What pulls the reader, half-willingly, half-apprehensively, inside the author's struggle with self-meaning is not only the power of Lewis's grief. It is as much the power of the reader's shared recognition that the person he takes himself to be is not immutably cohesive and can be overwhelmed by unanticipated shock.

Lewis's experience, however, despite his referring to it as his "mad midnight moments," did not lead to madness. His was a mind that could use his dissociative defense against trauma without rigidifying it into a protective fortress against the pain of yearning without hope. Despite his not knowing whether any given state might in *fact* last forever, he could let himself enter fully into his shifting self-states of violent rage, self-pity, longing, heartbreak, and cynicism without losing self-reflectiveness—an example of what I have called the "capacity to feel like one self while being many" (Bromberg, 1993, p. 186). In the following passage, Lewis's (1961) use of the metaphor of falling snow portrays his painful recognition that his mind was slowly anesthetizing itself by perceptually blanketing with tiny forgettings his image of H as a real person, and that only by accepting this blurring could the loss ever be bearable.

> Today I had to meet a man I hadn't seen for ten years. And all that time I had thought I was remembering him well—how he looked and spoke and the sort of things he said. The first five minutes of the real man shattered the image completely. Not that he had changed. On the contrary. I kept on thinking, "Yes, of course, of course. I'd forgotten that he thought that—or disliked this, or knew so-and-so—or jerked his head back that way." I had known all these things once and I recognized them the moment I met them again. But they had all faded out of my

> mental picture of him, and when they were all replaced by his actual presence the total effect was quite astonishingly different from the image I had carried about with me for those ten years. How can I hope that this will not happen to my memory of H? That it is not happening already? Slowly, quietly, like snowflakes—like the small flakes that come when it is going to snow all night—little flakes of me, my impressions, my selections, are settling down on the image of her. The real shape will be quite hidden in the end. Ten minutes—ten seconds—of the real H would correct all this. And yet, even if those ten seconds were allowed me, one second later the little flakes would begin to fall again. The rough, sharp, cleansing tang of her otherness is gone [pp. 31–32].

Unconstrained by the normal barriers that existed during daylight hours, Lewis, though in pain, could play with his self-states and the boundaries between them that defined reality. But what is it like when someone cannot play? Being in a room by oneself, especially at night, can be a dreaded experience if self-state permeability creates a felt risk of depersonalization, and in such a moment a person does not feel "held" by the environment. It does not become potential space in which to play with boundaries, but takes on the presence of a malevolent other, threatening to disintegrate boundaries and selfhood. At such moments, the room becomes grimly concrete in what it can offer as a potential anchor to reality, and in its extreme form it is an experience that a human being will desperately attempt to prevent at any cost.

Consider, for example, a passage from a different work, this one a horrifyingly evocative moment from Conrad Aiken's (1932) "Silent Snow, Secret Snow." It uses the same metaphor, falling snow, to pull the reader into what is here the total anesthetization of a mind already on its way to madness. Aiken's words embody the experience of uncontrollable switches in self-meaning during which an internal object-attack becomes unbearably traumatic. The need to prevent complete breakdown of self as defined by connection to the maternal object leads to a dissociative "snowfall" so obliterating that all perceptual, self-reflective contact with the world of real otherness is foreclosed.

> Not a moment too soon. The darkness was coming in long white waves. A prolonged sibilance filled the night—a great seamless seethe of wild influence went abruptly across it—a cold low humming shook the windows. He shut the door and flung off his

clothes in the dark. The bare black floor was like a little raft tossed in the waves of snow, almost overwhelmed, washed under whitely, up again, smothered in curled billows of feather. The snow was laughing: it spoke from all sides at once; it pressed closer to him as he ran and jumped exulting into his bed.

"Listen to us!" it said. "Listen! We have come to tell you the story we told you about. You remember? Lie down. Shut your eyes, now—you will no longer see much—in this white darkness who could see, or want to see? We will take the place of everything. . . . Listen—"

A beautiful varying dance of snow began at the front of the room, came forward and then retreated, flattened out toward the floor, then rose fountain-like to the ceiling, swayed, recruited itself from a new stream of flakes which poured laughing in through the humming window, advanced again, lifted long white arms. It said peace, it said remoteness, it said cold—it said—

But then a gash of horrible light fell brutally across the room from the opening door—the snow drew back hissing—something alien had come into the room—something hostile. This thing rushed at him, clutched at him, shook him—and he was not merely horrified, he was filled with such a loathing as he had never known. What was this? this cruel disturbance? this act of danger and hate? It was as if he had to reach up a hand toward another world for any understanding of it—an effort of which he was only barely capable. But of that other world he still remembered just enough to know the exercising words. They tore themselves from his other life suddenly—

"Mother! Mother! Go away! I hate you!"

And with that effort, everything was solved, everything became all right: the seamless hiss advanced once more, the long white wavering lines rose and fell like enormous whispering sea-waves, the whisper becoming louder, the laughter more numerous.

"Listen!" it said. "We'll tell you the last, the most beautiful and secret story—shut your eyes—it is a very small story—a story that gets smaller and smaller—it comes inward instead of opening like a flower—it is a flower becoming a seed—a little cold seed—do you hear? we are leaning closer to you—"

The hiss was now becoming a roar—the whole world was a vast moving screen of snow—but even now it said peace, it said remoteness, it said cold, it said sleep [pp. 258–259].

For both Lewis and Aiken the needed protection was against loss, but the nature of the loss differed; for Lewis it was object loss (the death of his beloved wife), and for Aiken's protagonist, it was loss of selfhood (annihilation of core identity).

For Lewis the unbearable affect was grief, the pain of remembering his beloved. The blanketing snowfall was the normal dissociative relief provided by the mind. If one's memory of a lost beloved were to stay as perceptually vivid as was the loved one herself when alive, the survivor would be condemned to a life of yearning without hope, grief without diminution, and perpetual torture without solace.

In Aiken's short story, the protagonist's unbearable affect was hatred; hatred toward the undifferentiated object of primary attachment; hatred that was no longer sustainable as a not-me experience; hatred that had entered consciousness as "me"; hatred that had begun to trigger an annihilating plunge into the abyss. The dissociative snowfall, by totally breaking his connection to reality, brought him peace; he no longer needed to need, nor did he need to hate.

It is that thin line between the unanticipated but containable shock and the unanticipated but uncontainable shock that separates what is perceived by most readers as potentially traumatic from what is perceived as safe but on the edge. The "right" author–reader dyad can stand, together, in the spaces between realities (Bromberg, 1996a) and move safely, but not *too* safely, back and forth across the line.

Freud (1908) wrote,

> In my opinion all the aesthetic pleasure which a creative writer affords us . . . proceeds from a liberation of tensions in our minds. It may even be that not a little of this effect is due to the writer's enabling us thenceforward to enjoy our own daydreams without self-reproach or shame. This brings us to the threshold of new, interesting and complicating enquiries; but also, at least for the moment, to the end of our discussion [p. 153].

And also to the end of mine.

4

"The Gorilla Did It": *Thoughts on the Real and the Really Real*[1]

A Shaggy Panda Story

I am starting with a shaggy dog story, except that this is a shaggy panda story. A panda walks into a bar, sits down on a barstool, and orders a tossed salad and a beer. The bartender serves him, and the panda finishes his meal, pulls out a gun and kills the man sitting on the stool next to him. He then gets up and starts to saunter out of the bar. The bartender, recovering from the shock of what he has just witnessed, shouts at the panda, "Hey, where do you think you're going? You can't just come in here, have a meal, shoot someone, and then casually leave!" The panda looks at him with self-righteous indignation and replies, "Hey, man, get off my back! It's no big deal. I'm just doing my thing. I'm a *panda,* for God's sake. Look it up!" And he walks out. The bartender, still in a state of shock, locates a dictionary, looks up *panda,* and, sure enough, it reads: Panda: A fur-bearing mammal indigenous to Asia. Typically black and white. Eats shoots and leaves.

One might see the panda's reaction to the bartender as a metaphor for a central aspect of dissociative subjectivity with which we are all familiar: the insularity and concreteness of each self-state as a black-and-white island of "truth" about who one is at a given moment. The defining hallmark of dissociation is the presence of a concrete state of mind, by which I mean that there is thought without a thinker or, rather, without the thinker's being aware of the other as a thinker in his or her own

[1]An earlier version of this chapter was published in *Psychoanalytic Dialogues,* 2001, 11:385–404. Adapted by permission.

right with whom it might be possible to share or reciprocate ideas. Thus, each self-state, insofar as it exists in dissociation from other self-states, is necessarily an island of concreteness. "Hey, man, this is who I am. It's no big deal." As we get to meet new and different parts of our patients, often unexpectedly, we are confronted with variations of the panda's reply with little regard for what *we* regard as reality, and we find ourselves in the position of the bartender in the story.

In the first three chapters I made it pretty clear that I view "reality" in analytic treatment more as an aesthetic concept than as a philosophic one. I commented in chapter 1 that I believe a therapist will enjoy the work most if he has a feel for the "aesthetics of incompletion." Here I follow Levenson (1972), who used the concept of aesthetics "not in the vulgate sense of beauty and light but more precisely, meaning sensitivity and perception, that is, concerned with the forms and organization of sensory experience, rather than content and meaning" (p. 211). This perspective is deeply related to my sensibility about the nature of reality, so much so that, were I a painter rather than a therapist, I suspect I would be an impressionist. So, at the risk of being dogmatic about reality, what I essentially discuss in this chapter is the idea that reality comes in shades of felt intensity. Reality has a gradient of intensity. Sometimes what is real to the patient so excludes the analyst's intersubjective participation that it borders on what I called in chapter 2 objectification of the self and other. At other times, when analyst and patient are able to come to a new, vital, and shared understanding of some hitherto sequestered part of the patient, they also share a feeling that the newly arrived part of the patient is "really real."

I confess that this distinction first occurred to me when I saw the catalogue for a 1981 exhibit at the San Antonio Museum of Art on contemporary American realism—"Real, Really Real, and Super Real." ("Super Real" never did find a place in my thinking, but who knows? Someday it might.) I have often thought we might use the same title for a conference on contemporary American psychoanalysis, as there may not be enough other differences between modern theories of psychoanalysis worth arguing about. But what really has made the distinction a permanent part of my inner lexicon is my reading of a wonderful children's book, *The Gorilla Did It* (Hazen, 1974), about a little boy, his parents, and a friend who shares the boy's bedroom, a friend who happens to be a gorilla. It is a story about a boy blessed with parents who, in the face of their own "grown-up truth," are able to be helped by their child to remember how thin the line is between the real and the really real and do not force him to surrender his imaginary gorilla companion to assure his continuing place in their hearts.

The tale begins with, "Just look! There's food all over the floor and grape juice under the radiator. . . . Don't tell *me* a gorilla did all this while you were sound asleep. . . . I want you to go back to bed and think about what happened. And when you've thought it over, I want you to come out and tell me what *really* happened." The story ends with the little boy's coming back out and telling his mom that he and his gorilla cleaned up the mess together, but that his gorilla said he was still hungry. "Can I take him a cookie? And can I have one too?" Mommy, with a look of loving resignation, provides cookies for both of them. The little boy, back in his room, looks into his gorilla's mischievously contrite eyes and says, "And he *really* means to be a good gorilla." The reader, whether child or adult, closes the book knowing that both the little boy and the gorilla are safe, sound, and well loved and will grow up enjoying each other's company for a long time.

Let us say the boy has different parents. Not brutal parents, nor parents who cannot tolerate their own helplessness for even a little while. Just ordinary parents who think that what they are doing is "right" and continue to insist on their rightness, because they cannot modulate what is real to their "grown-upness" by accessing another part of themselves that knows what it is like to have a gorilla for a friend. In other words, these are parents for whom the gorilla too long ago became "not-me." The little boy will then gradually have to dissociate his gorilla to preserve the attachment bond with his parents that defines his core sense of self. But the gorilla will not just disappear. No part of the self ever disappears; it will make its presence known in one way or another that will be experienced as not-me. Sometimes this part will make its presence known in ways that are painful enough to bring that little boy (often years later) into treatment. He will be escorted into a therapist's office by his adult self, who is ashamed of both of them—the boy and his gorilla. The therapist's job at that point becomes one of trying to restore the connection between the little boy and his gorilla notwithstanding the intense pressures by the now grown-up patient to keep them apart and to discourage the therapist from trying to bring them back from dissociation into the "really real."

In considering how to get the little boy back in touch with his "gorilla," I do not find it helpful to think of lifting "repression." I think of the gorilla as accessible to consciousness, but I do not believe we will get to speak with him this way. Mitchell (1995) put it this way:

> To understand unconscious processes in one's own mind or that of another is not to expose something that has a tangible existence, as one does in lifting a rock and exposing insects beneath. To understand unconscious processes in one's own mind or that of another is to use language in a fashion that actually creates new experience, something that was not there before [p. 8].

In normal mental functioning a person can access simultaneously a range of discrete self-states that, despite their contrasting and even opposing perspectives on personal reality, are able to engage in internal dialogue. It is this capacity that permits oppositional aspects of self to coexist in consciousness as potentially resolvable intrapsychic conflict. It is this capacity that allows patient and therapist to create, linguistically, what Mitchell called "new experience."

In other words, most people are able to bridge the gaps between their multiplicity of discontinuous self-states and are not exiled from the healthy experience of intrapsychic conflict and its potential resolution. I have referred to this "normal dissociative structure of the mind" (Bromberg, 1994) as a set of discrete, more or less overlapping schemata that, taken together, define who one is—each schema being organized around a particular self–other configuration with a distinctive affective flavoring.

The effect of traumatic experience is that the person surrenders self-state coherence to protect self-continuity. When the illusion of unity is so dangerous to self-continuity that coherence cannot be maintained, experience that is disjunctive with the ongoing self-state that organizes core identity is denied simultaneous access to consciousness. The person becomes unable to hold conflicting ways of seeing himself vis-à-vis his objects within a single experiential state long enough to feel the subjective pull of opposing affects and dissonant self-perceptions as a state of mind that can be taken as an object of self-reflection. As a consequence, inharmonious contents of the mind (affects, wishes, beliefs, etc.) are not readily accessible to self-observation, and the person tends to experience his immediate subjective experience as truth. Any response to his "truth" that contains the existence of data implying an alternative perspective is experienced as disconfirming and unempathic.

The patient is in a bind. The more he risks, the more he risks being misunderstood. There surfaces a more or less enduring penumbra of expected disappointment in the other. In the words of the 19th-century author George MacDonald (1858),

Alas, how easily things go wrong!
A sigh too much, or a kiss too long.
And there follows a mist and a weeping rain,
And life is never the same again.
Alas, how hardly things go right!
'Tis hard to watch in a summer night.
For the sigh will come, and the kiss will stay,
And the summer night is a winter day [pp. 130–131].

Of course, the analyst will experience his own affective version of his patient's complaint about "how easily things go wrong," and the meaning attributed to it by a given analyst will determine how he processes and uses it with his patient. An analyst's school of thought plays a significant role in shaping meaning. Traditionally, analysts were trained to hear such complaining not as the real stuff of the analytic work, but as the medium through which they could reach the "genuine" material by "analyzing" the complaint interpretively. Michael Balint (1968) eloquently addressed the flaw in this approach,

> If the patient's complaints, recriminations, and accusations remain vague and cannot be pinned down to something specific, it is nearly always possible to "analyze" the complaining—whatever it is really about—even to analyze it away for a time; in due course, however, the patient invariably returns with the same kind of complaints [p. 108].

Balint goes on to state that when a patient complains, especially when the complaints seem to be immune to interpretation and seem to go on interminably, an analyst sometimes "cannot appreciate the importance of the fact that the patient *is able to complain* (irrespective of what the complaint is about), nor the immense and unique therapeutic potentialities in the doctor–patient relationship which enable the patient to complain at all" (p. 108).

Transition from Dissociation to Capacity for Conflict

In a growth-facilitating treatment, there develops an increased ability to surrender the safety afforded by dissociation, and a simultaneous increase in the capacity to bear and process internal conflict. A patient becomes more able, mentally, both to play with and to struggle creatively with experience that before could only be *enacted* in the interpersonal field. In terms of clinical process, he becomes more able to "speak himself to you" in an intrapsychic/intersubjective process of cognitive self-resymbolization. This new ability will entail a pleasurable reconnection of mind to psyche–soma (Winnicott, 1949a) that employs the analyst's presence as a trustworthy, nonimpinging other. From behind the couch, the analyst, too, starts to feel something subtly different taking place that encompasses his experience both of his patient and of himself. His patient is more able to use the pleasure and security in what Winnicott (1958) called the capacity to be alone in the presence of another person—the experience of being alone in the presence of "someone available, someone present, although present without making demands" (p. 34). Because of this heightened ability, his patient is now doing more and more of the work internally rather than through enactment.

This shift is not without consequence for how the analyst manages his participation. Because a patient can relate to his analyst within a more coherent experience of selfhood rather than simply using the relationship as a means of *achieving* self-coherence, a new demand is now made of the analyst's use of his own subjectivity and of his definition of clinical judgment. First, because of the patient's greater capacity for internal processing of conflict and the concomitant decrease in enactment, the analyst's experience of the here and now no longer provides as reliable a key to what is going on in his patient as it had previously. His patient is more self-contained, and the analyst suddenly finds himself a "few steps behind," a development that brings with it the analyst's own vulnerability to an unanticipated shift in roles between himself and his patient. The analyst must become able to recognize and accept this unannounced change in the relationship—a shift that is sometimes greeted with denunciation by his patient because it is a shift that is most often more of a surprise to the analyst than to his patient. The shift in roles, however, is not always announced by confrontation. As illustrated in the first clinical vignette I present later, sometimes the shift in roles entails an experience in which the patient is taking on some of the analyst's functions and is glad for it. All told, notwithstanding any difficulties attending the shift in roles, the patient's dread of traumatic "shock" decreases, and, in general, surprise and spontaneity become more present and more pleasurable in the clinical process.

Second, the analyst must now be able to experience and respect his patient's need for privacy and his patient's new ability to take charge of it on his own, without the analyst's conceptualizing as resistance his patient's choice to participate less than before in the here-and-now exploration of their relationship (including exploration of the role shift itself). In a now quieter way, the analyst must be as fully engaged with his patient's immediate self-state as he was earlier on, when full engagement embraced vivid here-and-now interaction between subjectivities. If the analyst is more or less comfortably able to move in tandem with this silently developing capacity in his patient, the hallmark of this shift is not that collisions of subjectivity will cease; rather, when they do occur, the patient's self-experience, because it is less subject to disorganization by the dreaded return of unprocessed trauma, is less rigidly organized by the single "truth" of "Alas, how easily things go wrong and life is never the same again" (MacDonald, 1858). The experience that life *can* be the same again, and that relational ruptures can be repaired (see Safran and Muran, 2000) without losing the secure continuity of the attachment bond, begins to be trusted as reliable.

The Therapeutic Action of Psychoanalysis

In this context, analytic technique, regardless of the school of thought from which it is derived, is useful only if it is not held as objectively "correct." Historically, analysts influenced by a British sensibility (e.g., Winnicott, 1949b; Heimann, 1950; Racker, 1953, 1957) or by their work with severe psychopathology (e.g., Sullivan, 1954) have organized their use of countertransference and their use of themselves around the patient's need for safety; they have viewed interaction (as well as their own self-revelation) principally as a threat to impinge on a patient's internal reality. The British Middle School, for example, gives greatest emphasis to patients' being particularly vulnerable to their analysts' becoming "dangerous" (Winnicott, 1963) by forcing dissociated not-me concepts into them for which there is not yet a transitional linkage to their "imaginative" capacity (see Rycroft, 1962). At the other end of the continuum are analysts who emphasize the importance of a more interactive—sometimes systematically so—use of themselves (e.g., Little, 1951; Tauber, 1954; Levenson, 1972, 1983; Ehrenberg, 1992). These analysts tend to centralize the value of self-revelation of the analyst's own subjective experience within the analytic field.

Each of these schools of thought represents a different subjective sensibility that generates its own "technique," giving the analyst an internally valid place to stand when subjectivities collide (see Friedman, 1988). It is only when an analyst holds his preferred stance as more than simply a personal sensibility—that is, as Technique with a capital T—that he forecloses his ability to facilitate intersubjectivity and prevents his patient from using him optimally. The analyst must accept that his stance (no matter what it is) will eventually be met by a statement from some self-state of the patient that "This is not me" and "You are not understanding who I am and what I need."

My view is that following a particular school of thought provides a valid frame for treatment, but that the analyst's use of his subjective experience, above and beyond his theoretical loyalties, is the critical factor in promoting a patient's self-growth. In its most general (and, admittedly, oversimplified) form, my contention is that the analyst's use of his own subjective experience fosters a reciprocal process that, in turn, frees the patient's active involvement with the states of mind of the other. This reciprocity allows a patient to experience his self-states that are dissociated but are being held in the mind of an other. The heart of the work at that point is negotiation between subjectivities, not interpretation. Fonagy and Target (1995) speak to the diminished emphasis on interpretation in such a conception of therapeutic action:

> Interpretations may remain helpful but their function is certainly no longer limited to the lifting of repression and the addressing of distorted perceptions and beliefs. . . . Their goal is the reactivation of the patient's concern with mental states, in himself and in his object. We believe that the developmental help offered by the active involvement of the analyst in the mental functioning of the patient, and the reciprocal process of the patient becoming actively involved in the analyst's mental state, has the potential to establish this reflection and gradually to allow the patient to do this within his own mind. . . . The critical step may be the establishment of the patient's sense of identity through the clarification of the patient's perception of the analyst's mental state. . . . It seems that gradually this can offer a third perspective, opening up a space for thinking between and about the patient and the analyst [pp. 498–499].

Pathological dissociation can be said to exist to the degree that the patient cannot simultaneously access self-states that might modulate the "truth" being held by the self-state that is the "real me" in the moment. He is like the panda in my opening anecdote—he "eats shoots and leaves." What we want is that his self-experience become more complex by becoming safely enough linked to other self-states. And what we discover is that this linkage comes about through a process by which the patient uses the analyst's mind as a way of enlarging his own. We also discover that in many patients, perhaps all, this process will entail coming to recognize one's sequestered self-states as legitimate aspects of "me." In other words, the patient needs to get in touch with his "gorillas," such as they may be. In this sense, what I would call a gorilla is not necessarily a mischievous self-state like that of the gorilla in Hazen's book; it can be any self-state that has been disconfirmed, invalidated, or traumatically threatened because it is "making a mess" in the eyes of a significant other to whom the patient was attached in a primary way that defined his or her core sense of continuity as "I." To the degree that the attachment bond, and thus core self-continuity, was compromised by the patient's *particular* "gorilla," that gorilla lives out its existence as a not-me experience.

F. Scott Fitzgerald once wrote, "The test of a first-rate intelligence was the ability to hold two opposing ideas in your head at the same time and maintain the ability to keep functioning" (cited in Jefferson, 1999).[2] Although Fitzgerald was not much interested in the factors that might *impair* this talent, his observation was particularly astute as it applies to the effect of pathological dissociation on mental functioning. Someone who cannot, as Fitzgerald put it, "maintain the ability to keep functioning" while holding two opposing ideas in his head at the same time constricts the use of his mental capacity in a manner that not only can come across as a defect in intelligence, but is also interpersonally confounding to those with whom the person is engaged in relationships. In these terms, the goal of treatment is to facilitate an ability to hold two or more opposing ideas in one's head.

Independent of theoretical persuasion, almost every seriously held theory of therapeutic action holds that the creation of an authentic analytic experience depends on whether or not the analytic situation is able to facilitate and support a sufficient level of transferential intensity to sustain enactments and nourish their cognitive processing. Both classically and postclassically, this result is brought about through a treatment structure that permits the continuity of the ongoing *process* to become the most powerful organizing experience in the patient's internal world. Thus, regardless of the specific real-life issues with which a

---

[2] I thank Fran Scheff for calling the article to my attention.

patient enters treatment, there is an increasing shift in the patient's experience toward his own mind as an object of attention. That is why clinical psychoanalysis, regardless of the theory on which it is based, invariably has some "frame" that organizes and structures what an analyst does while being an analyst. The analytic stance deemed most appropriate to make maximum use of the relationship as the most powerful medium of therapeutic action—that is, to support an optimal level of transferential intensity—is thus linked directly to how a particular theory conceptualizes and implements its frame. But to make matters even more complicated, most of us know from our own clinical work that, within any single theoretical approach, the meaning of "useful analytic behavior" varies from patient to patient in the work of any one analyst. This is not to say that the effort to specify the relational source of therapeutic action is useless, but, rather, that any attempt to specify it abstractly is bound to collide with the reality that its specificity is tied to the uniqueness of each analytic dyad and thus to the unpredictability of the moment to moment context that gives it shape. Consider, for instance, the following clinical example.

"Helen"

Helen was a patient in her mid-30s whose history of severe trauma had led to a reliance on dissociation so longstanding that she was unable to experience herself with a past that felt like hers, a present that she breathed life into, or a future that she could imagine. To ensure that the protective function of her dissociative solution remained reliable, she had defined the scope of her existence in a manner so limiting that she allowed herself almost no interchange with the outside world other than her work. When not in her office, she secluded herself in her small apartment, saw few friends, had virtually no social life, and was sexually inactive.

To disguise her identity, I have given her the name Helen in the vignette, but the quotation marks placed around it in the section title are not meant simply to signal that the name is fictional. Primarily, the quotation marks are intended to convey the ambiguity surrounding the reality of her identity as it existed in her inner world. Her given name was Helena but everyone called her Helen, a name she loathed, and, in spite of what she described as clearly voiced objections, her family and friends continued to call her Helen. None of this would be worth mentioning here were it not that her despised name, like her despised life, was a diminutive. She experienced both of them as not simply *smaller* than the real thing, but as shrunken facsimiles of the person she was supposed to be. When I first met her, she could barely contain her unprocessed rage at knowing that she was somehow being shortchanged as a human being but did not know whom to blame or if she even had the right to do so. "Was I just born this way, different from everyone else, or could I have been a whole person if only . . .?" Further, she insisted that I refer to her only as Helen, because "that's who I really am. Helena is what I was *supposed* to be." And so I did. For more than five years I called her Helen.

Ironically, Helen was herself a therapist and was endowed with an extraordinary gift for healing others despite her own pain, which never went away. Being a therapist, she was aware that I wrote, and she made a point to read my work as it appeared in print. I was never quite sure of what she did with what she read because the impact of experiencing me as part of the "world out there" was held by different parts of herself in different domains of reality. I was privy only to those parts that were least likely to threaten the fragility of the attachment that she felt was always in danger of being irreparably broken. In this respect, her image of me called to mind the words of Kathryn Harrison's (1997) protagonist in *The Kiss:* "I cannot remember a time that I was not aware of my mother's fragility. It's part of what has convinced me of her surpassing worth, the way only the best teacups break easily" (p. 50). Helen, behind the scenes, did indeed take care of me as if I were a fragile teacup.

After about five years of work we reached the point where Helen was able to hold in conscious awareness the existence of moments when her thinking just stopped, when her sense of reality faded, and she was able to reflect on her own dissociative processes and the functions they served. Not surprisingly, she also began to share with me aspects of herself that were now safer to allow into our relationship, including her growing ability to make self-reflective use of some of my writings in a way that was dramatically different from her storing them away as a protection against discovering their existence unexpectedly and being helpless to prevent their assault on her mind.

On this particular day, she arrived for her session filled with undisguised enthusiasm—a state that caught me completely unprepared, as I had not before been allowed to be part of it. I blurted out both my surprise and delight, but withheld my confusion in the hope that she would not see it. She responded, however, with a mischievous smile. She said that, for a change, it was I who had to deal with being shocked and that it made her feel strong to have read my writing without feeling she was doing something bad either to me or to herself. "In fact," she went on, "I'm enjoying the disturbed look on your face; there's something about it that makes me feel closer to you." She then reported having just read my latest paper, thought about it, and experienced an exciting insight about herself, as she put it, "without help from *anyone*."

As I began to reply, I found myself aware of speaking from a strange state of mind in which I felt more like her patient than her therapist—a state that, uncannily, was as physical as it was mental. I clearly was not "myself"—at least not any of the selves I was accustomed to being when I was with her. Oddly, I was not anxious about the shift in our roles and was even aware of feeling "held" by her self-confident recognition of what was taking place. In retrospect, I am pretty sure that this was part of the reason I had not been anxious—*it felt good.* Is this, I wondered, what she is like in her own office? If so, small wonder her patients get better. As I allowed myself more and more to trust my "unboundaried" feeling of intimacy, I could sense that my own spontaneity was being matched by a new level of spontaneity in her and that we were, in fact, experiencing aspects of one another's selves with an immediacy that had not before been possible. Later, when reflecting on how much I had enjoyed the moment, I recalled a remark by Haley (1993) about Carl Whitaker: "He most enjoyed a treatment session when he could say afterwards, 'I never did that before'" (p. 15).

The paper that Helen had read was "Playing with Boundaries," which now forms chapter 3 in this book. Recall that I included a personal vignette illustrating the normal ability of the human mind (in this case my own) to go beyond the usual boundaries that define what we experience as "reality" and to hold multiple states of consciousness simultaneously if existing conditions are facilitating. I had written about how the room, because it was oval, had no corners and of how the unexpected absence of corners allowed me to play with reality.

"When I read it," Helen said excitedly, "I felt like I was in it myself. I knew what you were talking about because I could feel it. And I wasn't even scared. I could even feel that circles are *better* than squares. Corners stop you, so they're safe. If you can't go around the corner you can't be hit by the flood of bad stuff that is waiting there to get you, so you have to start all over again each time there's a corner. It's like beginning life over and over a thousand times a day. But now I'm realizing that this is why I can't live my life. The corners stop me as though each moment is another ending. It protects me from the bad stuff that might be around the corner but each time I start over I also lose what came before, so everything I do is for nothing.

"But my real insight isn't just that; its that I now understand why I'm always making pronouncements to you about how I'm going to be different but never act on them. It's a way that when I'm with *you* I can get past the corner but still be me—the me that's safe. While I'm with you in a session, what's around the corner is safe because you're there; so I make a pronouncement about how I'm going to be different tomorrow because today isn't tomorrow. But then when tomorrow comes I'm all by myself and I can't remember ever feeling safe because the corners are really still there."

Not long after, Helen asked that I call her Helena because she wanted to see how it felt. And so it went.

The Dizziness of Intersubjectivity

Attempting to talk about what happened during this session in terms of therapeutic action leads me to repeat my belief that its definition is tied to the uniqueness of each given analytic dyad and thus to the experience of unpredictability and surprise inherent in the moment-to-moment context that gives it shape. Why surprise? In 1936 Theodor Reik suggested that there is no "royal road" to the unconscious, and if there is indeed a road at all, it is to be discovered most vividly, not in dreams as Freud (1900, p. 608) suggested, but rather in the dizzying experience of surprise, for surprise allows an analyst to find something new that will then create its own technique. Translating Reik's insight into postclassical language, one might say that the road to the patient's unconscious is created nonlinearly by cumulative surprises. I would add that the royal road of surprise is no less surprising even if the analyst's own unconscious participation is abetting its construction while he thinks he is simply observing it.

In this regard, Jessica Benjamin (1995) makes the valuable and interesting point that

> intersubjectivity refers to the capacity of the mind to directly register the responses of the other. It is affected by whether the other recognizes what we have done and is likewise charged with recognizing the other's acts. Whatever breakdowns in recognition occur, as they inevitably do, the primary intersubjective condition . . . is that of experiencing the dizziness *together* [p. 183].

The power of this session with Helen was, in fact, located within the experience of dizziness to which Benjamin refers—an experience Helen and I each had, in different ways, as we made contact through self-states that permitted a temporary suspension of our familiar "corners." Benjamin draws on the work of the French philosopher George Bataille (1932, 1962), whose work addressed deeply, issues pertaining to death, merger, and the limits of intersubjectivity.[3] These reflections led Bataille to ask a penetrating question, the answer to which I believe determines how far a patient and analyst are ultimately able to go together: "Without doing violence to our inner selves, are we able to bear a negation that carries us to the farthest bounds of possibility?" (p. 25). How long can we hold the "dizziness" of intersubjectivity under stressful interpersonal conditions without having to dissociate some part of ourselves—what Benjamin (1995) calls the "breakdown into complementarity of doer and done to" (p. 185)—so that other parts of our selves may live.

What Bataille (1962, pp. 12–13) offered is no easy solution, but it does describe for me what feels most real in my own clinical experience. Bataille said, "I cannot refer to this gulf which separates us without feeling that this is not the whole truth of the matter. It is a deep gulf, and I do not see how it can be done away with. Nonetheless, we can experience its dizziness together. It can hypnotize us" (quoted by Benjamin, 1995, p. 182). I would say that his words come pretty close to the heady, hypnotic pleasure I felt in surrendering my fixed role as therapist, in suddenly experiencing a moment of intersubjective contact that had been foreclosed, in crossing the gulf that, as Bataille put it, the "isolates must cross to meet one another."

Reality and Shame

What does it mean to say that the analyst "works" with dissociation? If the experiential self—the boy and his gorilla—is indeed dissociated, where is it located so that you are not only "observing" it but often speaking to it? My answer is that the world of internal objects is as

---

[3] I want to acknowledge my personal debt to Karol Marshall, who first pointed me in the direction of Bataille's writing, and whose two essays (1996, 1998) elucidating Bataille's philosophy have informed my awareness that that the "unthinkable is always at war with coherence, identity, thought and theory" (Marshall, 1998, p. 7).

observable as that of real people, provided the field of observation is defined as intersubjective rather than as simply interactive and provided the analyst does not choose to avoid being pulled into the enactment of what is unsayable in words but exists as felt meaning. If the analyst does not avoid this pull, then the "observable" data are coming from the interface between the analyst's own shifting self-states and those of his patient. As an analyst, if you allow yourself to enter and participate in this field, you come to know the boy and his gorilla through what you are feeling, what you are thinking, and what you are doing, as long as you do not try (indefinitely) either to mask or minimize your *own* gorilla's part in the creation of this reality or attempt unilaterally to deliver meaning as if it were objective truth. A new kind of reality—a reality *both* "shadow" and "substance" (Bromberg, 1993)—can then begin to take shape and previously incompatible domains of self begin to coexist.

I do not take for granted the presence of intrapsychic conflict or even a patient's capacity to experience it, much less to reflect on it. Even for so-called good analytic patients, I believe that working in the transference is a matter of the degree to which the patient is able to access aspects of self-experience that have been dissociated. For those patients in whom the effect of trauma on the organization of psychic structure has been most pervasive, the reflective ability to work in the here and now is least likely to be there at the beginning. These patients tend to use each session to process the nonprocessible experience from prior sessions. That is, each session is a kind of commentary (through derivatives, dreams, and enactments) on the preceding session or sessions. The analysis often proceeds that way for a long time, the analyst's job being to try to enable the processing to be safer and safer so that the patient's tolerance for potential flooding of affect goes up; that is, the threshold for autonomic hyperarousal increases. Consequently, the patient can increasingly process, in the moment, the full complexity of the relational experience (in all its vivid here-and-nowness) with less and less need for dissociative processes.

Muller (1996) wrote about a patient who self-mutilated by scratching into her wrist the "gang name of a biker boyfriend, oriented so that the name faced the viewer as if it were a tag claiming ownership of her body and its pleasures, an identity tag for her self as the object of someone else's desire" (p. 85). I argue that sadomasochistic relationships are, in general, a perfect example of dissociative self-definition. When a person is behaving either masochistically or sadistically with regard to an other, the event often feels to the person, in the moment, as if it had a life of its own because some aspect of the person's self is watching the event and experiencing it as if at a movie. What I have found often described is something like, "I could stop it if I wanted to—I don't have to do this. But how he is seeing me now is right. I could end it if I chose to, but I can't/won't. If I did, I wouldn't be me any longer."

Because trauma cannot be narratively represented in memory, traumatic experience is unsymbolized by language and therefore cannot be spoken "about" as material. Attempts to do so invoke a reliving of it as part of the telling, which for the patient also involves the activation of intense shame that is typically dissociated to preserve the bond with the analyst. One of the most difficult aspects of the clinical approach to dissociated self-states, shame makes the most demands on the relationship; the analyst is frequently unable to recognize the patient's high level of shame because it too is dissociated. The reason that seemingly repeated enactments are struggled with over and over again in the therapy is that the analyst is over and over pulled into the same enactment to the degree he is not attending sufficiently to the arousal of shame. The patient is going to hear anything else the analyst is saying as though he really means, "The pain you are experiencing now is no big deal; it is just from the past; what you feel now isn't really happening now," translated by the patient into "You'll get over it; *I'm* not causing it." Even if the analyst is not feeling any of those things initially, the odds are that sooner or later he will be. If the analyst does not respond with genuine personal concern to the patient's pain at that moment, the patient will almost always experience his or her own pain as toxic to the analyst.

Nathanson's (1992) description of this therapeutic dilemma is worth considering here: "When affect is piled on affect, one magnifying the other continuously, all in the context of a social or interpersonal situation forbidding surcease or solace relevant to the affects really involved, the resulting affect density can be unbearable" (p. 424). He specifically identifies shame as a cause of such an unbearable escalation of affect in treatment:

> Central to treatment is the understanding that the patient, stuck alone in the shame experience, is unable to return to normal interpersonal interaction unaided. Therapeutic passivity—the decision to remain silent in the face of a humiliated, withdrawn patient—will always magnify shame because it confirms the patient's affect-driven belief that isolation is justified [pp. 324–325].

Nathanson's conceptualization of dissociated shame as a crucial component of enactment contributes to our understanding of the "unbearable" quality of such symptoms as "feeling like my head is going to explode from inside" when these symptoms occur during a session. Shame is also present in those patients who "disappear" during a session when what is being discussed touches unprocessed early trauma. Such moments enact an interpersonal situation with the therapist that mirrors the original event in which it was impossible to manage the pain within a relationship *before* the pain became unbearable and *before* they could no longer imagine surcease or solace.

A brief clinical vignette will put into high relief the reason I feel an inseparability between the therapeutic action of psychoanalysis and working with dissociation as a relational phenomenon. I have chosen this vignette precisely because the patient was not "classically" dissociative: that is, dissociation did not signal itself through dramatic symptoms but rather through the kind of characterological patterns of relatedness, at once concrete and elusive, with which we are all familiar.

James

James was an actor, successful, highly intelligent, witty, and chronically depressed as far back as he could remember. He was also a man of great warmth, and I, like almost everyone else in his life, was very fond of him even though in some ineffable way I was not sure I really knew him. He had been in analysis with me for about four years and had grown significantly during this time in both his personal life and professional life. As he was nearing the end of treatment—a seemingly mutual decision—he was telling me about a check he had unexpectedly received from his professional organization, which, besides other functions, monitors films on television and makes sure that the performers whose movies are shown get paid each time they appear. As I was listening to James's story, I found myself toying with the fantasy of how great it would be if, every time he had a positive life experience to which our work together had contributed, his inner world would be monitored by this organization and he would then automatically think about me. I would not exactly be getting "residuals" on my successful interventions—but something not too far from that!

Although this fantasy seemed humorous to me, even at that moment I could feel it connecting with something about him that was not funny, but I did not know what it was. Yes, I was going to miss him when he terminated, but my feeling was more than that. It had something to do with a need to stay alive in his mind after he was gone. I shared the fantasy with James and asked if he had any feelings or thoughts of his own that might relate to it. Haltingly, and with a degree of shame I had not seen in him before, he began to cry. He revealed that the need I had just described feeling in myself was one he had lived with all his life—a need that was still there and that he has been too ashamed to admit to anyone, including me. It could never change anyway, he said—it was simply a piece of childish irrationality, a wish to be so important that he could not be forgotten. We had already talked about one level of his wish—his seemingly unquenchable need for fame and recognition—but he was always too afraid to reveal the part of himself that cried in bed at night because no one knew how alone and scared he was. He was sure that, anyway, no one who knew it would believe it and certainly could never *really* know what it was like because he was so successful.

He allowed that he was feeling more and more empty and cut off as termination was approaching, but he said he believed this was just a natural reaction to ending and he never would have said anything if I had not revealed my fantasy. He said that he had told me about the residual check so that I would feel good about how much I had helped him be successful and so that when he left I would have good feelings about him. I told him that I did feel good about helping him be successful, but that my personal reaction to the story was more complex than just feeling good. I also felt something I was not used to feeling—something that had been James's constant companion. I told him I felt that, when he left, I would somehow disappear because I would disappear from his mind forever and that I felt a need to keep that from happening by a fantasy in which he would be forced to think about me—like his own wish to be so important that he could not be forgotten. I said that it was as if, at that moment, I could feel in myself a bereft part of him that had never been able to speak in our sessions, and perhaps this was the only way I could ever really hear that voice—by knowing, at least in a small way, what it personally felt like to look strong but to feel in danger of disappearing.

The termination phase did continue longer than either of us had anticipated, and it led to places that neither of us could have imagined before that session. James's "gorilla" had joined us in the room, more and more "really real" to James, because James's gorilla at last became "really real" to me and to my own gorilla.

PART II

COLLISIONS AND NEGOTIATIONS

5

Potholes on the Royal Road

Or Is It an Abyss?[1]

Jay Greenberg (1995, p. 6) has offered the view that "little of the familiar foundation of psychoanalysis remains unchallenged," and that "virtually all the traditional conceptual, clinical, and epistemological premises that guided psychoanalysis through its first hundred years are being called into question." If this statement is accurate, and I for one believe it is, where does that leave psychoanalytic authors now that they lack a theoretical "mainstream" to support or oppose? We are gradually eliminating what for some has been their greatest dread, and for others a call to arms: the potential for being deemed "unanalytic." It is becoming meaningless for an author to be called unanalytic when we cannot really agree on what it means to *be* analytic. If we less often write to present marvelous new "evidence," clinical or theoretical, that supports or undermines the validity of one sacred theory or another, perhaps the real test of an analyst's courage these days is not, like the opening lines of *Star Trek,* "to boldly go where no one has gone before" but, rather, to boldly go where *everyone* has gone before–to the office. Let our writing reveal, in our own clinical voices, the details of what happened in a particular treatment with a particular patient, in spite of what we did and in spite of our believing that we were doing it "right." Why does doing this take courage? The main reason, I suggest, is that some of the most clinically powerful material is what was unplanned by us when it took place. It can sometimes be a bit dicey to share what John Klauber (1980) called, too benignly I think,

[1]An earlier version of this chapter was published in *Contemporary Psychoanalysis,* 2000, 36:5–28. Adapted by permission.

> those moments that present themselves to the analyst spontaneously, and occasionally even interpose themselves *to his surprise* just when he was about to say something else, adding the dimension of a human encounter over and above that of professional and client working together to solve problems of transference and countertransference [p. 197, italics added].

Spontaneity and surprise! Sometimes these are the gateway to our most pleasurable moments of intimacy with our patients; sometimes they are a Pandora's Box we wished at that moment had remained shut. But each contributes a life force to clinical psychoanalysis without which our work would be as unproductive and uncreative as painting by numbers. All told, I share the view of Steven Cooper (2000), who writes that "at its heart, the analytic process involves risking saying and feeling new things by both patient and analyst" (p. 195), things that will be surprising when they emerge.

The centrality of spontaneity and surprise to the psychoanalytic enterprise was, in fact, recognized and openly stated more than 60 years ago. In 1936, Reik made the startling suggestion (startling only because it was so far ahead of its time) that there is no "royal road" to the unconscious. If there is, indeed, a road at all, Reik argued, it is to be discovered most vividly not in dreams, as Freud (1900) suggested, but, rather, in the experience of surprise, for surprise allows an analyst to find something new that will then create its own technique. As Reik (1936) put it,

> an analyst ought to have learned in the course of his practice that his own unconscious drags all kinds of things from the darkness. . . . It is not necessary for an analyst to be constantly occupied with his plan of campaign during the process. If he is a good psychologist, the blind urge within himself will teach him the right way [p. 91].

Reik, in other words, was proposing that what Freud (1900) called the royal road (p. 608) is not something that is traveled by the analyst, a solitary and objective interpreter of the patient's associations as observed text. Nor is the patient's unconscious a destination that is reached as a goal, like the pot of gold at the end of a rainbow. The road to the patient's unconscious is created, and it is created nonlinearly by the analyst's own unconscious participation in its construction even while he thinks he is simply observing it. As Reik well knew, the experience of surprise in an analysis is an event that is not just intrapsychic but inherently dyadic.

In contemporary terms, some aspect of what is unconscious in the patient is always present in what we call enactment, an intrinsic dimension of the ongoing field of shared affect, thought, and interaction constituting the analytic relationship. It is the enacted piece of each partner's impact on the other that makes the royal road a bumpy one and makes it all too evident that the raw material from which the road is constructed is drawn from the unconscious not only of the patient but also of the analyst. Smoothing the bumps and paving the potholes—that is, bringing the bumps and potholes from the level of enactment to the level of conscious perception and conscious thought—is at best a trying job, and with some patients it is an uncomfortably sweaty mess that stretches to its limit the analyst's capacity to endure it. Why do we have to go through all this? (Sometimes when I ask myself this question what I really mean is, "Who needs it?") The answer I have arrived at after many years of climbing out of potholes is that, like it or not, an analysis without potholes is, in the final analysis, a pseudoanalysis.

Out of everything I was taught while in training and learned in the years thereafter, I think what has most shaped my day-to-day work as a practicing clinician is the continuing echo of Harry Stack Sullivan's apocryphal, though often quoted, wish that God spare him from a therapy that goes well. This was Sullivan's way of dramatizing that a successful treatment does not merely perambulate smoothly along while you enjoy watching your patient grow. It is the bumps in the royal road—what Reik (1936) called surprises—that provide the greatest leverage for therapeutic action. They are the most powerful ongoing source of novelty, unpredictability, and spontaneity—the true wellsprings of the unconscious. They are also, however, the source of the greatest potential difficulty between analyst and patient because surprise sometimes crosses the threshold into shock, the harbinger of potential trauma. This threat, I suggest, is what leads to the stressful messiness of certain enactments, an inevitability at one point or another in most analyses, but an inevitability that for some patients can escalate into increasingly problematic enactments, long impasses, eternal therapeutic stalemates, and, often, terminations that both parties know are really escapes.

I have found that when an analyst tries to describe his experience of what it is like to be in such a treatment crisis—on a dimension ranging from "hard work" to "Oh, my God!"—key among the host of variables shaping this experience is almost always the degree to which early trauma was an issue. With some patients, those on the "easier" end of the continuum, as you both lurch along the royal road together you seem to be encountering an array of bumps or even potholes, some feeling worse than others, some lasting quite a while, but none feeling as if they will never end. The analyst is usually in touch with a sense of vulnerability, and with his own limitations, but he does not typically feel as if his very efforts to find a solution are in themselves putting his patient, himself, and the treatment more and more in jeopardy and leading things inexorably toward a yet unknown disaster.

But there is a different group of patients—those who typically have a history of severe trauma. With a patient in this group, the unrelenting repetitiveness of certain enactments is more likely to eventuate in the analyst's feeling that his patient is getting closer and closer to the edge of an abyss and that he himself is moving in the same direction. These patients do not experience the escalating problem between themselves and the analyst as simply bumps in the road—as "just" potholes. It is quite a different story for them, and, as it unfolds, the analyst's view of their relationship—and, worse, his very experience of reality—is destabilized in a manner that makes the term stressful seem grossly understated.

To the degree that such a patient hears the analyst trying to frame the event as if it were just a pothole, most gestures that would be felt by other patients as an effort to be therapeutically supportive—such as, "I'm pretty sure that things between us will get better eventually"—will make a patient in this group only feel worse. The reason, from my perspective, is that the analyst is unknowingly triggering increased feelings of emotional abandonment because he is dissociating an aspect of the patient's here-and-now experience in the room: the overwhelming pain and shame held by that part of the patient's self that is silently screaming for recognition and relief. At such moments we find ourselves groping for the "right" words. We try out our "best" interpretations. We mutter things about repetition of early trauma. We hint at parental neglect, maybe even parental abuse too early to remember. And, of course, there is always the likelihood of parental depression! Who hasn't had at least one depressed parent? All to no avail—the patient's silent scream goes on and gets louder.

"But it *must* be the parents' fault; surely it isn't mine. Look how hard I'm trying!" Over and over we are refused the privilege of passing the buck to the parents, those shadowy figures from the past into whom we wish desperately to transfer some of the heat from the not so shadowy fix we are in right now. The patient's anguish seems to be filling the room, and we are feeling more and more hopeless about ever finding a way to assuage it or, at least, help contain it.

A bulimic patient, whose dissociated acts of purging were starting to become a more fully conscious experience, began simultaneously to recall and to refuse to talk about experiences of abuse at the hands of her parents. She first described it as "having a pebble in my shoe that I can never get rid of." As she talked about what the experience of the pebble felt like, she began to recognize that the self holding the secret is able to keep the secret only because it is no more than a pebble. Feeling the pain in the room with me made it real "out there"; it magnified the pain, which threatened to betray the perpetrator and, of course, that part of herself that was identified with the perpetrator. Accusing a person to whom she was attached became tolerable only if the accusation came from an inadvertent not-me betrayal of the family secret through her symptoms. But she felt unbearable shame at betraying and hurting this person out of an ego-syntonic need to express her own reality with full awareness. "Why would I want to hurt the people I feel closest to?" she agonized. I, too, felt her agony, and I was beset with my own doubt–I wondered if my "help" was inflicting needless pain, hurting the person to whom at that moment I felt closest. Ridden with feelings of disloyalty at betraying not only her parents but also that part of herself for whom "goodness" was shaped by protecting the family secrets, she screamed angrily at me during a session following a particularly violent night of purging, *"You'll never get me to stop vomiting–I'll never spill the beans!"*

Along with many other contemporary theorists, I see the issue of affect containment as critical, but in my own view, as I have touched on in earlier chapters, the most powerful affect a person is unable to modulate is the experience of shame.[2] The patient is feeling overwhelmed not only by reliving such traumatic affects from the past as anger, fear, grief, sadness, and futility, but also by a dissociated here-and-now shame experience that is triggered by the analyst's lack of awareness and seeming indifference to the fact that his therapeutic "success" in bringing about the reliving of unprocessed traumatic affect leaves his patient both

---

[2]I have found some particularly interesting ideas on the topic of shame in the early writing of Helen Lynd (1958) and in the more contemporary treatments of shame by Helen Block Lewis (1971, 1987), Michael Lewis (1992), Donald Nathanson (1992), Andrew Morrison (1987, 1989), and Alan Schore (1994).

needing relief and unable to communicate the need. As in the original trauma, the person from whom a soothing response is needed is the person least likely to offer it *on his own* because he is also the person whose behavior is *causing* the pain. In other words, in the act of trying to help his patient find a voice for dissociated parts of self through reliving unsymbolized affect in the here and now, the therapist becomes a *player* in what is being relived. He is enacting the role of the original "other," by placing the patient in a situation whereby their relationship and the attachment bond on which it depends has become more affectively complex and dangerous to the patient than can be safely contained as internal conflict within a single state of consciousness.

To the degree that the patient's dissociated shame caused by this unaddressed and unprocessed aspect of their ongoing interaction remains unrecognized by the analyst, the threat of potential retraumatization is experienced as looming larger and larger to the patient. Because the patient will by and large tend to dissociate this "neglectful" aspect of the therapist, the therapist's own dissociative solution is reinforced, and he usually does not "get it" until matters escalate to the point where he is forced to feel it through the enactment, whether or not he wants to. The patient, from this vantage point, has simply employed what has come to be her most reliable response to a situation in which the person whose behavior is causing the pain is the same person from whom the patient needs soothing. It is a defense against an experience of being flooded with a level of affective hyperarousal that threatens the stability and continuity of selfhood in those persons for whom self-continuity remains endangered by the unprocessed residue of traumatic aspects of early object attachment.

The experienced pull toward an "abyss" in those patients for whom an abyss is a dissociated reality is due to the fact that the patient's and the analyst's dissociative processes continue to accelerate unless the analyst "wakes up" and begins to experience consciously the entirety of the situation. For the analyst, the feeling that the nightmare will "never end no matter what we do" is what makes it feel subjectively an invasion of his mental stability. For the patient, trying to talk *about* the nightmare has the horrifying effect of making it worse. She cannot safely talk "about" her here-and-now experience because its lack of symbolic representation will lead to *additional* associated shame no matter how much "holding" the therapist does. In the act of talking *about* it she will feel it as increasingly taking her over and will feel shamed by her own desperate need for recognition of this shame from the person with her, whose help is, in a sense, what is causing the pain to increase. To the degree that this need for relief through recognition is unmet—and it is invariably unmet because of its paradoxical nature[3]—it further triggers her shame that the person to whom she is talking experiences her as inflicting her need on *him,* and she thus enacts her experience that her need for soothing is shameful. She will take any and every sign, especially the analyst's "analytic" stance, as evidence that he is repelled by her unreasonable need to be soothed from the pain caused by the helpful thing they are doing together. Her experience is of being left alone in her distress (see Nathanson, 1992, pp. 324–325) and that it is her own fault.

The analyst is, of course, in an impossible bind because he cannot "do" anything about it. No matter what he tries, he is more and more taken over by the intensity of an invisible assault on his own sense of self-validity. Experiencing the pain and causing the pain begin to merge, and his escalating failure to *do* something about the patient's pain gradually leads him to *become,* in fact, the person that patient already experiences him to be. The analyst becomes immersed, dissociatively, in an effort to ward off his own shame, as if he were being covered with something ugly of which he feels uncannily a part. As he begins unwittingly to lose his boundaries, he becomes a part of the patient's shame dynamic.

The experience is not unfamiliar to most analysts. You feel the patient getting worse and worse right in front of your eyes. You cannot do anything about it, but you cannot not *try* to do something about it. The more you try, the more you feel as if you yourself are toxic and that it is the patient's pain that is making you that way. Your increased efforts to rescue yourself from the shame caused by this violation of your professional selfhood—to find some "correct" therapeutic posture—makes your patient ever more certain that she is overloading you with her awful stuff and that once again she is too much for anybody to bear.

As a rule, the therapist, in his desperation to find a solution, unwittingly perpetuates and often increases the patient's shame, because, through his efforts to get rid of his own negative affect by getting rid of *hers,* the patient can feel the analyst becoming ever more alienated from her. She knows experientially that he is unable to just be with her. And, indeed, this is so; he is unable to be with her without feeling contaminated by his own dissociated shame for causing the pain—his

---

[3]See Pizer (1992) for an illuminating discussion of paradox and its distinction from conflict.

warded-off experience of himself as hurtful, sadistic, or indifferent. It is only when the analyst "awakens" from his own dissociation that he is sufficiently freed from the enactment to address and process with his patient their respective contributions to it and the core affective issue it masks—the shadow of the abyss and its threat to selfhood and sanity. As the use of dissociation diminishes, there is, happily, a corresponding decrease both in behavior that we have come to call "acting-out" and in the repetitive treatment crises that evoke the shadow of the abyss.

The Real and the Really Real

In response to something festering in the treatment relationship for too long a time, however, the thought of psychosis can arise in a form that begins to penetrate the therapist's very being. This will happen despite the therapist's awareness that most traumatized patients, including patients diagnosed as borderline, will as a rule give the therapist a lot of latitude to "screw things up" interactively without their traveling too far south of the border. The reason an actual fall into the abyss seldom takes place is that a dissociative mental structure is designed to prevent trauma from occurring by always anticipating it. The felt danger to sanity is if the trauma fails to be anticipated and hits unexpectedly—by "surprise." So the scenario of escape from potential trauma is played out over and over with the therapist, as if the patient were back in the original trauma, which one part of the self, indeed, is. But this time there are other parts of the self "on call," watching to make sure they know what is going on so that no surprises occur, and poised to deal with the betrayal they know will happen.

Through this enacted scenario of escape from potential trauma, the patient relives miniversions of the original trauma with a hidden vigilance that protects her from having it hit without warning. Its effectiveness as an early warning system is dependent on the preservation of her dissociative mental structure, which is designed to preempt any potential for lasting trust, hope, or spontaneity. Thus, these patients seldom, if ever, actually fall into an abyss (nor does their therapist), but for a seriously traumatized patient the experience is frequently one of being dangerously "on the edge." So, I repeat, what makes all of this such a bloody mess is that, if the therapist does not allow himself to experience the danger as a real danger and protects himself indefinitely with thoughts like, "Oh, it's not going to happen because I know that traumatized patients, even 'borderline' patients, don't usually go crazy in therapy," then the patient will feel affectively abandoned, because experientially the abyss is really there and looms larger and larger. It is the difference between what I have come to call the "real" and the "really real," a distinction I raised in the previous chapter. For the patient, the abyss is really real. The analyst, to the extent that his theory gives him a place to anchor his sense of professional competency (and, of course, we all need such a place to stand), will not allow the abyss to seem really real until he absolutely has to.

Thus, until the analyst is forced to deal with the patient's experience as something that gradually permeates its way into his soul in spite of his theories and his logic, the iatrogenic threat of potential retraumatization escalates. This is why the royal road at that point is an abyss experientially for certain patients and why a pothole is not just a pothole. It is an abyss, even though the closeness to the edge is a retrospective falsification–a collapse of past, present, and future that is the hallmark of trauma. But it is not for the analyst to say that the abyss is false. As Davies (1996) has cogently put it, "It is not our task to impose meaning . . . but rather to stand ready to engage actively with the patients's internal self and object world and to recognize and confirm meaning when that meaning is offered to us within a shared context" (p. 216). Because the abyss is subjectively an abyss to an aspect of the patient's self that feels it as "really real," if we are personally to live with and know that part of who our patient is, the abyss must become a really real experience for the analyst too.

Using imagery that any analyst might well consider, Michael Greene (1954) discusses the work of the philosopher Georges Bataille:

> To assume what is not known is like the known, just not known yet, is to shirk an encounter with the radically unknown. . . . Knowledge is always from the outside, requiring a subject–object relationship. . . . inner experience attends to existence from within; it entails not knowledge of the abyss, but being in the abyss [p. 56].

And quoting Bataille (1932), the point is made explicit that "'communication' takes place only between two beings at risk–torn, suspended, and one and the other leaning over their nothingness" (Greene, p. 64).

Like it or not, we are often forced to experience the treatment as being in crisis, and we do not know what to do about it. Paul Russell

(1975) argued that treatment crises must occur in most analyses if the treatment is given a chance to develop, because a patient will choose the treatment crisis, even if it entails a potential rupture of the therapy relationship, to try to convey what is most important to him. A paradoxical situation will arise, Russell asserts, in which the need for some kind of understanding and containment is at its greatest and is least likely to occur. My own take on this seeming paradox is that it enacts, in essence, an attempt to force the analyst to repair the irreparable. The paradox is not simply a compulsion to repeat the past; it is a need to repair what is indeed irreparable, a frozen past. Of course, the past cannot literally be repaired, but it is only through the patient's determination that it be recognized and known by an other that the present can be repaired. That is to say, the past-as-present must come to be known by the analyst, who "hangs in" while being forced to go through the no-win situation of failing the patient most at those moments when he is trying hardest to be helpful.

In other words, the analyst's own repeated efforts to relieve his patient's distress must fail in order for the analyst to know the patient's experience for what it is. But knowing is not enough; the irreparable must somehow be repaired, and the only way the past-as-present can be repaired is within a relationship that repeats the failure of the past but somehow does more than repeat it. Something new must occur—something that has to emerge out of what patient and analyst do in an unanticipated way. Raising the spirit of Reik (1936) once more, we might think of this kind of unanticipated relational event as potentially a safe surprise,[4] a newly coconstructed space between spontaneity and safety.

---

[4]Edmund Burke (1757) considered the phenomenon of "safe shock" (see Edmundson, 1997, p. 30) to be a form of aesthetic experience associated with the "sublime." Burke (1757) wrote, "When danger or pain press too nearly, they are incapable of giving any delight, and are simply terrible; but at certain distances, and with certain modifications, they may be . . . delightful . . . [p. 86]. Whatever therefore is terrible . . . is sublime too . . . for it is impossible to look on anything as trifling or contemptible that may be dangerous [p. 101]. If the pain and terror are so modified as not to be actually noxious, if the pain is not carried to violence, and the terror is not conversant about the present destruction of the person . . . they are capable of producing delight; not pleasure, but a sort of delightful horror, a sort of tranquility tinged with terror. . . . Its highest degree I call *astonishment;* the subordinate degrees are awe, reverence, and respect . . . distinguished from positive pleasure" [p. 165].

The patient's potential for full aliveness slowly increases as the dread of retraumatization decreases and trust gradually finds its place as part of his ever-shifting configuration of the multiple self-states that embody the experience of me-ness. In my own metaphor, the patient can more resiliently "stand in the spaces" between realities and, in Stuart Pizer's (1998) metaphor, build bridges between dissociated self-states that formerly were islands of incompatible truth.

That is why, for an analysis to be more than a pseudoanalysis, the relationship must feel safe but not perfectly safe. If it were even possible for the relationship to be perfectly safe, which it is not, there would be no potential for safe surprises because it would never be surprising that the analyst was *not* behaving, as expected, like a bad early object. In fact, it is not unreasonable to offer this as a plausible explanation for why, historically, all attempts by analysts to cure patients through the technical stance of trying to be a good object have failed, including Ferenczi's mutual analysis (see Bromberg, 1994, pp. 262–263). A patient needs a human being as a partner, a human being who can accept (eventually) his own limitations and failings, and, most important, a human being who can tolerate not having seen his failings when they are pointed out. Only from an interchange between human beings can something new develop as a relational event. In other words, whether or not the abyss becomes a clinical issue, the work with *any* patient must leave space for "messes" and repair to occur, and, as most of us are aware, in analytic work there are plenty of such opportunities. No matter which school of thought organizes one's basic stance, the inherent structure of the analytic situation—the inevitable tension between the treatment frame and the human relationship—pulls for relational collisions. Enactments are what we count on to make the analysis of transference possible; it is only when seemingly unresolvable treatment crises emerge from enactments that we even question the role played by the relational collisions in the therapeutic action of psychoanalysis.

Repetition, Relational Repair, and "Safe Surprises"

I offer the view that what we experience as a treatment crisis takes place when an enactment begins to become personally problematic for the analyst by arousing feelings that are not comfortably containable within his basic professional stance. Such discomfort leads to the analyst's hypnoidal disconnection of consciousness from whatever aspect of the relationship is creating the problem by dissociating that part of himself that is already engaged in it. I have observed that treatment crises are regularly preceded and accompanied by this kind of hypnoidal dissociation in the analyst, in which a part of himself that is connecting to a discomfiting aspect of the patient does not allow awareness of this connection into his perception of what is taking place between them. Consciously, the analyst may feel bored; he may feel that there are "issues that can't be addressed yet"; he may be worried about his patient's "real life." Whatever he feels, he does not allow what is hypnoidally dissociated to inform the ways he is otherwise being with his patient. On this account, he is unable to be fully himself with his patient, and, to secure his dissociation, he increasingly tries to "manage" the relationship as a substitute for participating in it. His management efforts become directed, dissociatively, toward trying to restabilize himself by finding a "solution" to the disruption in the relationship, and trying to do so, of course, escalates the enactment.

The patient is trying, equally dissociatively, to force recognition of her own experience into the analyst through an enactment that leaves the analyst no place to stand except in his version of the same mess in which the patient is trapped. The felt crisis, one might say, occurs when the analyst is finally crowbarred by his patient out of whatever professional context of meaning he has been using to keep at bay the disjunctive affect held by his own dissociated self-state. The patient escalates her part of the enactment until the analyst cannot, despite his best efforts, comfortably maintain the professional frame he relies on to understand what is going on. Underneath all this lies the analyst's continuous hypnoidal dissociation from a part of himself.

So, from my perspective, a patient's need for repetition (the historical repetition compulsion) includes as a central element the need to get the other (in this case the analyst) to experience his own part in the treatment failure. That is, the patient requires that the analyst fruitlessly try to help until he is forced to recognize himself as failing her in the same way she was failed by her primary objects. In other words, the repetition of the crisis is fundamentally the enactment and reenactment of a failed communication that has the potential to become a successful communication if the oppressiveness of the repetition eventually affects the analyst's communication with his own internal objects and draws the analyst's inner world into the enactment. If this takes place, the crisis will make room for "something new" that will bridge past and present. Words will be allowed the opportunity to symbolize what is taking place between and within each partner in a way that is safe enough and immediate enough for the unsymbolized dynamics of the patient's early developmental trauma not simply to be repeated but to undergo repair in the process of repetition.

Highly relevant to this last point is Tronick and Weinberg's (1997) illuminating research finding that it is not affective synchrony between infant and caretaker that is the salient factor leading to sturdy personality development. Rather, "*reparation of interactive errors is the critical process of normal interactions that is related to developmental outcome rather than synchrony or positive affect per se*" (p. 65, italics added).

> With the experiential accumulation of successful reparations and the attendant transformation of negative affect into positive affect, the infant establishes a positive affective core. . . . Specifically, the infant develops a representation of him- or herself as effective, of his or her interactions as positive and reparable, and of the caretaker as reliable and trustworthy. These representations are crucial for the development of a sense of self that has coherence, continuity, and agency and for the development of stable and secure relationships [pp. 65–66].

The significance of this cannot be overemphasized because it bears directly on the *centrality of collisions and negotiations* as a nonlinear process that enables our patients to grow, heal, mature, change, or whatever words we prefer. An example of this occurred in a session recently reported to me in supervision. The patient had reached the point in treatment where words no longer seemed hollow and she could reflect on her experience of what had until then been possible only to enact. "I'm going through all this pain and you're sitting there looking so peaceful," she accused. "I feel like you have it to give and you're withholding it. You could make it better, but you won't. I feel victimized." Then her state abruptly shifted. "Now I feel like I ought to apologize for feeling that way about you. I don't blame you. Who would want to go through what I'm dumping on you! Maybe I shouldn't come for a couple of weeks until I stop being like this."

The analyst at that point offered his opinion that a part of her still needed to preserve her safety in believing that only by finding some way to soothe herself, all alone, could she keep the connection between them from being unexpectedly destroyed. He said he thought that she was feeling, as a real possibility, that he *might* finally give up on her and would protect himself from knowing this by sealing off (maybe behind an artificially "peaceful" façade). Then it would be all over, and she would not be able to change it and would feel it happened because of her. The patient then responded in a way that was for her something new—she genuinely linked a real present with a real past. "I get like this," she replied, "I got like this a lot as a kid. I would go to my room and hope someone would find me. But no one ever came."

The paradox is that, until the enactment begins to undergo at least some degree of repair, all the analyst's efforts to deal with the patient's communications at the level of words, conflict, verbal meaning, and genetic reconstruction are experienced by the patient as signs that the analyst really does not want to know. The patient's experience is that the analyst is offering empty words and concepts as a facsimile of recognition while leaving her even more alone and hopeless than before. The internal experience is that of being once more failed, and that there is no way to communicate this feeling without escalating the pressure on the relationship and increasing the kind of intense shame that for many people threatens the very existence of selfhood by threatening to destroy the self–other attachment bond on which selfhood depends. Sometimes repair, in fact, fails to happen and the treatment does indeed fail, but I have found that if the analyst hangs in, even if he is not sure he wants to learn or *can* learn, most treatment crises can undergo repair because he does learn.

Nevertheless, until repair begins, the analyst's professional stance, his most reliable asset, is no longer a flexible means of relating to his patient. It has become a dissociated self-state—a "truth" to which he clings at least for a time, thereby compromising his ability to experience other realities about their relationship and keeping himself and his patient isolated in their separate islands, treating each other as objects to be managed. To the degree that the patient's shame is not recognized and addressed by the analyst, the patient's already impaired capacity to bear shame is increasingly burdened. There is no way the patient can, on her own, point out the analyst's inattentiveness to the mental destabilization being caused by his efforts to help her talk about what needs to be talked about, because the analyst is attending only to the material (the content). In our vernacular, he is preserving the treatment frame. The patient responds by needing more and more to obliterate the treatment frame so as to make it impossible for the analyst to use words, ideas, and concepts as substitutes for *being* with her. The analyst then is gradually forced to feel at a personal level what it is like to be talking to someone and causing her this much pain by pursuing what he holds is right and necessary.

Not a pretty picture of an analyst, I suppose, and at those moments when we are most in touch with other parts of ourselves that are "nicer," it will seem to be an unfair caricature. The unfairness that we feel in the characterization, in fact, speaks to why the capacity to dissociate is simply part of being human and why patients and analysts in this regard are no different from one another. In a relationship we value and are trying to enhance, preserve, and protect, when we are simultaneously being forced to experience ourselves as damaging it or being damaged by it in a way that is too disjunctive with our self-experience at the moment, the mind's capacity to dissociate defensively goes into action. Trapped within a shared dissociative cocoon, the analyst is now being forced, little by little, to relinquish his confidence that what he is doing as an analyst has validity. The enactment will continue or escalate until the analyst runs out of ways to "understand" it and runs out of techniques to deal with it. A classical interpretive stance in such a situation is doomed to fail because it is frustrating without being validating. That is why such patients have been considered by some classical analysts to be unanalyzable. But what stance does work? Does any? And if not, why not?

Alec

Let me offer a clinical vignette that I hope makes thinking about these questions more interesting even if it does not provide answers. Imagine this scene. A patient I will call Alec[5] has been in analytic treatment with me for about one year, on the couch. He has come regularly to sessions four times a week and has for several months been more and more openly dissatisfied that the treatment is not moving fast enough. He cannot describe the details of what "fast enough" means or what the sessions feel like to him, other than to say it feels pointless to just lie on the couch and discuss how pointless the sessions feel. He also asserts that, despite his wishing not to come to sessions, he has every intention of staying in treatment even though he does not quite know why. All he does know is that he wishes he could get something out of it. I do not feel consciously uncomfortable with

[5]Interested readers are referred to an essay on a related theme—"Love and Hate in Psychoanalysis" (Bromberg, 1986)—in which an earlier version of this vignette appeared.

this development (yet) and maintain my curiosity in trying to address this new "material" with Alec. I use my own feelings as a source of data as well as my patient's difficulty in articulating his. I anticipate that as the transference–countertransference context becomes clearer, the "work" will move along.

No such luck! Alec arrives for a session and tells me that he has joined a group run by a student of Albert Ellis. He informs me, with more enthusiasm than he has shown in months, that he wants to see if he can help the analysis move along faster and expresses some concern, which he attributes to his own insecurity, that I might disapprove. I am taken completely off guard by this development and experience some anxiety and mild irritation, but I realize that whatever is going on between us, if it can be explored, might start to provide the clarity I have been hoping for. Determined to maintain empathic contact with my patient's viewpoint while inquiring into the interaction between us, I shift my perspective on the situation to one that sees Alec's behavior as an act of self-expression requiring respect and acknowledgment, though not necessarily agreement. I now feel able to encompass, at least consciously, what I experience as going on in myself at that moment, including my negative feelings toward Alec as simply more grist for the analytic mill, and I am more curious about my irritation than threatened by it. I say to myself something like, "Okay, Alec will either stay in this rational-emotive therapy group or he won't, but whatever he does we will have a chance to explore the meaning of it to him, along with his experience that I didn't invalidate the importance of it to him. Perhaps it is even 'good' that he goes." My anxiety and irritation are, at least for the moment, held in a professionally containable framework of meaning. I then ask Alec to tell me in more detail about the feeling of disapproval he is anticipating from me; I expect that his doing so may start to make some sense of both my own and my patient's feelings in the same context.

Alec, however, responds by saying that the additional cost of the group makes him now unable to continue paying for four sessions per week, at least for the next year, and he is going to have to cut back to three. I can now feel myself getting hot under the collar. My anger is now personal. I am even able to recognize that my patient's infuriatingly *impersonal* manner must be a corresponding part of the same context as my own feelings, but the awareness does not seem like "material." The concept of setting limits, usually an idea I employ only with great reluctance, suddenly is like a weapon I am almost tempted to use.

I realize that it would be useful to have my own feelings under better control before I say anything further, and I decide to wait and remain silent as I think about what is happening. Alec breaks the silence by saying that he feels I am very mad at him right now and that using the couch feels "wrong." As I am considering how to respond to his remarks, Alec sits up and tells me that he feels much better sitting up and being able to look at each other. In fact, he wants to try sitting up for a while. "Perhaps," he says, "between the group and sitting up, the analysis may move faster."

I'm now on the ropes. I can feel my own hatred in my body and in every sentence I formulate in my mind but reject saying. I also know that my feeling shows in my face and that Alec, now sitting up, can probably see it. I then decide that, if I were able to communicate what I was feeling to Alec, it might be useful because he might then be freer to deal more openly with what he already sees but cannot fully use. I want to place what I have to say in a therapeutic context rather than just "unleash" it, so I say to Alec, "I don't know what to make of what is happening between us right now, but I'd like to see if we can make some sense of it from both of our perspectives. How are you experiencing what is going on?" Alec, ignoring my gesture toward what seemed to me a more intersubjective stance, replies that he does not know what there is to look at and that now he is totally confused and upset because he feels like nothing he said was understood. "But," he goes on, "I know that I have so many problems it makes me wonder if I'm seeing this all wrong. After all, I did come to you because you're the expert. Maybe I should have a consultation with another analyst to get clear on that. Would that be all right with you, and would you give me someone's name since I don't know any other analysts?"

At this point I am feeling totally "possessed" by the out-of-control quality of my own feelings. Alec no longer seems to me like a patient. He has joined a group representing a rival approach to treatment, is sitting up, has rejected the transferential context as a valid medium for the work, and now wants me to agree that a consultation might be useful and to recommend the consultant. I ask you to keep in mind that I considered myself an experienced clinician; I was accustomed to dealing in a flexible way with unanticipated "breaks in the frame." The variable use of the couch, adjunctive types of therapy, medication, changes in frequency of sessions, outside consultations, and so on were all familiar to me and in most situations were used successfully, when needed, as part of an adaptational analytic context. The affect I was feeling here that was so disturbingly overpersonal resulted from Alec's having left me no way to respond to what was happening between us as part of any analytic frame that had meaning for me. I was without a place to organize and address my subjective experience within a conceptual frame of reference that could hold my identity as an analyst.

My affect felt completely irrational—a not-me experience in which every form of response I could think of felt either deceitful, hopeless, punitive, or submissive. I experienced my patient's behavior toward me as somehow hatefully motivated and a successful personal attack on my very being. I was forced out of my professional identity, now hated my patient in a totally personal way, and was unable for the moment to regain access to my "therapist self." What started as a therapeutic enactment had become a potential abyss. My state of consciousness now held the power of a personal truth: "I'm simply doing my best as a good therapist, and Alec is behaving as though everything I offer is either poisonous to him or irrelevant." "Clearly," I told myself, "Alec has lost his observing ego." I was feeling totally misunderstood and the unfairness was getting to me in a big way. I was held captive within our shared dissociative cocoon, and in this kind of situation either we escape together or neither will escape alone. Some slight temporary relief is, of course, always at hand if the analyst tells himself that his patient is in the midst of a "psychotic transference," but this is a dangerous path to take because one might never get off it.

I could go on to describe the other options I considered, how I discovered each to be "wrong," and how, when I finally ran out of techniques (yes, I did run out) and gave up trying to do the "right thing," Alec and I ultimately made personal contact and openly worked with our respective experiences, including the extent of our undisclosed anger toward one another and the warded-off shame it masked. But going into detail would take me too far from the central point of the illustration, which is that, within the analytic relationship, enactments are not worked through by the unilateral application of proper analytic technique, no matter which school of thought it represents; they emerge from each unique relationship as a solution that is not repeatable, even by the same analyst. So, even though I know its not a very "relational" thing to do, I am going to let the story of Alec and me end here, with the treatment crisis unresolved, rather than enact the vignette by attempting to tidy things up with a "relational miracle" tacked on at the end so that you won't be frustrated by my leaving you with the mess.

But now that I have said that, I just cannot resist adding one little piece more—a seemingly minor event that occurred shortly after Alec and I began to relate more fully as human beings. I was feeling deeply moved and personally changed by Alec's willingness to hang in while forcing me to see what I could not before acknowledge: that my out-of-control anger had protected me from experiencing the dissociated shame held by another part of myself, which I could now own. I spontaneously thanked Alec. Undramatically and straightforwardly, he said simply, "You're welcome." It was a nurturing moment for me (I felt wonderful) and a powerful statement of Alec's growth. At that moment Alec revealed that he felt deserving of being acknowledged for having just given me something valuable, his help, and that I was not above being personally enriched by his acknowledgment in the same way that Alec felt enriched by my thanks.

The point I am trying to emphasize is not about the technical issue of saying thank you. It is that shifts in state of mind, whether the patient's or the analyst's, provide the core context for a genuine analytic experience to take shape. Moreover, a shift in the analyst's own affective experience within the ongoing field is not his private property but belongs to the intersubjective space they share equally. Gratitude toward a patient may or may not be something an analyst routinely will attend to in himself, but it is only one feeling among many about which this is true. Feeling sorry that your patient is in acute distress during a session, even though you may also feel that the pain is inevitable, is another.

If an analyst cannot recognize that he has been protecting himself against feeling the unprocessed pain being evoked in his patient by what they are doing together, then he cannot feel personally sorry—as opposed to being professionally sorry—about that aspect of it, and his patient is forced to sequester his unrecognized feelings as though they do not exist. And, indeed, they do not exist as part of the self, because dissociated aspects of self will not be "real" unless they come to exist affectively in the mind of the other. *If they are not personally real for the analyst, then they are not personally real for the patient either.* Thus, these feelings continue to remain beyond the self defined by human relatedness, and the patient continues his desperate need to press into the analyst's mind the dissociated aspect of self that the analyst is ignoring. This process is what makes the "repetition" of the past not a literal repetition, but an effort to rework the past by forcing the therapist to succumb to that domain of the patient's personal reality for which words do not exist.

The Personal, the Professional, and the Analyst's Self-Revelation

A word about the analyst's self-revelation, which I discuss at greater length in chapter 7. Can it be misused? Can it sometimes be intrusive? Sure it can. But I do not at all believe that the analyst's self-revelation has a defensive meaning inherently packaged with it. I believe that, used judiciously, telling one's patient in words what one is feeling has to do with something quite different. Simply put, if an analyst tells his patient what he is feeling so that this patient can respond in his own way, the coconstruction of new meaning is enhanced by bringing what is being dissociated in the here and now into the mix, adding to the experiential material needed to symbolize the unspeakable. In many, if not most, cases of an escalating treatment crisis, if the therapist does *not* do this, then the patient will increasingly feel closed out of what he must possess of himself in order to feel whole and real.

I have found in my own work that what I am advocating here addresses the analytic necessity of heeding Nathanson's (1992) caution that helping a patient manage his or her affect cannot be done without addressing the moment-to-moment impact of your efforts, and that disregarding the here-and-now effects of your behavior as though it were just a technique being applied can have the effect of pushing the patient into a far greater degree of negative affect. No soothing techniques, as such, are required. What becomes soothing is the analyst's availability to having the patient enter his mind in a personal way. It is the analyst's genuineness in revealing his experience of their relationship and simultaneously attending to the impact of this disclosure, that provides the safety that leads to soothing the dread of runaway affect (cf. Fonagy, 1991; Fonagy and Target, 1996; Target and Fonagy, 1996).

In my experience, most instances of an analyst's destabilizing his patient's reality through his self-revelation stem from the analyst's feeling unsettled with regard to his own ability to sort out on his own what is real and what is not real. He is trying to ground himself by attempting to define reality for his patient in his own (the analyst's) terms. It is at such times that an analyst is most inclined to bolster his mental stabilization by selecting his favorite version of the different ways that a therapist can convey to a patient, "It's *your* problem," which adds to the patient's shame without the analyst's even knowing that he is doing so. He has, in effect, abandoned his patient by abandoning his involvement with the patient's subjective experience and replaced it with a total involvement in his own while, I might add, seeing himself as being helpful. It is this kind of "helpfulness" that invariably accelerates the enactment. The patient reacts to his dissociated sense that his therapist has left him and feels more and more as if his own need-state is toxic because the therapist has to defend himself against it, a perception that is, in fact, accurate.

All in all, I think that the value of self-revelation ultimately hinges on whether it is an act of authentic sharing–showing where one stands–rather than a means of exerting control over the relationship and over what the patient is feeling or thinking. In any treatment, whether a given act of revelation by the analyst is experienced by the patient as helpful or as controlling is an issue that is engaged again and again as part of the ongoing collision of multiple subjectivities contained within and between patient and analyst. It is important to remember, however, that, when the analyst does choose to be open about his subjective experience, there is a responsibility that comes with it. It is simply not enough to hope that the patient will then be equally open about his or her own subjectivity. The analyst must actively inquire into his patient's reactions, including how it feels to her that her therapist is so open.

In other words, self-revelation, used relationally, is not a technique–an act designed to produce a certain outcome. The therapist is not attempting to put something into the patient as a substitute for the patient's own reality but is offering an invitation to consider the therapist's experience as part of the evolving exploration of intersubjective space. Why do I believe this so strongly? Because experience does not become symbolized through mere words; it is symbolized through words that become consensually meaningful in a here-and-now perceptual context. It is when that perceptual context is relationally open on both sides that the coconstruction of a transitional reality will take place most richly, most safely, and lead to the most enduring personality growth; but that is going to take place only by going through the "mess" in which realities collide, and sometimes collide and collide and collide again. As Davies (1998a) observed, "associative and dissociative processes exist along a psychic continuum, a nonlinear, nonhierarchical mode of organizing consciousness and unconsciousness that oftentimes determines the direction of our clinical interventions" (pp. 205–206).

There are times, for instance, particularly at the ends of sessions, when the therapist thinks he has had a good hour and the patient leaves but comes back feeling awful and the therapist does not know what happened. From my perspective, other parts of the patient's self feel unacknowledged. The part that is committed to self-preservation and the protection of the dissociative structure is feeling unappreciated, alienated, and endangered by all this new and "wonderful" change that is going on. It feels to that part of the patient's self as if the therapist does not want her around, so the therapist hears a voice from this dissociated self-state reminding him not to get too carried away by his own therapeutic skill. This voice is, in effect, saying, "*You* think that everything is okay because you had a good session, but *I* am not okay; I am very scared." I believe that this viewpoint facilitates the work of every analysis, even those we look at as more or less routine.

For example, a patient came into a session complaining about her stepfather, how bad he was, and how her mother was brutalized by him. The theme of that session opened up the idea that the patient's hate might not be only an expression of her own feeling but also that of her mother. The next session she came back in tears, overflowing with gratitude. "I walked away from the last session" she said, "feeling like I finally understood something that reached right down to my soul. It's something that years and years of previous therapy had never reached. I can't tell you how freed I feel by the insight I had last session." Right! The following session she came in again complaining about her stepfather in the same way she had before. She had only a vague memory of the previous session and denied feeling liberated by what she had "understood" the last time. She claimed that anything she might have felt was just an avoidance of the "real truth." I was somewhat stunned to find myself being accused of not being interested in her problems, not wanting to hear how depressed she really felt, and not recognizing that she felt she was getting nowhere in therapy. Oddly, I felt startled and unprepared for the switch, despite the fact that this sequence of events had happened before. Not willing to attribute this "pothole" simply to my denseness, I began to recognize it as a reminder that, whenever dissociation is operating in a patient, it is frequently operating also in the analyst.

Russell (1975) proposed that the ambiguous and urgent tension between the present, the past, and the transference creates at times a "critical grey area of ambiguity that includes *the therapist's own grey area*." At those times, the "patient impacts upon the therapist in a way that necessitates that they struggle it out together again and again. The uncertainty," Russell writes, "is a mutual and shared uncertainty."

Any technically organized posture, no matter how empathic or reasonable it is, will be obliterated at such points because these situations are organized by something that overrides reason—the increased tenuousness of a person's (any person's) psychic stability when dissociated aspects of reality collide. It is at these times, Russell asserts, that the "therapist's sanity is most shaky." I agree. I also find it fascinating to think about a treatment experience that, because it shakes up an analyst's sanity, carries the potential for the deepest and most far-reaching analytic outcome, if the therapist allows himself ultimately to enter it rather than control it.

When I am in the throes of such an experience and can find enough space to breathe a little, I sometimes find myself wondering if it's crazy to believe that this process actually has some *rational* piece to it and that maybe I am making it up so that I can write papers. But then, if I have not lost my sense of humor, I can hear another part of me murmuring, in a voice that sounds reassuringly like Polonius talking aloud to himself about Hamlet, "Though this be madness, yet there is method in't. And, don't worry, Philip. On some days you might actually be able to tell which is which."

6

Treating Patients with Symptoms, and Symptoms with Patience[1]

If we were to place our difficult patients into one group and our so-called good patients (more and more difficult to find) into a second group, there is one particular characteristic of most patients in the first group that transcends the individual personality traits that we normally use in making differential diagnoses. Put simply, what our difficult patients most require from us for growth to occur is, paradoxically, the same thing that is most difficult for us to provide—interpersonal engagement that combines affective honesty and safety. Although it is certainly true that this same combination is needed by those in the good-patient group, with that group its provision is part of the natural give-and-take of the relationship and is largely taken for granted as, so to speak, background music.

For patients in the difficult group, this natural give-and-take is minimal, sometimes totally absent. Most of them, with good reason, have come to mistrust signs of genuine relatedness from another person as though these signs were really omens of potential betrayal. Such patients *are* difficult, and they *feel* difficult to a therapist because they

[1]An earlier and briefer version of this chapter, "Out of Body, Out of Mind, Out of Danger," was published in *Hungers and Compulsions,* edited by J. Petrucelli and C. Stuart (Aronson, 2001). A different and more extended version was published simultaneously (2001) in *Psychoanalytic Dialogues,* 11:891–912, and is the foundation of this chapter. Adapted by permission.

deprive the therapist of what he most counts on to sustain hope—a working relationship that will grow in depth and security as the work progresses. With these patients, such a relationship does not as a rule exist, at least for a long time, because their mental structure has been shaped too extensively, or for too long, by the effects of trauma and dissociation. Their capacity to trust a human relationship must first be slowly restored—in some cases built for the first time—and without this restructuring taking place, any attempt at psychoanalysis results in a pseudoanalysis.

If such a person is ever truly to feel recognized within a relationship, the therapist must comprehend that, when his patient behaves as if the only self that she feels is really her is the one present at the moment, his patient is not being merely capricious, inconsistent, or resistant. The therapist's task is to allow himself slowly to discover all her selves or self-states and to form relationships with each, while honoring that each holds its own truth, its own reality, and its own treatment agenda, which must be discovered and taken seriously.

Self-States and Symptoms

Difficult patients are not new to psychoanalysis. Some years ago, at a conference celebrating the centennial of the publication of *Studies on Hysteria* (Breuer and Freud, 1893–1895), I was invited to discuss the case of Emmy von N. I was struck with her intractability and how she coerced Freud into numerous negotiations about her symptoms and even about the method he should use in treating her. I was also struck by Freud's great patience with Emmy as a person and his impatience with her symptoms, which he initially thought he could dispel with hypnotic suggestion (see Bromberg, 1995b). Freud's refreshingly honest assessment was that the "therapeutic success on the whole was considerable; but it was not a lasting one" and that the "patient's tendency to fall ill in a similar way under the impact of fresh traumas was not got rid of" (Breuer and Freud, 1893–1895, pp. 101–102).

My perspective (Bromberg, 1996b) on what Freud described as Emmy's continuing "tendency to fall ill in a similar way" was that she, like any trauma survivor, was highly dissociative and lived in the present as if it were the past. In this context, the continuing return of her so-called hysterical symptoms is not an illness but part of a dissociative mental structure that automatically and unreflectively, perpetually reinforces itself. It is her mind's attempt to protect itself, proactively, from reliving unprocessed affective experience associated with self-destabilization. Thus, to certain of Emmy's self-states, her "symptoms" were not symptoms at all. They were not pathological, nor were they experienced as alien when they were present. They were functional, adaptive, and, at certain moments, vital to survival. When these parts were at center stage, they were not felt as things she was *doing,* because they were dissociated aspects of who she *was*. Most interestingly, they were parts of Emmy that seemed to emerge particularly vividly during moments in treatment when Freud was working hardest to erase them. *No one will allow themselves to be cured of who they are.* Emmy's "symptoms" had minds of their own, and it is not too difficult for a contemporary reader of that case history to hear Emmy's body voicing protests that her mind could not process as thought. Freud's efforts to help were being frustrated, and, despite his determination to succeed, he grew a bit impatient with what he referred to as Emmy's "unruly" self. One hundred years later we call this enactment.

To understand why Emmy's cure was not a lasting one is to understand that we do not treat patients such as Emmy to cure them of something that was done to them in the past; rather, we hope to cure them of what they still do to themselves (and to others) in order to *cope* with what was done to them in the past. Emmy's real illness was the plundering of her life by foreclosing the here and now on behalf of the there and then: a self-cure that effectively prevented her from participating in life with spontaneity, pleasure, or immediacy. And so I concluded my discussion with an observation that led to the title of this chapter: a clinician's success in treating patients with symptoms depends, at least in part, on his ability and willingness also to treat symptoms with patience.

I believe that this point can be made validly with regard to most symptoms, including those associated with eating (which, by the way, Emmy had to no small degree). That is, they represent the basic adaptational function of dissociation in avoiding the necessity of holding in a single state of consciousness two incompatible modes of relating. As Freud put it, in discussing Emmy's aversion to food, "it is impossible to eat with disgust and pleasure at the same time" (Breuer and Freud, 1893–1895, p. 89). In its most general form, a person is protected from the felt impossibility of responding self-reflectively with feelings of fear and security toward the same object at the same moment.

In this chapter, I focus on symptoms associated with eating because these offer a familiar avenue for thinking about the treatment of difficult patients and the struggles in which analyst and patient typically become entangled. Moreover, symptoms involving eating take us readily into issues of appetite versus desire and of the difference between control and regulation. On the basis of my own clinical observations and those of others (McCallum et al., 1992; Gleaves, May, and Eberenz, 1996; Katz and Gleaves, 1996), I offer the view that most of the symptoms associated with eating disorders can be best understood as an outcome of dissociation. The ability to act from a cohesive sense of self-agency is not destroyed but is "repackaged" in unlinked states of mind, leading to a personality dynamic whereby certain self-states are dramatically purposeful—often stubbornly intractable—and others seem inhibited but are simultaneously on alert. The unlinked quality inherent in defensively dissociated states of mind has been noted by many as characteristic of eating disorders such as bulimia.

> A temporary cognitive narrowing is experienced during a binge as the bulimic refocuses attention on to the immediate stimulus. This refocusing allows a reduction in negative affect or a general reduction in self-awareness. . . . This pattern of "escaping from awareness" appears to involve cognitive processes similar to those that underpin the concept of dissociation [Everill, Waller, and Macdonald, 1995, p. 155].

Freud never followed through on his early insights about the incompatibility of unlinked mental states, and in his war with Janet[2] ended up minimizing the significance of trauma and dissociation in human mental functioning. In this context, Havens (1973), in a wonderful book, *Approaches to the Mind,* has some things to say about Janet and Freud that are highly relevant:

> It was obvious to both Janet and Freud that the *conscious* ideas of the patients did not encompass the phenomenon of hysteria. Freud then searched, first by hypnosis and later by the method of free associations, for unconscious ideas and was led forward to the idea of unconscious yearnings, attitudes, convictions, and expectations. Janet searched for what besides ideas was

---

[2]See Breger's (2000) breathtakingly honest biography, *Freud: Darkness in the Midst of Vision* (Wiley, 2000), for the most comprehensive understanding of Freud's "anti-Janet" stand and its constricting effect on the evolution of psychoanalytic theory over the past 100 years.

> dissociated, and in what ways. He left behind the old conception of single ideas, resulting from trauma, and splitting off from mental life, for that of dissociated functions or systems within which many sensations, acts, fears, and ideas were included—separate, organized centers of attention, receiving impressions and able to be communicated with; in control of the personality (as in the somnambulisms and fugue states) or capturing a leg, arm, or the function of eating. . . . Each hysterical function had its own consciousness, organizing principles, and capacities for communication [pp. 59–60].

For patients suffering from eating disorders this issue is particularly salient, as was Janet's contribution. For the person who is anorectic, wrote Janet (1907), the act of eating is an amnesia, a "somnambulistic phenomenon which can only be effected in the . . . somnambulistic state . . . [and] is lost to the normal and waking consciousness" (p. 243). The most powerful and enduring significance of Janet's work in this area, Havens (1973) asserts, is not simply in recognizing the centrality of dissociation, but in demonstrating that dissociation involves an organized system of self-experience rather than just a single idea or sensation, and that in the case of anorexic illness this cutoff system has captured and redefined the meaning and function of eating (pp. 49–50). Anorexia is a hypnoidally isolated complex of physiological events, fears, movements, sensations and ideas that work together as a *separate center of attention that is able to be communicated with and is in control of the total personality when it needs to be.*

What Janet (1907) discussed under the rubric of somnambulism is what I see as a dissociated self-state, or a self organized by its own dominant affect, its own view of social phenomena and human relationships, its own moral code, its own view of reality that is fiercely held as a truth, and, for patients suffering from eating disorders, its own relationship to food and to the body.

In the contemporary analytic community, Janet's ideas have begun to take hold only during the last 10 to 15 years. Analysts have been influenced in part by hard data provided from outside psychoanalysis. At this point in time an increasing number of analytic clinicians, researchers, and theoreticians are arguing that, and presenting evidence that, the human personality begins and continues as a multiplicity of selves or self-states, each with its own dominant affect and sets of characteristics, which are always shifting in configuration and moment-to-moment availability to one another. This is not, however, the same as saying that everyone really has a multiple personality or, as we now term it, a dissociative identity disorder. Why not? Because the discontinuities between one's different states are, for most people, subjectively concealed by the developmentally adaptive illusion of being one self. That is to say, if all goes relatively well early in life, one's own self-state shifts are normally as unobservable as the beating of one's heart, and self-state coherence goes on without disruption. Most of us can access a broad range of self-states that can participate in even the most emotionally complex and psychologically conflicted situations. But not everyone is so lucky. In the face of psychological trauma, self-continuity is threatened, and this threat, for most human beings, is countered by the use of dissociation as an evolutionary response that is as important to survival as certain genetically coded response patterns of lower animals to a life-threatening attack by a predator. The responses of lower life-forms to overwhelming threat sometimes make instructive analogs to what happens to the human self in the face of trauma.

For instance, there is a strange-looking sea creature, the holothurian, that is best known for its disconcerting ability, when attacked, to divide itself into unlinked parts and regenerate from that part which escapes death. "*Non omnis moriar*—I shall not wholly die!" Consider the following brief excerpt from a poem by a woman awarded the 1996 Nobel prize for literature when she was in her late 70s, the Polish poet Wislawa Szymborska.[3] The poem's title, "Autotomy," is the biological term for the capacity of certain living things to give up wholeness in order to preserve life:

> In danger the holothurian splits itself in two:
> it offers one self to be devoured by the world
> and in its second self escapes.
>
> In the middle of the holothurian's body a chasm opens
> and its edges immediately become alien to each other.
>
> On the one edge, death, on the other, life.
> Here despair, there, hope.
>
> To die as much as necessary, without overstepping
> the bounds.
> To grow again from a salvaged remnant.

---

[3] I thank Dr. Marcel Hudon for making Wislawa Szymborska's writing known to me.

> Here a heavy heart, there *non omnis moriar,*
> three little words only, like three little plumes ascending
>
> [Szymborska, 1983, pp. 115–116].

I shall not wholly die! With these words in mind, now contemplate a piece of advice offered almost 150 years ago by George MacDonald (1858), the Scottish clergyman and author whom C. S. Lewis acknowledged as the primary source from whom his own capacity to bridge fantasy and reality was shaped. MacDonald wrote that the "best way to manage some kinds of painful thoughts is to dare them to do their worst, to let them lie and gnaw at your heart till they are tired, and you find you still have a residue of life they cannot kill" (p. 55). MacDonald's words sometimes come to me when hope seems far away with certain patients. But sometimes it is just too damned difficult to do what MacDonald proposed. It is difficult even for those of us who were not seriously traumatized as children. And for those who have been traumatized, trying to hold painful thoughts, letting them "gnaw at your heart till they are tired," and surviving without dissociating is an outright impossibility. And this is the conundrum faced by analysts working with difficult patients who are symptomatic. For these patients, parting with a symptom, whether it concerns eating or some other vital avenue to staying "alive," is not possible without an involved other who can hang in during the long process of collisions and negotiations.

Laurie

Laurie, age 26, had been obese as a child and became bulimic during adolescence, when she shed most of her weight and for a brief period became anorectic. At the point I first met her, she appeared slightly underweight but not anorectically thin. Her older sister, who had also been obese as a child, remained that way, never having developed a bulimic solution. She became for Laurie the apotheosis of greed—an object of contempt and a constant reminder to Laurie of who she was *not.* Laurie entered treatment with a variety of symptoms along with the eating disorder. Some were classically dissociative, such as fugue states manifested in such things as her history of "forgotten" appointments, not going to class, not coming to work, all without her awareness. She also suffered from flashbacks, traumatic nightmares, and a body experience sometimes blurred and always unstable. She would frequently start sessions by asking me either, "What do I look like today?" or, "Do you think I look different from last time?"

During sessions, she was also prone to sudden state-shifts preceded by attentional disturbances in which she seemed to disappear from whatever interaction was taking place between us. She also presented with other symptoms, less classically dissociative, but often found to accompany those that are. The major ones were migraine headaches so severe that they could virtually incapacitate her and a compulsive "hair-twirling-leading-to-hair-pulling" habit that started at age 14, when she also developed amenorrhea, which lasted until she left home at age 20. She described the bingeing and hair pulling as reducing tension because they "make my mind a blank."

On this particular day Laurie began her session, as she frequently did, sitting silently and staring, trancelike, into space. She then began to talk blandly and without affect about having pulled out her hair the night before, "I discovered I haven't stopped. *You* thought I had." As I listened to her I became aware of my own feelings—an odd blend of apathy and irritation. I might have ignored it and just launched into another dead-end inquiry about the details of what had led to the hair pulling, except that I noticed her sitting back contentedly like someone settling in to watch a movie. I commented on this, and she responded by telling me the dream she had had the night before—a dream in which she was at her sister's birthday party, which, interestingly enough, was taking place in an insane asylum:

> There was a big, gooey birthday cake—my sister loves cake, I hate it—and she's getting mad at me because I don't want any. I finally start yelling at her to "shove it." I woke up just as I had my face up against hers, screaming, "I don't have that body. It's yours, not *mine,* you pig!"

I asked Laurie what thoughts she had about the dream, and she said in an offhand manner, "None! I don't like to come up with ideas. I'd rather wait for *you* to have some. That way I can either agree or disagree and I don't have to risk being wrong." There was a look in her eye as she spoke that made me feel she was trying to pull me into a battle. But, as was not the case earlier in the session, I could vaguely sense she was conscious of what was going on between us at least to some extent, and, contrary to feeling apathetic and irritable, I was not put off by her manner this time. In fact, I was feeling kind of playful, and I found myself saying to her,

> Actually, what you usually do is agree and disagree *at the same time,* so I never can really be sure what you feel. It's like I slave over a hot couch all week. I cook you my best interpretations. Do you eat them? No! You taste a piece here, a piece there. I throw out three quarters of what I cook. There are starving patients in Europe who would be grateful for what I throw away that you don't eat.

Laurie, although not a "couch" patient, began to laugh, and I could feel the atmosphere shift, lending some support to Michael Lewis's (1992) observation that laughter is a mechanism by which shame can be reduced or eliminated. "Laughter," Lewis writes, "especially laughter around one's transgression as it occurs in a social context, provides the opportunity for the transgressing person to join others in viewing the self. In this way, the self metaphorically moves from the site of the shame to the site of observing the shame with the other" (p. 130). Unlike Lewis, I do not see the shift as metaphorical. In my own preferred idiom, laughter allows more of one's selves to get into the act. A part of Laurie that was lively, animated, and almost enthusiastic was now clearly participating.

I said to Laurie, "At this stage of our work, the odds of each of us being wrong are pretty high because there's so much we don't know yet. But the odds get better when we compare notes about what each of us is feeling about what we are doing and saying. It reduces the amount of guessing."

After a moment of silence she replied, "I think the insane asylum was your office. Sometimes I feel you want to make me fat like my sister. All these interesting things you say to me make me afraid to hear more. Yeah, I guess I was sitting back like I was getting ready to take in a great movie—like a great meal I could have without getting fat because I didn't even know I was eating it. I think I know what made me start pulling my hair out again."

She then described an event that took place two days before this session. "I was walking to a restaurant with my father, and he holds my hand in this weird way—he won't let go. I had to pretend I was fixing my hair to remove my hand." This, incidentally, was her first concrete association that could potentially shed some light on the hair-twirling/pulling behavior. Then, suddenly, in the voice of a preadolescent child, she said, "He never touches mommy that way. I wonder sometimes if people who see us think I shrunk."

"Who would they see?" I asked her.

Now, again in the other voice, she said, "They'd see a 10-year-old girl walking with her father. My husband lives with her most of the time. Most of the time he likes it. But he doesn't like it when I change. He says, 'Why do you have to be different people on different days?'"

"Well, I'm glad I had a chance to meet her," I replied, "even if it was only very briefly."

"Yes," she said pointedly. "She went away again as soon as you asked me to *tell* you about her." A bit dazed as the end of the session approached, I mumbled what I hoped would be a supportive response and a "good" note on which to stop: "Maybe if I talk to her more directly she will stay longer. Do you think so?"

Naively anticipating that this would be our "marker" for next time, I was shocked when she ignored what I thought were my obvious cues that the time was up, and she began a monologue that seemed nonstop. She began to talk about how afraid she was of offending people at whom she secretly scoffs, people who think that what they say matters to her when it really does not. "It's so strange," she went on. "Even though some people don't seem to get angry about it, I crash when it's over. I go home and binge and vomit."

I felt paralyzed at this point. Even though I believed she was talking about *us* and about what it feels like for her after she leaves sessions, I also wanted to end the session. I kept hoping that if I gave her just a little more time I would think of the "right" thing to say, so I let her go on . . . and on . . . and on . . . hoping against hope that if I did not stop her before she stopped herself, it would end in the "right" way. Well, I finally abandoned that hope and stopped her 10 minutes past the end of the session.

She said, sounding a bit miffed, "I haven't finished yet." I replied, probably sounding a bit contrite, "I know, but our time is up for today and I'd love for us to have a moment to reflect on what just happened here." She retorted, "I never reflect on what I'm saying when I'm like this." I answered, now a bit more composed, "But later when you get home, a different part of you does think about it–all alone. And then you decide you were horrible and end up bingeing and vomiting." At that moment, something clicked into place for me, and I added, "But in a funny way you only did what I asked you to do, didn't you? Remember when I said 'Maybe if I talk to *her* more directly, she'll stay longer'? I just didn't expect it to happen *now!* But why wouldn't it?" And then, shifting realities, "After all, you were just being you. 'Longer' means until you've finished, right?" She stood up, grinned, and left. I breathed a grateful sigh of relief.

Eating Disorders, Affect Regulation, and Desire

> Psychosomatic dissociation can be seen as the core of eating disorders. It results in the separation of the mind from the body, with the absolute hegemony of the mind and the negation and abandonment of the body in anorexia, and in bulimia with either a continuous struggle between the mind and the body, with their alternately prevailing cycles, or eventually a consolidated withdrawal so that the mind is no longer able to control the body or keep in touch with it [Ciocca, 1998, p. 52].

In the context of the preceding vignette, Ciocca's statement underlines the intricate relationship among trauma, damaged capacity for affect regulation and self-observation, and the need for a resilient analytic relationship that will survive the repeated collisions and negotiations on which the patient's growth depends. As we know, successful interpersonal transactions between infant and caregiver mediate, at the brain level, the capacity for affect regulation and secure human relatedness. One could, if one wished, translate this finding into the language of attachment theory, whereby the phrase "secure attachment bond" could substitute for the phrase "secure human relatedness." When these early patterns are relatively nondisruptive and, most important, *reparable* (see Tronick and Weinberg, 1997), they create a stable foundation for internal affect-regulation that is largely nonverbal and unconscious.

Much adult psychopathology may thus be the end result of the prolonged necessity of an infant to control physiologic and affective states while lacking an experience of human relatedness and trust in the potential for reparation. An early foundation of reparability in relationships allows for further successful negotiation of interpersonal transactions at increasingly higher levels of adult self-development and interpersonal maturity. This foundation not only affects the richness of one's life, but also determines the relative ease with which a person will attempt to negotiate and use a psychotherapeutic relationship. It is the absence of trust in reparability that is most closely associated with what we call difficult patients, and for these patients the experience of trust in the continuity of human relatedness must be restored as part of the analytic process.

With regard to people for whom this state of affairs has led to an eating disorder, Boris (1984, 1986) has proffered the view that eating disorders arise when the dysregulation of desire is linked in infancy with the dysregulation of appetite. The result is what Boris calls an "unevolved state of mind," in which one wishes and hopes to have everything all the time—a state of mind commonly known as greed. Greed in an eating-disordered patient attempts to eliminate the potential for traumatic rupture in human relatedness by replacing relationship with food, a solution that is largely self-contained and thus not subject to betrayal by the other. But it is by no means a perfect solution. The problem with greed is that its presence is inevitably tarnished by the existence of choice and the shadowy pressure of the need to choose. To make a meaningful choice, one must feel meaningfully related to others. The realization of the need for choice, Boris writes, either stimulates a refusal to endure it, leading to the decay of appetite back into greed and an experience of vast frustration, or stimulates the making of the choice, leading to the satisfaction of appetite but always accompanied by the feeling of profound loss of what was not chosen. Loss, too, if it is to be felt as tolerable, presumes relatedness to others. In Boris's (1986) words,

> appetite . . . makes manifest the infant's first encounter with actuality and, as such, makes actual experience for the first time a player in the process. The quality of the appetitive experience will now play a role in whether the feeling of loss is modulated by compensatory and consoling experience—or is not [pp. 48–49].

Boris is saying, in other words, that the essence of the human condition is having to recognize one's insufficiency, and that the degree to which one draws satisfaction from human relatedness will keep one from seeking nonhuman solutions (e.g., food) as a means of compensating for the experience of loss. For some people, because the recognition of insufficiency is unbearable, choice becomes unbearable; in the infant who later in life develops an eating disorder, the capacity to make a choice is additionally impaired because the experience of loss connected to appetite is not modulated by the compensation and consolation of human relatedness. That is, what in adulthood might have developed into appetite and healthy, regulatable desire, instead, because it is denied the relational context on which that transformation depends, freezes the experience of being an affectively out-of-control infant within a dissociated self-state that takes on an imperious life of its own. The person who eventually shows up at a therapist's office, no matter how she chooses to define her presenting problem, is someone whose real problem is that she is at the mercy of her own feelings, someone who is enslaved by her felt inability to contain desire as a regulatable affect. What cannot be regulated must be controlled, by total renunciation if necessary. Boris (1984) writes,

> By the simple expedient of declaring "less is more," greed for the breast is metamorphosed into a gluttony for punishment, yearning into abstinence, retention into elimination (in bulimia) via each and every alimentary orifice, indeed, by exercise and sweating, through the very pores themselves [p. 317].

The renunciation of desire is what we see as the hallmark of anorexia and, in a different way, of bulimia. But at its core, it is a loss of faith in the reliability of human relatedness.

I have found that in patients with eating disorders, the transmutation of desire into renunciation is most frequently mediated through the mechanism of dissociation. Sands (1994) suggests that "dissociative defenses serve to regulate relatedness to others. . . . The dissociative patient is attempting to stay enough in relationship with the human environment to survive the present while, at the same time, keeping the needs for more intimate relatedness sequestered but alive" (p. 149). This dual function is the reason that a dissociative mental structure is organized psychodynamically rather than as an impermeable suit of armor. Even though a patient might prefer *total* insulation from potentially destabilizing otherness (Bromberg, 1995a, pp. 194–195), she cannot escape human interaction because the adaptational function of a dissociative structure is not that of escape from people; its function is to anticipate potential dysregulation of affect by anticipating trauma before it arrives. Therefore, from the perspective of its evolutionary value as a survival mechanism, if the person is to stay vigilantly alert to danger cues in order to *anticipate* trauma, a dissociative structure cannot perform its function unless the person, simultaneously, is part of the human community. A dissociative mental structure thus provides insularity, not through eliminating interaction but by maintaining partial permeability without which the patient's mind could not be as attuned to danger, but equally important, the patient would be totally shut out of the human community and become vulnerable to psychosis. So, in serving its adaptational function, the same blend of qualities that gives a patient the ability to anticipate potential trauma also allows a dissociative mental structure to be accessible to self-state negotiation in analytic treatment. But this negotiation is never easy.

As treatment progresses, the patient will often reveal the existence of an inner life dominated by a never-ending war between parts of the self, each denouncing the other around the issue of appetite and desire. It is a war that more often than not manifests itself experientially through the presence of internal voices, often sadistic and unrelenting, that the patient desperately needs to still by finding ways to give each some of what it wants. And the war between self-states never ends, because desire, as Boris (1984) writes, is undeniable and durable. For someone with a severe eating disorder, everything else but the internal war is obliterated.

Symptoms, Internal Warfare, and Analytic Treatment

In the analytic relationship, the patient's internal war is manifested dissociatively, and this takes place in part through the analyst's relational encounter with the patient's symptoms. As Zerbe (1993) states, "Given the frequency with which dissociative states and eating disorders may occur together, it behooves clinicians to keep an open eye to making both diagnoses if one or the other is found" (p. 321).

In bulimia, for instance, bingeing and purging as a cohesive act is by and large done in a dissociated not-me state. Muller (1996) argues that bulimic patients "are attempting to set a marker at the edge of the self so that they can experience a limit and not become fragmented in a diffuse unnamable scatter" (p. 85). The trance state, through dissociation, allows this marker to be set between areas of self that trauma has made incompatible. This purpose could not be served if the bulimic patient were fully conscious, because it would be an experience of something being done *by me to me,* and thereby unable to ward off autonomic hyperarousal of affect. But this protection comes at a huge price because it forces the self to severely limit what can be experienced as "me" at any given moment.

How are we to account for a solution that can be so fiercely self-destructive? To begin with, the patient may not intend self-destruction. There is something I find convincing in a comment made almost 40 years ago. Erik Erikson (1968) wrote of such patients as creating a "self-decreed moratorium, during which they often starve themselves, socially, erotically, and last but not least, nutritionally, in order to let the grosser weeds die out, and make room for their inner garden. But often when the weeds are dead, so is the garden" (pp. 41–42, quoted in Muller, 1996, p. 81). How do we keep the garden alive? As Ciocca (1998) has put it,

> we must find the reasons for her intolerance of a . . . conflict related to . . . being herself. The aim of every therapeutic encounter . . . is to lead her to a meeting with herself, as that which she is, and that which she could become. . . . [F]oremost in therapy is her impossibility to deal with the dissociation itself. In such a situation it is useful to highlight the way in which her mind works, and how it influences the way in which she is living [p. 54].

If a therapist is to work with a patient's here-and-now experience of safety by negotiation within the enactment—*while* he is highlighting the way her mind works—it is essential that he be especially attuned to his patient's potential for dissociated hyperarousal of affect created by the therapy itself. This means addressing each patient's ongoing experience of emotional safety as an intrinsic and inseparable part of the analytic interchange. For those patients in whom the effect of trauma on the organization of psychic structure is most pervasive, the self-reflective ability to work in the here and now is least likely to be present at the beginning of treatment. These patients tend to use each session to process unprocessed experience that occurred in prior sessions. In other words, each session becomes for at least one part of the self a kind of commentary (through derivatives, dreams, and enactments) on the preceding session or sessions. The therapy proceeds that way, with the therapist's job being to try to enable the processing to be safer and safer so that the person's tolerance for potential flooding of affect goes up. The patient's threshold for "triggering"[4] increases, allowing

---

[4]Here I use the term *triggering* to refer to the sudden opening of subjectivity to affective hyperarousal, by more or less intended analogy to neurological "triggering." There is another sense of triggering of which I also make use, that is, in describing the instantaneous switch from one self-state to another that is seen in some patients. Here, too, there is a presumptive neurological substrate, about which I can say nothing further. This kind of triggering occurs when a patient suddenly switches to a different self-state without warning, without conscious awareness, and without subsequent memory of the switch itself. The two types of triggering represent successively activated components of a coherent

her increasingly to hold on to the ongoing relational experience (the full complexity of the here and now with her therapist) as it is happening, with less and less need to dissociate; as the processing of the here and now becomes more and more immediate, it becomes more and more experientially connectable to her past.

To reiterate, in any treatment where trauma is an issue—and I believe trauma to be a factor for every patient in at least some areas of personality—the patient will attempt to talk *about* the trauma, though always with hidden shame because "talking about" evokes "reliving." The patient, however, will usually reveal enough data to stimulate the therapist's curiosity, setting off a process in which the therapist's accelerated attempt at exploring events for which the patient has no narrative memory leads to an enacted reliving of the trauma, into which the therapist is drawn like a moth to a flame. As the enactment continues, the patient's dissociated shame escalates, and the therapist finds himself feeling things about his patient and about his own role that make him increasingly uncomfortable, often triggering his own dissociative processes. I believe this collision of subjectivities to be inevitable, not a sign of a technical error. It draws the work into a dialectic between the here and now and the there and then and allows the mutual construction of a transitional reality. Both the patient's and the analyst's dissociated experience have an opportunity to coexist as a *perceived* event different enough from the patient's narrative "truth" about relationships to permit internal repair to take place and the patient's reliance on dissociation to be gradually surrendered. To be fully in the moment is to fully allow new (as yet unprocessed) experience to interface perceptually with *episodic* memory, thus optimizing the potential for integration of unprocessed experience into *narrative* memory and, ultimately, into an enriched self-narrative—the goal of any form of treatment. We are at those moments, in effect, "standing in the spaces." Dissociation short-circuits this possibility.

In this regard, it is worth noting that the term "eating disorder" can become a real handicap to therapy if it is embraced unreflectively by the therapist as simply a handicap to the patient. The therapist must simultaneously recognize and respect as an achievement the means by which a patient has constructed her "disorder" so as to preserve its

---

process in which the triggering of self-state switching occurs as a dissociative response to the sudden triggering of emotional flooding (potential or actual) when the threshold of affective containment has been exceeded.

dissociative structure and thereby give each part of self some of what it wants without unbearable conflict.

Mr. Hyde Meets Ms. Hide

Elsewhere I have described a case presented to me in ongoing consultation (Bromberg, 1994, pp. 247–250). The patient was a woman who had been in treatment for quite a few years; she had made major changes in her life and her self-experience, except with regard to the issue that had brought her into treatment in the first place, her obesity. The analyst, having had as much as he could handle of "getting nowhere" no matter how hard he tried, stopped addressing the issue of her weight, in the hope that she would eventually bring it up on her own. The war over desire entered a new phase. He allowed long silences to develop in which he hoped that she might ultimately put what she was feeling into words, which she did, but not in the way that he had anticipated. As he began to find the silences increasingly difficult to tolerate, she started to take him to task for his "failure" to mention her weight, even though she herself was not mentioning it. Without the least regard for logic, she told him he had no right to stop trying to find out what she was feeling about her weight. "What did you think you were doing? *You* ought to know," she insisted, "that when I'm talking about anything else, as long as I'm still fat it's only my good self that's talking and I'm doing something self-destructive that you're not even caring about." It was in the course of their dealing with the apparent no-win quality of his "failure" that he was able to begin to find a small island of shared experience on which he could plant at least one of his feet.

"Only in my silence," the patient declared, "do I feel real." Then she added, speaking of her inner world (and perhaps the office also), "The only way I can get out of here is to be silent for a year." How could it make any sense that the only way she could release herself from the trap of her dissociated mental structure was without words, by remaining silent for a year? Her point was not that silence *in itself* was what mattered, but silence in the presence of her analyst. Why? Because her silence in his presence could have a communicative effect *as long as he had not given up trying*. The analyst has to get fed up. It is important that he get fed up. He *should* get fed up. But he should not become so detached from his own "fed-upness" that he cannot perceive the retaliatory component of his behavior. If he is open to that, he will feel the communication from his patient as it is pressed into his soul through her silence as well as into his brain through her words. This patient was ultimately able to put into words a remarkable insight:

> When I'm not talking to you and you don't realize that my silence is talking, I feel like I'm hurting myself and you don't care. I hurt myself by being fat in order to call attention to the inside "me." And if you don't notice or seem not to, it's like you're mad that I'm still fat and will let me hurt myself because I'm fat instead of putting why I'm fat into words. But if I do talk, it's not my fat self that's talking. So you have to find her by noticing the fat and not pretending you don't. If I get thin, no one will ever look for her because if I stop calling attention to her existence, you will settle for my good self, which looks healthy because it is thin, and you will never know it isn't real to me. I'm like Dr. Jekyll and Mr. Hyde.

In other words, by the analyst's "noticing" through the impact of forced involvement with what the patient needs to call attention to without communicative speech, the dissociated self can start to exist, and a transition begins to take place to engage what this patient so evocatively described as a growing awareness of "Ms. Hyde." But the success of the transition depends on the patient's ability to destroy successfully the analyst's unilateral experience of "what this is really all about"—a piece of "pathology" that has become an adversary—and thus destroy the analyst's limited image of the patient in which Ms. "Hide" is imprisoned. The problem for the analyst, of course, is that his own self-image, which is a part of all this, is also dismantled, and it is this destruction he must "survive" in Winnicott's (1969) conceptualization of object usage.

The analyst's own dissociative processes enter the picture in this context. If the patient's eating behavior is held by the therapist for too long as simply a piece of pathology to get rid of (and the patient, of course, makes it very easy for us to hold that view) nothing much changes, and what we have come to call "resistance" starts to fill up all the space. It becomes very easy for the analyst to grow to hate the patient's eating disorder, and then, without recognizing it, to hate that part of himself that is trying but failing to "cure" it. The analyst begins to feel victimized by his own desire and then feels the patient's "pathology" as an adversary.[5] The mortal enemy of an eating-disordered patient, as Boris (1984) cogently observed, is desire. Because she does not wish to want, her solution is to stimulate desire in the other, to become object not subject, ultimately to be the object of other's wants. In treatment, this "solution" leads to a situation with which we are all painfully familiar. Desire becomes the enemy of the analyst, as the patient–analyst relationship is pulled into the patient's internal drama, which has become a substitute for living. The war over who shall hold the desire is externalized as an interpersonal war and fought out dissociatively, calling into play a constantly shifting array of the patient's and the analyst's self-states. It is a war that, in one respect, the analyst has to lose in order to win. A transitional reality has to be constructed in which the patient's trust in human relatedness begins to become possible, and this can happen only through the analyst's surrender to his own dissociated self-experience.

For the analyst to surrender in this way is not so simple and especially not at those moments when a dissociative patient pulls the rug out from under him. For example, after a session that seemingly went well, a depressed patient with a longstanding eating disorder left a message on my answering machine late that night: "Memories are beginning to come up that I've never had before, and its very disturbing. Its like I'm watching them from a different part of my brain," she said. "It's very weird." Her voice sounded upset, but not in a panic.

Next morning, someone I hardly recognized showed up for her session, and growled menacingly, "*I'm* the one you need to ask the permission from! Who do you think is going to pay the rent if you keep going the way you are going? You said that I would be able to carry on with my life and my work if we agreed to do this therapy. This is bullshit! There is nothing to be gained from this. This work changes nothing. It's expensive and a waste of time.

"You remind her of how alone she is, how alone she has always been, and this is supposed to be of help? She's nothing but a fat, ugly, poor kid in pain, and she has suffered enough! I won't let her suffer anymore! She knows that no one will support her if I don't. Not even the shrink will be there if the bills don't get paid. *Who do you think pays the bills anyway???*

[5]It is not unreasonable to wonder if some of Freud's zealous determination to permanently *erase* Emmy von N's symptoms, as well as his impatience with an "unruly" part of Emmy that was standing in his way, were both fueled by an increasing experience of her "pathology" as an adversary.

"*I* won't allow this! I will *not* allow this! *I will not allow this!!!* As long as you threaten to disable me, I will not allow this. I am not nice and I don't care what you think of me."

As an example of working with state-change phenomena, this incident is not as dramatic as it may sound. I selected it because it puts into high relief the point made by Stechler (2003) that the "possibility of the emergence of new states and new organizations arising during times of disregulation and apparent disorganization or chaos has become one of the hallmark principles of contemporary theories of self-organizing systems" (p. 716). In therapy, Stechler wrote, the "work often consists of a renegotiation of old patterns, facilitating the creation of new organizations and new states" (p. 718).

> Whether that new state is a richer, more complex, and more appropriate foundation for further development, or is the less advantageous choice in the sense of narrowing through toxic adaptation, may depend on whether the partner in this self-organizing system biases it in one direction or the other. The more toxic adaptation can stem from an interactional partner who reacts as if the destabilization were toxic. That is, if the therapist's . . . primary aim is to reduce his own destabilization and its accompanying anxiety as if it were toxic and intolerable, the partner's aim and choice will be biased in the same direction. If the therapist can stay connected with his own and with the patient's destabilization and can bias his own subsequent state choice toward openness and affective authenticity, then the patient's will be similarly biased. On the other hand, if the patient feels the freezing or the pretense of the therapist at these critical moments, the work of the therapy cannot proceed well [p. 723].

What Stechler called openness and affective authenticity require an abiding respect not only for a patient's autonomy, but also for what might be called, more poetically, a patient's autotomy—the dissociative unlinking of parts of the self in the face of potential trauma so that *non omnis moriar*—"I shall not wholly die!"

7

The Analyst's "Self-Revelation": *Not Just Permissible, but Necessary*[1]

> I prithee, speak to me as to thy thinkings,
> As thou dost ruminate, and give thy worst of thoughts
> The worst of words.
>
> —William Shakespeare, *Othello,* act III, scene 3

Because Othello cannot not see that Iago's diffidence is a conscious pose, he innocently urges him to reveal the secret that Iago pretends is too terrible to disclose but also too painful to contain. Pleading with Iago to share what is on his mind with complete honesty, Othello exhorts him to give his "worst of thoughts the worst of words." He thus, unwittingly, entangles himself in Iago's masquerade and falls victim to his friend's duplicity (Shakespeare, 1604). The fact is, however, that, even when a person is not being consciously two-faced, speaking with complete affective honesty in a human relationship is not possible because we all contain parts, each doing its own job, that are relatively unknown to one another at any given moment. That is to say, it is not possible for anyone to obliterate all motives other than candor; honesty

---

[1]Incorporated into this chapter is material adapted from "Ev'ry Time We Say Goodbye, I Die a Little: Commentary on Holly Levenkron's Case Study, 'Love (and Hate) with the Proper Stranger'" (Bromberg, in press) and from "Speak to Me as to Thy Thinkings: Some Reflections on 'Interpersonal Psychoanalysis' Radical Façade' by Irwin Hirsch" (Bromberg, 2002). Adapted by permission.

is always modified by various other aspects of self and self-interest even in the absence of conscious duplicity such as Iago's.

In psychoanalysis, the spirit of Othello's request to "speak to me as to thy thinkings" continues to remain an implicit injunction, even if not a "basic rule" (Freud, 1913), that an analyst hopes his patient will take to heart. It is not, however, a principle that is intended to organize an analyst's *own* stance–not if he hopes to relate therapeutically to his patient. As an unmodified and unmodulated analytic posture, free disclosure of the analyst's thinking will create an atmosphere that is inherently so unsafe, affectively, that the patient will minimize access to his unconscious processes in the interest of maintaining attachment. In some cases such a posture can be even a recipe for affective retraumatization of the patient.

From a postclassical perspective, however, it does not thereby follow that the analyst should avoid self-revelation. In fact, a recent emphasis in the relational literature has been on the therapeutic power of the analyst's self-revelation, affective openness, and affective honesty. In light of the obvious potential for free disclosure to lead to hyperarousal in the patient, how is this new turn to be understood? The answer is that the emphasis on the analyst's affective openness has been consistently balanced in these writings by an equal emphasis on the analyst's simultaneously demonstrating his overriding and explicit concern for his patient's emotional safety. In other words, the analyst is shown to be involved with the affective impact of his openness and demonstrates this involvement as an intrinsic aspect of what he is revealing in his self-revelation. Notable examples of such papers are those by Aron (1998), Davies (1994, 1998b, 1999, 2004), Frank (1997), Gerson (1996), Hoffman (1994, 2000), Levenkron (in press), Maroda (2000), Mitchell (1998), Renik (1996, 1999), and Slavin and Kriegman (1998).

Ironically, the new emphasis on the analyst's subjective openness has been attacked by some as though it endorses an analytic stance equivalent to what Othello asked of Iago, as though it were a version of giving one's "worst of thoughts the worst of words" while believing it to be psychoanalysis. Clinical vignettes in which the analyst's limited self-revelation was straightforwardly described by the author have been targeted as if the analyst were endorsing a naive invasion of the patient's psyche. To some critics (e.g., Bernstein, 1999; Greenberg, 2001) these vignettes by relational analysts threaten to open the door to undisciplined analytic behavior and seem to sanction an "anything goes" attitude because of the analyst's ease with the open use of his own thoughts and feelings. To other critics, the self-disclosure in these vignettes seems to simply represent illegitimate analytic technique. In my view, invoking the issues of legitimacy or permissibility deflects awareness away from the importance of these papers as a breakthrough in clinical theory. I refer especially to a growing recognition that the psychoanalytic theory of therapeutic action must be rethought in terms of the mind as a nonlinear, self-organizing system, and that this rethinking is leading to a reconceptualization of the analyst's self-revelation as not simply permissible but *necessary*. I believe that it is no longer useful to frame the topic of the analyst's self-revelation in the context of analytic technique (see Bromberg, 1994, pp. 261–266; 1998b, pp. 315–316), and indeed that it is time to revise the basic premise of what analysts call technique.

A friend of mine had just returned from a summer vacation at a music camp—a musician's version of the MacDowall Colony—where the members were sorted into trios, each of which would play together all summer. Although there were no formal auditions for acceptance into the camp, each applicant had to perform for a panel that then evaluated his or her level of musicianship to assure that each trio would comprise individuals of comparable ability. I asked my friend how this had worked out for her, and her reply fascinated me because she is a woman who, by nature, always sees the cup half full: "I met a lot of people who had good technique but there was no music coming out." When I asked what she meant by "no music coming out" she shrugged and answered, "It's something hard to describe, but it doesn't get better by learning better technique."

Technique is something that one *applies* with the experience of command over it. In classical psychoanalysis, technique has traditionally been framed as a set of rules to guide the therapist's behavior—a set of rules that organizes an analyst's conduct in a way that, if the rules are followed, should allow an authentic analytic process to take place. Early classical analysts were not unaware of the danger of "painting by the numbers," and, although the rules were framed as a technique, analysts tried to apply them with sufficient humaneness that the patient wanted to remain a patient. Thus, technique has served as a baseline of analytic behavior from which certain strategic, but analyzable, departures (parameters) may be acceptable under predefined conditions with certain patients. Further, as prescriptions for behavior, the rules seem to have had the added benefit of allowing the analyst's unconscious deviations from them (countertransference) to be assessed in terms of their seriousness.

Freud's (1923) view of mental functioning was premised on the idea of a psyche that is self-contained. Given this view of the psyche, a patient's productions under optimal clinical conditions are held to be generated endogenously while the analyst works with the implied (but one-sided) interaction between the patient's psyche and the analyst's presence as a fantasy object of projected imagery. It follows naturally that the subjective contents of the analyst's mind should as much as possible be kept from the patient for two reasons: (1) because such revelation is an *interference* with the analytic process, and (2) because it is *unnecessary* to the analytic process. The second reason, historically, has been a relatively minor theme in classical Freudian writing because its logic has always been implied in the first reason, but, in postclassical analytic theory and practice, a vigorously discussed issue in the literature is whether or not the analyst's self-revelation may be indeed *necessary* to a patient's psychological growth.

Postclassical theory is moving increasingly in the direction of a psychoanalytic model of mental functioning in which our view of what is conscious and what is unconscious is informed by a conception of the mind as a nonlinear, relational process of meaning construction. This model is organized by the shifting equilibrium between stability and growth in one's range of self-representation; that is, by a dialectic between the need to preserve self-meaning (the ongoing experience of safely being oneself) and the need to construct new self-meaning in the service of relational spontaneity and creativity. In this model, the analyst's presence as a real person is not intentionally diminished, because the concept of endogenous unfolding of transference projections has no clinical meaning. Because unconscious material is held to be coconstructed rather than revealed, the analyst's role is not to avoid personal participation in the process, but continually to monitor and use the immediate and residual effects of his personal participation as an inherent part of his stance.

I argue that the analyst's existence as a real person is not only inevitable, because it is not something under his control, but is *necessary*. Why? Because the analyst's experience while with his patient is linked to his patient's experience as part of a unitary affective, cognitive, and interactional configuration that is at once subjective and intersubjective. Some aspects of that configuration are dissociated in each person and must be processed jointly in the immediacy of the analytic interaction to achieve cognitive symbolization through language.

I fully recognize that I am risking criticism from those analysts who define "wild analysis" as allowing what is in your mind to come out before you have worked on it and "cleaned" it up, and from those who believe that there is a correct analytic stance and that this is not it. To be sure, even among analysts who work from a more conservative stance, the latter allegation today has few sponsors. But I go further here. I assert not only that the analyst's *self-revelation* is permissible but that it is a necessary part of the clinical process if the therapeutic efficacy of analytic treatment is to be most enduring and far-reaching. I submit that the most effective psychoanalysis is inevitably a process of living through and working through enactments, some of which can be volcanic. Further, I submit that the analyst's self-revelation, from a postclassical stance, is not inherently an intrusion of the analyst's subjectivity into the patient's psychic processes.

Intrusiveness Reconsidered

At this point in the history of psychoanalysis, how one approaches the issue of the analyst's self-revelation and the centrality of the analyst's affective aliveness is highly dependent on whether or not one accepts that the movement from classical to postclassical theory is based on clinical observation as well as an understanding of the mind that is challengingly different from Freud's. It is from the vantage point of this current understanding that a postclassical position on self-revelation must be considered. Self-revelation is equivalent to intrusiveness only if the frame of reference is that of an analyst trying to change a patient. If the analytic rationale is that of the analyst's sharing his experience to facilitate the goal of intersubjective negotiation, then self-revelation is quite another matter.

Intrusiveness, within the classical model of a self-contained mind, means that the analyst is interfering with finding what is inside the patient, as though what is inside can emerge in a relatively pure form (if the analyst does not contaminate it) largely uninfluenced by the context in which it emerges. Intrusiveness, in a postclassical model, means temporarily interfering with the process of intersubjective negotiation provided the intrusiveness is understood to be a therapeutic part of the analytic process as long as it does not foreclose intersubjectivity or shut it down for too long. Relationally, when an analyst is being "intrusive," he is not forcing his input into the patient's mind and thereby preventing him from accessing what it unconscious. Rather, he is forestalling, temporarily, the coconstruction and use of intersubjective space—a process that is based on the analyst's responsiveness to his patient's subjectivity, which allows it to then interact with his own. The concept of intrusiveness, to an interpersonal/relational analyst, has to do with the analyst's *temporary* inability at a given moment to retain his own subjectivity and allow it to be modified in response to his patient's subjectivity.

How, then, does a relational analyst maintain self-discipline without renouncing the spontaneous use of his own subjectivity? Hoffman (1994) addresses this question through his concept of "throwing away the book," a clarifying frame of reference that speaks to what he calls "psychoanalytic discipline in a new key" (p. 193). In the context of this chapter, the "new key" to which Hoffman refers is a clinical stance that, in conjunction with Renik's (1999) formulation of the analyst's "playing his cards face up," makes it easier to comprehend the emphasis among relational writers on the value of the analyst's self-revelation. Both Hoffman and Renik recast the clinical application of technique within an overarching process of relational negotiation—what Hoffman calls a dialectic between ritual and spontaneity. "Technique," from this vantage point, boils down to what is useful to a particular analyst's work with a particular patient at a given point in time.

The complex meaning of Hoffman's phrase "throwing away the book" has been well articulated by Slavin and Kriegman (1998), who write that "there are inevitably times when, as Hoffman (1994) says, the therapist must 'throw away the book' in order to demonstrate a genuine willingness to place the patient before some of the rules of therapy" (p. 277). However, they continue, it is inevitable that any new therapeutic approach, including one that sponsors spontaneity and self-revelation, will inevitably become biased toward the needs and views of those who advocate it.

> Hoffman seems to be addressing some of the problems introduced by this tendency toward bias when he recommends the maintenance of a "dialectic" between the therapist's acceptance of ritual authority and anonymity, on one hand, and spontaneous deviation (including self-revelation) from those rituals on the other. . . . We believe that if we appreciate Hoffman's paradoxical dialectic, we are likely to practice with a new sensibility rather than a new set of rules and technical guidelines [Slavin and Kriegman, 1998, p. 278].

What Slavin and Kreigman describe as a new sensibility I would portray further as a *process-based* (rather than a content- or outcome-based) conception of therapeutic action, a central aspect of which is the joint processing of collisions between the patient's and analyst's subjectivities. I hold that a therapeutic posture that systematically tries to avoid collisions of subjectivities is eventually experienced by a patient as disconfirming. The patient feels that the analyst is not holding him in mind, and comes to feel this because the analyst is not feeling, *personally,* the impact of the dissociated parts of the patient's self that are trying to find relational existence. Because the analyst is not reacting personally to them they are not being held in mind, and these self-states are thus robbed of a human context in which to be recognized and come alive.

Since, from my vantage point, optimal processing should thereby include the analyst's private experience (what constitutes his "self-disclosure"), the analyst must be especially attuned to a patient's shifting equilibrium between affective safety and affective overload. If the analyst's commitment to this attunement is honored, a transitional reality can begin to take shape between patient and analyst that has room for the subjective experience of each partner and space for relational negotiation that is affectively alive. This in turn enhances the patient's capacity for intersubjective functioning in areas of personality where the capacity to bear intrapsychic conflict had been preempted by dissociation. The analyst's self-revelation is, in this sense, an ingredient in the source of therapeutic action that advances the all-important therapeutic climate of *affective honesty*. Holly Levenkron (in press) makes essentially the same point in an illuminating paper to which I will recur repeatedly in the rest of this chapter. She argues that this climate has been achieved "when the analyst can state her point of view by offering her experience of the patient." I would add that an analyst must also try to offer, when possible, his "experience of his experience"—which frequently is a key factor making such revelation palatable to the patient. When the analyst reveals the elements of his internal struggle that went into deciding what to say, he is revealing even more clearly that the motive for the disclosure is more one of sharing than covert indoctrination designed to *look* like sharing. I am suggesting, in other words, that the value of affective honesty is enhanced by one's openness to sharing the full complexity of one's subjectivity, including any self-doubt about whether to share it. But not every confrontation can or need take that form.

However, I cannot overemphasize the importance of Levenkron's statement concerning self-revelation that the "analyst's ability to do this with someone has to be earned." To an analyst holding a relational view of mental growth, the right to reveal his subjectivity is *earned* by struggling with his own limitations. It is earned by struggling with the humbling fact that he cannot, alone, find the right response. It is earned by struggling with the patient's experience of him while not foreclosing her own view. As Levenkron makes clear, it is in all this that an analyst's ability to survive intense affective confrontations and make use of them as enactments takes place. Put in these terms, earning the right to this analytic stance is what this chapter is about.

If one does not believe that the labyrinth of considerations attending the analyst's self-revelation is avoidable by endorsing either absolute prohibition or unrestricted freedom, then it is easier to recognize the intricacies of self-revelation as part of a broader question: what principle should most influence an analyst's judgment about how to make best use of his own existence as a real person? The specific conditions for analytic growth always differ for each analytic couple, and each dyad must strike its own balance between safety and risk. But for any patient confrontation with the analyst's existence as a real person, including the analyst's deliberate self-revelation, is experienced as affectively safe enough only within the window of the patient's capacity to process the evoked affect cognitively. When the analyst does choose to openly and knowingly reveal his thoughts and feelings about his patient, at that moment he is simultaneously revealing himself as a real person. Other things being equal, for his patient to experience this disclosure as both safe and enlivening, the analyst must *authentically* believe that the patient's knowing will facilitate the clinical process even though the analyst himself does not know in advance how this will take place. If the analyst remains genuinely curious and does not try to figure things out on his own, he will not be intruding in the classical sense of intrusiveness, because he will not be trying to get his patient to accept his subjectivity as a substitute for the patient's reality. Honoring this principle, I think, allows many seemingly fragile patients to hang in while facing an analyst's seeming intrusion; they can tolerate reflecting on what is taking place as both not-me and as me, because their own subjectivity is not at risk by their having to trade it off for the 'truth" being offered by an other. Nevertheless, for some patients the experience of otherness is a prelude to affective turmoil no matter how negotiably the analyst believes he is presenting his own view, and with these patients the work is especially difficult and strenuous.

Enactment and Self-Revelation

Enactment is a phenomenon that is not about denial or avoidance of internal conflict; it is part of the natural functioning of a mind that is simply doing what evolution has adapted it to do in two discrete modes of information processing. One mode, the "subsymbolic" (Bucci, 1997a), is organized at the level of body experience as "emotion schemas" that make their presence known affectively, through a person's "ways of being"; the second mode, the "symbolic," is organized at the level of cognitive awareness and is communicated through verbal language. When emotional experience is traumatic (more than the mind can bear), it remains unsymbolized cognitively, and the mind recruits the normal mental function of dissociation as a means of controlling both the triggering of unprocessed emotion schemas that were created by trauma and the release of ungovernable affective hyperarousal that could threaten to destabilize its functioning. Enactment in psychoanalysis is a dyadic dissociative process through which the patient's trauma-derived emotion schemas make themselves known and potentially available to consciousness. When enacted dissociated experience is processed relationally, internal conflict and its potential resolution increasingly become possible.

This postclassical understanding of mental functioning and therapeutic growth is especially relevant to Levenkron's (in press) observation that the analyst's "revealing is often a relief to the patient even if it opens up rage and painful feelings, because it makes things clear; 'being real' and connecting with another person cannot always occur through loving gestures." I believe this statement to be not only accurate, but also a significant aspect of the relational process through which cognitive control over hyperaroused affective experience becomes regulated by the patient's self-reflective functioning. Self-regulation of dissociated, and thus potentially out-of-control, affective experience can take place only by activating and cognitively symbolizing in the session itself what Bucci (1997a) calls subsymbolic experience that formerly could be only enacted. It is relieving because it increases a patient's trust in her own capacity to think about an otherwise overwhelming experience without the experience itself threatening to possess her. It is not, then, too difficult to comprehend why the analyst's self-revelation, even if it opens up rage and painful feelings, is relieving if it leads to increased self-reflectiveness.

In Levenkron's (in press) words, the "clinical craft . . . lies in contacting a part of ourselves which we can eventually own, that enables us to reflect upon, either verbally or nonverbally, what we have discovered about our own participation from within these interactions." The analyst's self-disclosure is thus as negotiable as any other aspect of his communications. I would put it that the relationship between what is enacted nonverbally and what is put into words during the processing of an enactment, including the analyst's revelation of his own subjective experience, touches on what Leston Havens (personal communication) has amicably referred to as "Bromberg's Common Property Principle": *that is, the analyst's feelings about his patient are not his personal property* because they are part of an unsymbolized context within which the analyst and patient hold pieces that are linked subsymbolically but not yet by language. Recognition that an analyst's personal feelings and thoughts about his patient are not his personal property does not lead to an "anything goes" stance as a technique, but it does indeed speak to an inevitability, namely, that the dissociated experience being relationally enacted is "known" subsymbolically. Bucci (1997a, b, 2001, 2002) has described the workings of subsymbolic communication in both clinical and nonclinical situations:

> The basic forms of emotional communication that operate in the analytic context also underlie all interpersonal interaction. In normal functioning as in pathology, we are constantly sending out and receiving subsymbolic signals; these often occur without accompanying verbal messages and are difficult to make explicit. A fundamental difference between normal and pathological functioning is that in the former, the subsymbolic communication is connected, or readily connectable to the symbolic components . . . whereas in pathology *the subsymbolic representations are largely dissociated from the symbolic modes that would provide meaning for them* [Bucci, 2001, p. 68, italics added].

During the analytic process, a main part of the analyst's job is to find words to get his own experience of enacted communication out on the table in a manner that facilitates the patient's ability to do the same. In his groundbreaking work, Levenson (1972, 1983, 1991) took Sullivan's (1953, 1954) original illumination of the interpersonal bridge that links affective experience and language to a place that showed how working in the moment with transference and countertransference experience provides the most powerful context for therapeutic growth. Levenson was the first "perspectivist," illustrating in his writing how the analyst's being pulled into an enactment is not a technical error but an inevitability. He showed how working one's way out of the mess of an enactment is a core ingredient of therapeutic action, and how neither patient nor analyst can free himself from the grip of a "mess" without the other's help. Levenson delineated the way an analyst's personal participation in enactments—even as the analyst simultaneously seeks a mutual language with the patient to symbolize therapeutically the experience—provides the most powerful context in which self-representation and representation of other are enriched and expanded in analytic treatment. Most relational analysts now accept this frame of reference, and many nonrelational analysts have adapted it to their own metapsychology.

The process of consensually finding the "right words," language that symbolizes a new shared reality, is the basis for the development of intersubjectivity where it did not exist. Finding the right words can be considered one aspect of interpersonal engagement. But other aspects of interpersonal engagement, including both spontaneity and the analyst's abiding respect for the patient's experience of safety, are no less important. It is the blend, not any single ingredient, that is unique to each analytic couple, and it is the affective aliveness that is generated by mutual spontaneity in a human interaction that holds it together as part of a relational analytic process.

I thus argue that what has been labeled the analyst's self-revelation, if used as a negotiable element in the ongoing relationship, is not only permissible but also necessary: a part of the developmental process that Fonagy (Fonagy and Target, 1996; Fonagy et al., 2002) calls mentalization, through which subsymbolic experience is allowed to become a part of the relational self rather than being interminably enacted. There is no technique for accomplishing this change in the "contents" of the mind. If one sees the mind as a nonlinear, self-organizing system, facilitation of mutative change is inherent to the process, not to the content, a clinical observation that is consistent with the research conclusion of the Boston Process of Change Study Group (Lyons-Ruth, 1998; Lyons-Ruth et al., 2001) that it is the process of communication ("implicit relational knowing") rather than the content of the communication that is the foundation for the therapeutic action of psychoanalysis.

Contrary to the long-held axiom of classical theory about making the unconscious conscious as a necessary condition for change, the Boston group's findings support the view that "process leads content, so that no particular content needs to be pursued; rather the enlarging of the domain and fluency of the dialogue is primary and will lead to increasingly integrated and complex content" (Lyons-Ruth et al., 2001, p. 16). When patient and analyst can each access and openly share their dissociated experience that has been too dangerous to their relationship to be formulated cognitively, the *process* through which this takes place begins to enlarge the domain and fluency of the dialogue and leads to increasingly integrated and complex content that becomes symbolized linguistically and thus available to self-reflection and conflict resolution. How much self-revelation by the analyst is enough and how much is too much cannot be known in advance, and it is the ongoing and often painful effort to struggle with its unpredictability that defines affective honesty, not simply the analyst's subjective assessment of the honesty with which his words are spoken at a given moment.

Developmental Trauma, Nonrecognition, and Shame

The early developmental history of certain patients with whom I have worked suggests that the psychodynamics of parental nonrecognition plays a key role in creating a seriously dissociative mental structure in adults. I am speaking about the early failure of responsiveness by the mother or father to some genuine aspect of the child's self, not necessarily open disapproval or abusiveness (which communicates that this aspect of the child's self is "bad"), but a masked withdrawal from authentic contact that leaves the child experiencing part of herself as having no pleasurable value to a loved other and, thus, no relational existence as part of "me." Nonrecognition leads to a *structural* dissociation of a part of the self. If too broad a segment of the core self is encompassed, there will be impairment in the early attachment process and in the capacity for mutual regulation and "implicit relational knowing" (Stern et al., 1998). In my view, the prolonged experience of nonrecognition best defines what is called developmental trauma or relational trauma.

Most frequently it is the parents' dissociated shame, generated by their own damaged self-experience, that makes it impossible for a parent to provide recognition of qualities in the child that the parent has disavowed in his or her own self, and in turn leaves the parent unable to modulate the shame the *child* feels in the face of his nonrecognition.

Thus, in domains large and small, the parent begins to dissociate from the immediacy of the relationship and from the shared pleasure that it potentially holds. And we should be clear that a powerful developmental casualty is in the offing when a parent dissociates his or her shame to such degree that the dissociation shuts down the parent's ability to take pleasure in being with the child. It embodies an act of nonrecognition that is as traumatizing as the pain caused by a parent who is actively abusive, and sometimes it is *more* debilitating.

Donald Fridley (2001), a contemporary traumatologist, explicitly acknowledges that "in many ways it is the blunt denial, disavowal, or dismissal of the child's emotional states which contributes to the child's confusion, shame, and feelings of worthlessness that has as much or more impact on the future than the fact of the physicality of the trauma itself" (p. 5). If the other systematically disconfirms (Laing, 1962) a child's state of mind, particularly at moments of intense affective arousal, by behaving as though the self-meaning of the experience to the child is irrelevant, the child grows to mistrust the reality of her own experience. The child becomes correspondingly impaired in her ability to process cognitively her own emotionally charged mental states in an interpersonal context—to reflect on them, hold them as states of intrapsychic conflict, and thus own them as "me." Dissociation, the disconnection of the mind from the psyche–soma, then becomes the most adaptive solution to preserving selfhood. The child's own need for *loving* recognition becomes despised and shame ridden. The need becomes a dissociated "not-me" aspect of self that, when triggered, releases not only the unmet hunger for authentic responsiveness, but a flood of shame, the affect associated with failure in who one *is,* not failure in what one *does.* Failure in what one does leads to anxiety and lowered self-esteem or to guilt and depression, but failure in who one is leads to shame, the signal of impending self-destabilization, the shock of no longer being "me."

Dissociation as an Interpersonal Process

As I stated at the start of this chapter, speaking with "complete affective honesty" in a human relationship is not possible, nor would it be desirable if it were possible. In psychoanalytic treatment, affective honesty is achieved through the analyst's struggle to communicate, not by a self-granted license to "tell it like it is." Affective honesty must be balanced with affective safety, and it is this balance that ought to be the organizer of one's analytic stance. Attunement to your patient's safety, in other words, must be experienced from *within* the relationship, rather than by trying to empathically "provide" it as a technical stance (see Bromberg, 1989). What organizes a postclassical analytic stance is the analyst's comprehension that his subjective experience does not tell him what is "really" going on as though it had some objective truth value, and thus places self-disclosure within the context of negotiation between subjectivities.

It ought to be clear from the foregoing that an analyst wrestles equally with issues of disclosure and nondisclosure. And here I would like to return to Levenkron's (in press) paper, specifically to an incident she describes with her patient that makes this unusually clear. Levenkron describes an event that took place with her patient Ali that I believe was framed by a major dissociative switch in self-state that took place in Ali and, as so frequently happens during enactments, led to a dissociative reaction in her therapist. The incident followed Levenkron's telling Ali, unexpectedly, that she was going to take a weeklong break and apologizing for the short notice. The reason for this break, unknown to Ali, was that Levenkron wished to give herself space to deal with her feelings surrounding her impending divorce. Ali, however, seeming to have missed all the nonverbal cues that her therapist was in a distressed state, behaved as if she were being gratuitously abandoned. Levenkron writes that Ali "got in touch with the aspect of herself that, when insecure and envious, becomes filled with rage." I hope you do not feel it is unsporting of me to second-guess Levenkron's reported experience, but I feel that this characterization does not give quite enough weight to the magnitude of what appears to me to be a dissociative switch in Ali.

What I read has a different feel than someone's simply becoming filled with rage, which would better capture the experience of a *mood* change. Ali's response seems much more a switch in self-state—fundamentally a dissociative phenomenon and not simply a change in affect. And that is what I believe made Ali's response especially upsetting to Ali's therapist. An affective change in itself is seldom that destabilizing to the other person; for it to have the kind of impact described by Levenkron, it almost always embodies a switch in the self-state that holds the affect. Levenkron observed Ali at that moment "turning her face to the wall and saying a few sentences that were tangential; she spoke in a slow, halted, breathy voice." This is the kind of description analysts give when they are trying to depict the nuances of what it is like to be with someone who is no longer feeling like the same person.

Levenkron writes that her own reaction was to get angry, but that she "wasn't aware of it." Why wasn't she aware of it?

> As an enactment begins, an analyst will inevitably shift his self-state when the patient shifts his. Dissociation is a hypnoid process, and inasmuch as analyst and patient are sharing an event that belongs equally to both of them—the interpersonal field that shapes the immediate reality of each and the way each is experiencing himself and the other—any unsignaled withdrawal from that field by *either* person will disrupt the other's state of mind. Thus, when an enactment begins (no matter by whom it is initiated), no analyst can be immediately attuned to the shift in here-and-now reality, and he inevitably becomes part of the dissociative process, at least for a period of time. The analyst's dissociation is not a "mistake" on his part; it is intrinsic to the normal process of human communication [Bromberg, 1996a, p. 285].

Levenkron (in press) states that she began to get angrier and angrier and did not want to soothe Ali. "At that moment," she recalls, "I wanted it out on the table where I could see it." Levenkron confronted her patient angrily. Ali stood her ground, "I can't stand the way you talk to me! You are so fucking mean! Who do you think you are, Levenkron? No one talks to me that way, only you! You're sorry for the short notice, well what about me?" As Levenkron then puts it, "it was out on the table."

Am I saying here that I think Levenkron should have done something different? Do I think that Levenkron should have soothed her patient? Do I think she should have taken a different stance? Actually, I don't. I think that the analyst entered a dissociated state of her own that was reciprocal to her patient's and that, when she did so, something unpredictable happened that ultimately became quite therapeutic. But at that moment, patient and analyst were in a dissociative cocoon together, so they could not access anything other than the dominant affect that organized their respective self-states. Levenkron is explicit about that fact; she describes it "as if we were a couple who was having a fight." I would argue that it was not "as if" they were a couple having a fight, but that in their dissociative cocoon they *became* a couple having a fight.

What is most important, however, is that they were not just having a fight. They were participating in an enactment that had a powerful therapeutic function because it opened a space through which an analyst can come to know her patient's "not-me" self-states firsthand, and vice versa—a personal channel that is frequently very painful for both at first. Levenkron, in the heat of the "unfair" attack by Ali, found tears welling up in her eyes because she was feeling tortured by having been accused of abandoning her patient in order to have a good time. She was unable to reveal that it was just the opposite—that she was taking time off to try to heal her wounds. She felt an intense need to be understood but was not allowed that solace. At that moment she was as close as she had ever been to feeling Ali's own pain of separateness. Levenkron writes, "I had a powerful urge to tell her every bad thing that ever happened to me; that is, just how hard my life had really been and, certainly, how hard it was at that time." The urge was poignant, and Levenkron struggled with it, but she chose not to act on it. By writing about what went into the struggle, she takes out of the shadows what an analyst frequently faces at such a moment unless the analyst "handles" her destabilization by invoking a prescriptive rule that provides either a license to reveal or a prohibition against it. Either allows the analyst to sidestep the painful but affectively honest experience of struggle, ambivalence, and conflict.

It should be pointed out that Levenkron's dissociated state was as complexly organized as Ali's. Because she was "containing" some of Ali's pain, Levenkron could not escape her own pain without affectively abandoning Ali, and this she would not do. Pain and confusion reigned for the analyst because she was forced to process simultaneously two experiences of their relationship and two self-states of her own that were incompatible and unresolvable by conflict resolution because the combination was too affectively intense to be either internally or externally negotiable. She writes,

> I thought I was protecting her from feeling guilty for attacking. I was also avoiding what I imagined to be a sadistic retort from her. . . . At that time I could not formulate what was a pull I fought against to tell all, as when the emotional and articulated demands of your patient to intrude into your privacy are so great that you "have" to tell—for the wrong reasons.

Sometimes, containing a patient's experience of threatened annihilation takes an analyst to the brink of knowing the patient better than one *wants* to know her.

The Analyst's Right to Privacy

Levenkron, in the preceding vignette, did not "self-disclose," but she was not pleased with herself for having "used nondisclosure as a foil to avoid an abuse of my privacy and admission of my vulnerability." Levenkron comments, "Although nondisclosure here was a clear expression of my subjectivity, I am not advancing a 'technical mandate' of nondisclosure. . . . In my withdrawal and silence, I was unaware of how I was enacting my self-protection and my right to privacy. I dissociated my ability to voice my boundaries—to talk to her about why I could not talk to her." Such a dissociative moment is part of the natural clinical process for any analyst who knows that spontaneity and aliveness ebb and flow relationally. But in her willingness to reflect on what contributed to her dissociation, and to think about the various meanings of what it meant to her personally (including a wish to avoid an abuse of her privacy and admission of her vulnerability), she is here openly stating that the implications of not revealing are as significant as those clinical moments in which an analyst *does* disclose.

I see this as quite a service to all therapists. In this regard, I think it important to note that an analyst's "dissociative moments" often, as in this case, reflect not only the analyst's self-protection but also a concomitant protection of the patient. I would argue that the emotional state that Levenkron was in when she dissociated and became thereby unable to reveal to Ali why she could not talk to her was too affectively intense to be therapeutically usable. If she had tried to speak from that state, it would have probably elevated even further Ali's already hyperaroused affect and reinforced Ali's dissociated "tough-kid" self as her only reliable means of controlling fear and shame that would otherwise have been unregulatable. So one could hypothesize that Levenkron's dissociation at that moment was not just a protection of her own right to privacy, but an adaptive relational solution to what she described as "being unable to remove myself from the explosions going off inside of me that would give me the distance I needed to speak to her in a calm way." Such a dissociative moment often provides an opportunity for things to calm down and is problematic only if the analyst, unreflectively, uses it as a permanent hiding place rather than a temporary sanctuary.

Privacy, most simply, is a dimension of the ongoing process of negotiation between incompatible domains of self-experience. From this vantage point, the right to privacy is part of the human condition. Privacy can be surrendered by choice, but the *right* to it cannot, and this is as true for the analyst as for the patient. Privacy and self-revelation are parts of an overarching configuration that defines the analytic relationship for both parties through an inevitable dialectic that takes place intrapsychically and interpersonally. My view (see Bromberg, 1997) is that, except for very rare instances, patients respect the analyst's personal right to privacy with regard to his history and life experiences. Almost any situation where that seems not to be true represents a transference–countertransference enactment in which the analyst has been unable to recognize and reveal his own dissociated experience of the patient, who then, often desperately, tries to penetrate the analyst's mind to find herself within it. Let me repeat: I believe that a patient's pressure to force the analyst to give up his right to privacy is organized not simply by a need to know the analyst, but by a wish to know what the analyst knows about the patient but has dissociated. When an analyst is successful in dissociatively "privatizing" some aspect of his experience of the patient, the analyst is, in fact, depriving the patient of her potential to discover safely her full relational existence. The enactment then increases in power, and, as the analytic space becomes filled with energy generated by the enactment, the patient more and more *becomes* the self that had been excluded from their relationship. That self gradually forces its way into the analyst's perceptual consciousness (Bromberg, 1998b) and finally ignites in him a personal response to a part of the patient that until then existed only in the enactment.

Personal and "Really" Personal

What we discover about our own participation from within these interactions at times may include the vivid emergence of memories from our own past—childhood relationships or "forgotten" events—that suddenly appear like ghosts that we thought had been exorcized in our own analyses but that we suddenly realize are very much *alive* in the moment and are quite relevant to what is taking place with that patient. What is it about such experiences that makes them such a source of debate about how to use them? Do they fall into a category austerely separate from "process" thoughts and feelings, a category so potentially dangerous that they should be ipso facto exiled from revelation, even by an analyst who might comfortably share his *process* experience? Or, if not, then how does an analyst decide whether or when to reveal personal biographical information? Obviously, it is a choice more complex than that entailed in the revelation of process feelings and, justifiably, calls forth greater concern not only about the welfare of the patient and the treatment, but also about the analyst's own personal privacy.

In my view, an analyst's disclosure of such information should be in response to a deeply felt sense that it will deepen an *ongoing,* affectively alive relational context in which here-and-now process experience is already being shared, and the analyst can feel this added element as consistent with that context. I believe strongly that such disclosure should not be made to *create* affective aliveness. Like any other choice an analyst makes with a given patient, self-revelation derives its meaning from the ongoing context of the relationship in which it takes place, not from its utility as a technique. Its usefulness to the analytic process is organized by the quality of its openness to negotiation, particularly the degree to which the analyst is free of internal pressure (conscious or unconscious) to prove his honesty or trustworthiness as a technical maneuver designed to counter the patient's mistrust. The value of an analyst's revelation of personal history rests on its spontaneously surfacing in the analyst's mind as part of the moment. That is, its value rests on its being something from his personal past that enters unbidden and very much alive into the present. Often it is something that the analyst recognizes emotionally—sometimes cognitively as well—as having contributed to a dissociative state of his own that increased his difficulty in experiencing and responding to an emotional state of his patient that was enacting its existence.

The patient does not need a dramatic act of self-disclosure by the analyst. For the analyst, the issue of whether, when, and what to reveal is mostly a matter of the analyst's feeling that, if he does share his experience and invites his patient to do likewise, a useful exploration of the relational context is likely to be enhanced at that moment. Do conditions seem to exist that could lead to something "new but not new" being constructed, or is the patient at that moment too affectively destabilized to use his mind in *thinking* about what is taking place intersubjectively because his brain will not process what is too emotionally risky?

When the analyst is revealing personal history, I believe it is his obligation to be attuned even more sensitively than when revealing his process experience. He has to try to be aware of the even greater complexity of the patient's response to his possible motivation for the revelation than of the content of what was revealed. He must consider particularly closely whether the patient is currently dissociating her own response to his behavior in order to keep from feeling affectively overwhelmed by what is taking place between them. It is almost always necessary to address that question *openly* because an analyst's self-revelation can sometimes, in subtle ways, increase a patient's dissociation. It is not an analytic error when this happens unless both analyst and patient, for too long a period of time, fail to process such moments together. In fact, the postclassical reconsideration of "error" as applied to clinical process bears directly on understanding why the wisdom of the recent psychoanalytic admonition to "strike while the iron is cold" is no more valid, prescriptively, than "strike while the iron is hot"; more often than not, it is only by *failing* to know when the temperature is right that the analyst learns when the iron is too hot. And it is only through this dialectic that the patient comes to know that the analyst is learning from *her* and, most important, cares about what he is learning. Simply put, by recognizing the nonlinearity of what we call mutative change, we also accept that it takes place not through thinking, "If I do this correctly, then that will happen," but, rather, through an ineffable coming together of two minds in an unpredictable way.

Clinical Transition from Dissociation to Capacity for Conflict

As the analyst is forced to experience and respond to those aspects of the patient the analyst wished to disavow, the patient begins to inhabit a self that feels whole in the analyst's mind and thus starts to feel simultaneously more whole in her own. At that point, a comfortable dialectic between the experience of insideness and the experience of human relatedness begins to replace, for both partners, the issue of the right to privacy. I have called this phase of the work the transition from dissociation to capacity for conflict. The essential quality of the transition is that the patient's self-experience is less subject to disorganization by the return of unprocessed affect. As a consequence, the patient's personality is less vulnerable to the single dissociated "truth" that relational ruptures can never be repaired, and thus the continuity of the attachment bond on which selfhood depends begins to be trusted as more reliable, and thereby becomes more secure.

A brief discussion of Levenkron's report of a later session in Ali's treatment illustrates this point. It is a session again marked by their personal reactions to one another, but it demonstrates the kind of therapeutic shift that can take place when an intersubjective space that has been fought for and earned now allows the open processing of collisions between subjectivities. In the face of Levenkron's impending vacation, Ali was talking about the painfulness, as a bodily experience, of the separation, but this time she was not holding Levenkron as an objectified other; Levenkron, in turn, remained exquisitely attuned to Ali's affective state without needing to give her own destabilization special priority. She was able to communicate to Ali from within their cocreated space without her thoughts being felt by Ali as unbearable. That is to say, Levenkron was able to stay, experientially, in this transitional space and at the same time reflect on her own and on Ali's subjectivity:

> No one ever talked to you about being separate, but what is more important for us is that no one ever separated from you in a loving way. At this point in the session I was able to tell her that I hadn't realized how frightening it had been for her, but this time as she left for vacation I did feel it, and said I was sorry for not understanding how scared she was of losing me. We had not talked about this openly before. I had the strangest remembrance at that moment. I recalled that when my own mother was dying, she would not let me cry; furthermore, she would not even consider that I needed to be protected in any way. She just denied her own death and wouldn't let me in on it. I was terrified, and when I later saw that I could survive her death, I wished I could have shared more with her.

That, to me, is a fascinating moment because it addresses the issue of the difference between self-revelation of process experience and self-revelation of biographical data. It is one of those moments when the line between them is especially permeable. Levenkron, apparently, did not share with Ali the spontaneous remembrance of her mother's dying, but I could easily imagine that sharing this remembrance at that moment might have been quite therapeutic. This is one of the few clinical vignettes I have read where I was able to feel how arbitrary the distinction can sometimes become between an analyst's disclosure of process experience and disclosure biographical data, and why whether to reveal or not to reveal is such a difficult judgment call. Had Levenkron chosen to reveal that remembrance, she *might* have had a very positive effect in underscoring, without making explicit, the degree to which she was in close emotional contact with Ali's dissociated desire for emotional contact and was not put off by it. That is to say, her revelation could have been potentially quite shame reducing. But, then again, maybe not!

One last time, I want to insist that self-revelation is not a technical issue but a relational one. It has to do with the process of facilitating the development of new mental representation, a process that is coconstructed by the participation of two minds that are alive to each other, each allowing the experience of the other to be known—a point vividly made by Alvarez (1992) in her book, *Live Company*. Whether or not an analyst chooses to reveal is not a debate about whether or not it is reasonable to deliberately reveal something because the patient already, at some level, "knows" what you feel. If analysts accept the view that patients already know what we are feeling about them as part of shared subsymbolic experience, then the primary clinical question is whether or not openly revealing our feelings will advance the symbolization process and lead to the construction of new mental representation. From this frame of reference, as Ginot (1997) has argued cogently, "self disclosure is not . . . a way to promote a sense of intimacy through seemingly similar shared experiences. Rather, the emphasis here is on revealing emotional data growing from and organically related to the intersubjective matrix" (p. 373). The subjective reality of a patient's unsymbolized states of consciousness, especially with regard to the patient's experience of the analyst, must be felt and, in some useful way, acknowledged by the analyst. If there can be said to be an interpersonal or relational analytic technique, it is mainly in the ability of the analyst throughout the course of each analysis to negotiate and renegotiate the meaning of what constitutes useful acknowledgment. Levenkron (accepted) writes,

> Over time, Ali and I discussed our interactions with increasing comfort, partially because the development of candor is a natural evolution of any successful negotiation, and partially because we both learned that articulating what we experienced did not lead to unreparable ruptures in attachment. In this light, disclosure of our thinking becomes collaborative and therefore negotiable, rather than power-based.

Levenkron is here saying that increased analytic collaboration depends on two principles: first, *being candid is a natural part of negotiation* (it is most definitely not the application of a technical procedure implemented by "telling it like it is"); second, *in the process of negotiated confrontation, the two partners learn that their confrontations do not lead to their breaking apart,* and thus the patient can more and more safely trust that relational ruptures are reparable (see Tronick and Weinberg, 1997).

Levenkron concludes her account thus: "I hope I have shown that the process of what we call 'working through an enactment,' ideally, does not take place through post hoc analysis, but rather, that the working through *is* the analysis and occurs as we live it: this is the negotiation." To this I can only say, Amen.

PART III

SAFE BUT NOT TOO SAFE

8

One Need Not Be a House to Be Haunted

A Case Study[1]

> One need not be a chamber to be haunted—One need not be a house. Far safer, through an abbey gallop, than unarmed, one's self encounter in a lonesome place. Ourself behind ourself, concealed, should startle most. Assassin hid in our apartment, be horror's least.
>
> —Emily Dickinson, "Poem 670"

What makes Emily Dickinson's imagery seem so right? Why should one part of oneself be terrified of meeting another part in a lonesome place? How does a person come to feel "haunted"? And how does one's sense that another person, one's patient perhaps, is haunted? And what does a therapist do about the patient's haunted feeling, that is, if the patient becomes able to speak of it? Being "haunted" entails the feeling that something strange is hovering about. So let me start there, with the experience of strangeness.

Some decades ago, David Schecter (1973), an interpersonal analyst from the William Alanson White Institute and a member of Sybil Escalona's infant research team, developed the concept of strangeness anxiety. Schecter foreshadowed the discovery by attachment researchers of

[1]This chapter materially expands and revises a version that appeared in *Psychoanalytic Dialogues,* 2003, 13:689–709. Adapted by permission.

the basic significance of the interpersonal context in the shaping and reshaping of the meaning of trauma in human personality. Schecter asserted that an infant's sense of "continuity of being" can be traumatically disrupted if the mothering person fails to help render the strange into what is engagingly novel or even familiar. Schecter's is a particularly important formulation insofar as it accurately defines trauma not according to its specific content, form, or objective magnitude, but by the degree to which it cannot be held or contained by a person without a flooding of unintegratable affect. He observed that, to cope with oncoming psychological disorganization, the infant "freezes" (one of the hallmarks of a dissociative response to trauma), leading to what he called "dys-recognition of me-ness" and disruption of the subjective continuity of "I." Trauma, in these terms, is caused by the "shock of strangeness" in an interpersonal field on which the security of selfhood depends and is relative to the developmental threshold at which the person can accommodate the strangeness at that point in time.

Helping a person to accommodate the strangeness is a task often left to a therapist or analyst years later. The problem, of course, is that in the intervening years the person has developed a repertoire of adaptive interpersonal strategies that have, as one of their purposes, the avoidance of strangeness—an avoidance that paradoxically leaves them haunted. In this context, therapy is and is not a welcome opportunity to change things. Dynamically-oriented therapy, as Schecter observed, "constitutes a radical rupturing of patterns of responsive interaction that have had their fundamental structuring way back in infancy"; and, because of this link, some dissociated part of the patient's self frequently experiences the analyst as an "unfathomable stranger whom he dare not trust" (p. 27). Schecter was underlining that inherent to the analytic situation is a genuine threat to the patient's learned patterns of social reciprocity—in effect, his experience of core selfhood based on what attachment researchers now call implicit relational knowing (Lyons-Ruth, 1998; Lyons-Ruth et al., 2001). Accordingly, the analyst must incorporate into his mode of relating his awareness of this disruption and the shame it generates as a result of the patient's feeling his dissociated affect as too much for the other to bear were it to be expressed. What is too shockingly strange to be held as "me," becomes what Sullivan (1953) called "not-me," and it is here that the haunting begins to be felt in the treatment. This is a ghost that not only evokes fear; it also generates *shame* when it emerges in the patient–therapist relationship. Speaking to this point, Nathanson (1996) remarks,

> The entire system of psychotherapy, as we had been taught it, worked only if we overlooked the shame that we produced day in and day out in our therapeutic work. No wonder there was so much shame left in the case failures that Helen Block Lewis (1971) studied. It became clear that post-Freudian society had been treated for almost everything *but* shame, and that the degree and severity of undiagnosed and untreated shame problems far exceeded anything we had ever imagined [p. 3].

Residual shame left over from childhood is a part of everyone's emotional makeup, and invariably some portion of it remains unassimilated. I suggest, then, that what makes Emily Dickinson's words hit home is that, to one degree or another, we all know the experience of feeling haunted. The presence of trauma and dissociation is to be found in the personality functioning not only of persons whose history is linked to massive physical violence or sexual abuse, but also of those who grew up without such a history. Increasing support for this view is coming from many quarters, including ongoing research by attachment theorists who have found that a secure attachment relationship offers a buffer against what Schecter called strangeness anxiety and against trauma generally. Indeed, one of the earliest findings of Bowlby (1969) was that the loss of the primary attachment relationship in itself constituted a severe trauma, whose impact on the small child could be charted through stages beginning with protest and ending, chillingly, in a state of detachment. Interestingly, Barach (1991) has argued from his reading of Bowlby's work that the detachment Bowlby describes "is actually a type of dissociation [and that] although Bowlby uses the term detachment in describing how children respond to abandonment, he is really describing a dissociative process" (p. 118).

In recent years, attachment theorists have gone further and elucidated how dissociation, in the sense of dissociative responses, can become an integral part of ongoing, troubled attachment relationships. Dissociative responses in both the child and the parent have been described by attachment theorists who are studying the relationship between disorganized/disoriented attachment and the presence of adult dissociative pathology (e.g., Barach, 1991; Liotti, Intreccialagli, and Cecere, 1991; Liotti, 1992, 1995; Main and Morgan, 1996). A key feature of this research, so striking to an analytic clinician, is the observation of the moments when an attachment figure who should be the source of safety does something that the child finds frightening, thus placing the child in an intolerable bind.

Main (1995) reports that she and her colleagues have been able to provide some support for Liotti's hypothesis that a disorganized/disoriented pattern of early attachment (type D) may be a prelude to dissociative pathology in adulthood. Main calls particular attention to "phenotypic similarities among some disorganized/disoriented infant Strange Situation behavior, some lapses in discourse and reasoning observed in the Adult Attachment Interview, and dissociative phenomena" (p. 456). Main adds, however, that she sees this proposal as still largely speculative. At least for the present, she sees disorganized infant attachment as approaching the status of a necessary but not sufficient condition for the subsequent development of adult dissociative pathology. That is to say, an early childhood marked by encounters with an attachment figure who has become inexplicably frightening may predispose one to the wholesale use of dissociation as a basic structuring principle of the psyche.

Childhood attachment patterns are in part designed to evoke soothing from an adult in an emergency. Thus the failure of the interpersonal pattern to provide the needed soothing in the face of trauma leads to profound impairment in affective self-regulation. In this light, current research in neuroscience is particularly relevant to understanding the residue of attachment disregulation and separation distress and the dissociation that may come in their wake. Van der Kolk (1987a) for example, writes of changes in the neurotransmitter systems of the brain:

> It is likely that certain childhood experiences make people vulnerable to disorders of these neurotransmitter systems, which may later be activated under stress, *particularly after the loss of affiliative bonds.* The nature and severity of childhood stress may determine which neurotransmitter system is most vulnerable to later disruption [p. 46, italics added].

Especially interesting is van der Kolk's mention of the unanticipated research finding that the "separation cry" in a variety of species is mediated by endogenous opioids, and that the areas in the brain with the highest opiate receptor density

> are precisely those that have been found to be involved in the maintenance of social bonding. . . . Thus, there now is some evidence that pain perception, separation distress, and affiliative behavior are all mediated, at least in part, by the brain opiate

> system, and that all three are related to discrete and interconnected neuroanatomical areas. It is conceivable that unalleviated separation distress during infancy makes a person more likely to seek the comfort of actions that stimulate the opioid system to cope with adult separation distress [pp. 40–42].

The implication is that addictive behavior, including actual substance addiction, might be directly linked to affect dysregulation related to attachment disruption. If this is accurate, it would further illuminate the issue, discussed at length in chapter 6, of why psychotherapeutic intervention seems to be most effective when embedded in a relational context rather than a context that is primarily symptom oriented. Even among clinicians who treat posttraumatic stress disorder from more behavioral models, the therapeutic emphasis is shifting away from the simple eliciting and deconditioning of a recallable traumatic event. The contemporary emphasis is on making more clinical use of the patient–therapist relationship through the enacted reliving and processing of unsymbolized interpersonal patterns that originated early in life. One can expect to see issues of addiction as well as of haunting as this processing goes forward.

Dolores

Let me now share some of my clinical work with a patient whom I call Dolores. Her pseudonym, I must confess, came to me without too much thought. Her pained, haunted look was barely concealed beneath her fixed smile. Even in repose, Dolores looked worried, but she claimed not to have a problem in the world except for her bad judgment about people.

Mostly, Dolores could not figure out why someone as bright, pretty, and loving as she kept finding the wrong boyfriends. That concern, which, in her words, was interfering with her finding the "right" man to marry, had escalated when she turned 31 shortly before she came to see me. It finally reached a level of urgency that led her to seek help. Marriage to the right man was why she was here, she announced, and married she would be. She clearly meant business.

We began a three-sessions-a-week analysis with Dolores on the couch. She seldom failed to arrive punctually, never missed an hour, worked hard, and was totally committed to the process despite her pragmatic opening declaration. But there was a part of me that could not shake the feeling that I had agreed to something that I would regret later. I subliminally felt I was playing Faust to her Mephistopheles. Sooner or later I was going to have to deliver on my end of the bargain, and somehow I felt I had not read the fine print. I, too, would come to know the experience of being haunted.

Dolores lived alone and worked in the sales department of an advertising agency. She was the younger of two children raised in Chicago in a lower middle-class Jewish family. Her brother, two years older, was the "bad" child, and she was the "good" one—good except for two issues that drove her parents to distraction: she was still single, and she was a binge eater. The latter problem would not have bothered her parents particularly, except that, when she was not dieting, she would be about 25 pounds overweight for relatively long periods of time (which they saw as the reason she was not yet married). In fact, seemingly unknown to them, she was also a part-time bulimic, using purging mainly to keep her weight from escalating to a point that could obliterate her status as the good child and her father's favorite—a tenuous position she had, in fact, achieved by default when her brother fell apart in adolescence.

It gradually became clear from the description of her day-to-day life that 30 minutes with her was about all that most people, especially most men, could take before they found one excuse or another to back slowly to the door in the hope of making a clean getaway. She revealed her bulimia to me, shamefully, during our fifth session together, along with the admonition, "It's not why I'm here, and I don't want it turned into a big deal because I don't do it all that much. But I know I'm not supposed to hold anything back, so I'm telling you about it right away." Other patients had said to me that they knew they were not supposed to hold anything back so they were telling me about such and such right away, but there was something so impersonally contractual about the manner in which Dolores said it that its chilling impact on me remained throughout the first phase of our work.

Even as I write this, I can reexperience both her tone and my response to it. I can sense the shadowy presence of a part of my self backpedaling away from her, just like the other men in her life, and I can still feel the residue of my wish to disown the existence of that part. To paraphrase Emily Dickinson, I did not want to confront that particular self "behind myself concealed." At the time, my wish to backpedal away from her was too destabilizing for me to contain it and reflect on it conflictually, so I dissociated a part of myself I was not yet ready to accommodate. I attributed my internal reaction to an unanalyzed repugnance toward vomiting that was unexpectedly surfacing in me, that is, an aversive reaction to the bulimia itself. It was not until later in her treatment that I began to recognize and accept that my reaction did not have to do with *what* she was talking about. It was a reaction to Dolores, not to her eating disorder. It was a reaction to a level of disingenuousness that was so ego syntonic that I experienced it as foreclosing the possibility of authentic contact with her.

Her disingenuousness took the form of emotional distance masked by a facsimile of relatedness. In one way it came across as pretense, but in another way it claimed the right to be taken as sincerity. The impact of her personality, at that moment, evoked feelings in me so incompatible with one another that I found myself in a state of emotional deprivation but seemingly without reason. Needing to find an escape from what felt like too much to think about, I drained the moment of its personal immediacy by dissociating the part of myself that felt deprived by Dolores's "inauthenticity." She became for me at that moment, and remained for a while thereafter, my "good" patient toward whom I could access only positive feelings, mostly associated with how hard she was working. My self-protectiveness was in response to an aspect of Dolores that was not yet processable by me relationally, but that I could sense hovering over us, threatening to destroy our still fragile connection if it became thinkable. I told myself I simply was respecting her need for affective safety. But part of me knew, even then, that I was also fleeing from the shame of my unanticipated negative reaction toward a dissociated part of Dolores—her disingenuousness—a reaction that made me feel as if our relationship would not live to see another session if I were to let this "inauthentic" part of her remain in my consciousness. There was something about her that was hard to define, something perhaps more absent than present, something missing from her here-and-now presence that was not easily identifiable. I continued to be aware, quite uncomfortably aware, of feeling deprived, alone, and needful of something I was not getting. But it was not easy for me to deal with my feeling so empty while *with* her ("needy" might be more truthful) since Dolores was such a "good" patient and always trying so "hard."

Although I knew full well that Dolores made some contribution to what went wrong in her relationships with men, I prevented myself from "getting it personally." In every situation she described, the other person seemed to reveal in himself—just in time to save Dolores from getting badly hurt by trusting the wrong person—some major character flaw that totally overshadowed whatever might have been contributed by Dolores. The harder I tried to see her through their eyes, the more I felt I was unfairly trying to perfect someone who was already good enough, someone who by rights should be getting more out of life than she did. Yet I knew there had to be more to her even if I did not know what it was, and I wondered when, if ever, I would get to experience it. But even while I was wondering when I would meet the Dolores everyone else ran from, I had isolated from consciousness the part of me that, like these men, was backpedaling self-protectively away from that very aspect of Dolores I told myself I wanted to engage. I was making my own clean getaway through dissociation.

How might my clean getaway be most usefully conceptualized? Dissociation as a process does not function as a hermetically sealed cocoon. It is designed to allow a necessary exchange of information while protecting against affective shocks that might threaten self-continuity. My dissociative reaction did not keep me from knowing *about* my disjunctive reaction to Dolores; it kept me from fully experiencing my reaction as happening to *me*. I robbed the experience of personal immediacy by dissociating the self-state that was holding the feelings I was then too ashamed to own. The self-state I had dissociated became for me, in Emily Dickinson's language, a haunting presence that I could not shake for a long while. It was a forbidding ghost that linked me unconsciously with Dolores's own ghost in ways that were yet to be discovered. And still, in spite of the narrowness of my mode of relating to Dolores being very much in my own self-interest, I also believe that, during the first year of treatment, it served a positive function with regard to stabilizing Dolores's affect tolerance.

After that first year, space began to exist for other self-states in each of us through which reference could be made to what had been formerly unspeakable, without the dangerous sense that our attachment would be threatened with potentially irreparable rupture. But getting there was not easy. And it sure wasn't easy on my ego, particularly my male ego. The following is from a session about two years into treatment. At this point we had a track record together and could say things that earlier on were not possible. Although it was still very difficult for her to confront, self-reflectively, her here-and-now experience of our relationship, several different parts of her were now trying to have a voice, one of them, as frequently happens, through a dream. In this case, however, the dream was less reported than lived—entering the session and taking it over as if it had a life of its own.

I could tell something was brewing even as the session began:

> Any man who's nice to me is a schmuck. Why am I still interested in *Stanley*? For some reason I'm not depressed. *Why are you writing this down? I don't like it!* It feels like you are making it into a problem of *mine*. All it means is that I'm becoming more independent. My bosses at work don't really help me. They have nothing worthwhile to add to what I think so I'd rather they don't say anything.
>
> It's weird having my father and mother visit me in New York. They're leaving today. When I got home from work last night they all had eaten and hadn't waited for me. I screamed, "Get out–I don't want you in the house for another second." She wanted to know if the reason I was mad was because I was hungry, and that she would make me something. I felt like killing her. I told her I wasn't hungry, and that all she cares about is food. I said that I couldn't care less about whether they waited dinner for me and I wouldn't eat her food if I was starving to death.
>
> She then started criticizing my father for having walked out of the room to pack their suitcases. My mother said, "I know him. He's going to do it all wrong." I shouted, '"For God's sake, he's only going to pack a couple of lousy suitcases." She said, "Everything will get wrinkled.'" I said, *"If you give him back his balls maybe he'll do things right!"*

I seem to remember a random thought about her father's balls, and *my* balls–that maybe we are each acting as though they were not our own. But I "packed" the thought away for future use without realizing that I was, at a different level, participating in an enactment of the very dynamics being described. Dolores went on,

> My mother didn't like that. She whined, "Leave me alone already." I said, "I'll leave you alone if you leave *me* alone." But I didn't know what I meant, because she didn't really do anything to me. It just felt like she did. My father came back and he looked sorry for me, but he was too much of a weak schmuck to say anything to her. Why am I still interested in Stanley? Any man who's nice to me is a schmuck.

At that moment her voice did not have the usual tone of unrelatedness that I found so difficult to be with in the room. It was as if I could sense some other part of her trying to find a way in. Was I being defensively hopeful? I did not think so because I was feeling a kind of tenderness toward her that was new. But I was not without some trepidation about whether I was about to offer myself up as just another schmuck who liked her. I said, softly, and probably a bit awkwardly, "Yes, it must be unbearable to feel your mother so totally walled off from what matters to you, and for you to feel so alone, so ashamed, and also so angry that there's no way to get through to her." I knew full well that I was speaking also about how it felt for me, at least until this moment, to be with her–including the shame of my own neediness.

It was here that the dream entered and took over. She suddenly shifted her position on the couch and her voice got very small:

> I had a dream last night where I was on the street at a payphone, talking to Stanley, but I was more interested in looking at the restaurant across the street. All I can remember saying to Stanley was "I have to get something to eat. I have nothing at home." I go across the street but for some reason the phone was still in my hand and Stanley was still on the line. I don't know how that could be because the cord isn't that long. As I approached the store, I could see it was closed, which was a shock because it seemed to be open when I was away from it. This was the worst part of the dream. It was like a nightmare. I felt like there was nothing for me anywhere. I was desperate, and I screamed over the phone, again "It's closed, and I have nothing to eat at home," hoping that Stanley would invite me over. But there was only silence on the other end. I said, "Are you still there?" He replied, "Yes, I'm still here," but didn't say anything else. It was horrible. I woke up in a panic that he would get off the line.

I said, "That must have been terribly frightening–the possibility that the connection could be broken. It *is* like a nightmare. I know its scary to get back into the dream, but do you think you might let yourself feel just enough of it again so you can you tell me more about what that silence is like?"

She curled up on the couch and began to sob:

> It's like . . . it's like, I have to hold my mind together to keep from going crazy. Its not just being alone. I stopped feeling real. There was nothing for me anywhere . . . inside me too . . . not just outside. Not just food. I felt like I had just brought this on myself, like Stanley was so disgusted by my neediness, and he didn't

> want to show how much he hated me clinging to him . . . I couldn't even hang up the phone even when I went to the store. If he had gotten off the line I would have gone crazy. I *know* it. Thank God I woke up.

The powerful transference–countertransference aspect of this dream was inescapable to each of us. She was afraid I would hang up in disgust if I "really" saw her neediness. And I was afraid I would hang up to avoid the neediness she evoked in me. We were on the threshold of being able to process a ghostly "not-me" presence that had haunted Dolores's inner world since childhood. It was a presence so annihilating to her early, attachment-based self that she developed a dissociative mental structure designed to insulate her from the thing she "knew" she inevitably would encounter in a needed other if she permitted herself to trust. A key piece of this self-state configuration was her ability to *reverse* in her relationships what had been done to her as a child; thus she left the *other person* in a destabilized state. Her principle was "Do unto the other before the other could do unto her."

If one translates our relationship into dream language, it is not difficult to imagine my experiencing Dolores as a kind of store that seemed open and available when I was away from it and mystifyingly closed when I approached it. This dissociated aspect of Dolores had left me, relationally, in a state of need that I could feel but not "think." I was unable to communicate any of this from my own dissociated state that I felt as shameful because I feared that she, like Stanley, might break the connection and, like Dolores in the dream, I would feel that I had brought it on myself.

During the next several years, as the analytic work became safer, more alive, and more open, Dolores began to *be* parts of herself that had been less available in the here and now of our relationship. She also showed some pleasure in taking her mind (not simply her life) as a focus of attention. To Dolores, all this felt like a mixed blessing, including the fact that the more I emerged from my own dissociative cocoon, the more I took on a presence of my own. Indeed, for at least one part of Dolores, this new development in the work was experienced as a betrayal of what was supposed to be our "bargain": that she would lie on the couch, be a good patient, have many dreams, and leave married. This was not the direction in which things were moving, and to say that she was distressed would be an understatement. Part of her distress was because of her growing recognition that I was beginning to matter to her, and this realization, in turn, threatened long-standing patterns of seeking comfort and soothing through food rather than relationship. She was beginning to gain the capacity to experience all this as conflictual, and she needed to process the transition from dissociation to conflict more slowly. The following dream describes both her predicament and the potential space to begin processing it:

> I was in my office doing some work and my boss Phil came in and out, disturbing me with his suggestions. You probably think his name means something about why I put him in the dream, but I don't. In the dream I put a chair against the door and leaned on it with all my might but it wasn't good enough. He kept finding a way in. So I decided to get out through a secret door. I crawled through it but I still wasn't outside. I was in a space where there was a lot of food stored. All kinds of food. Meat that was wrapped and some of it unwrapped. And jars of soup. It looked like my mother's lentil soup. I kept looking behind me to see if Phil had found the door and was coming through after me.

We discussed the dream, of course. So it was time for the other shoe to drop. Dolores arrived for the next session in a very belligerent state of mind. She said, "Everything feels like it's out of my control. I don't know if analysis is worth it." Half angrily and half shamefully, she admitted how afraid she was of "letting go." She was terrified that doing so would affect her work and the other areas of her life that had been running well. "All I want from analysis," she said, "is to work on why I can't find the right man."

I was starting to feel more than a little tense. Her demeanor became increasingly accusatory as she began telling me how she felt betrayed by me and that what was happening was not what she had bargained for. I was there to help her find a husband, and not only was I failing at what she hired me for, I was starting to ruin everything else in her life.

Part of me was wishing that the "good girl" I liked would return. Where was the Dolores who knew that, unlike her father, I was not a "schmuck" and would have the balls to appreciate how smart and pretty she was and show it by removing whatever blind spot was keeping her from recognizing the "right" man? I found myself wondering if perhaps her father was right. Maybe if she just lost those 25 pounds Stanley might stop being a workaholic and notice her. Maybe I should address her weight more forcefully. But I was also, equally strongly, in touch with another part of myself that felt ready to engage directly the Dolores I was avoiding. I could feel myself emerging more completely from our shared dissociative space.

As long as I continued to remain even partly dissociated, I would be imprisoning myself, and the work would stagnate. I would be continuing to anesthetize that part of me that perceived things about Dolores in our relationship that still evoked distress in me, even though I no longer feared that our relationship might be torn apart irreparably. To the extent that Dolores and I sustained this remaining area of collusion indefinitely, she would be losing an important part of me and losing what that part could provide to help her grow. I felt I could no longer allow her self-protective insulation from the mind of the other to remain unexamined because I was unwilling to experience and cognitively process what was now containable by me as *internal conflict.* I could not allow myself to remain affectively walled off from this part of her personality and know "about" it only from her relationships with others. I knew I could no longer hold on to my affectively insulated, and thereby bewilderingly sympathetic, view of her continued rejection by all who crossed her path.

As if reading my mind, she said, "*You* think I'm fighting off marriage and want to stay a child. I don't care. I'm over 30 . . . I can't afford to wait five more years to get married . . . Maybe therapy isn't the answer. I just have to get married and you aren't helping me do it. *So . . . what should I do?*"

Unlike similar moments in the past, I felt myself free of the pressure to be different from everyone else in her life and free of the need to grope around for some response even though I knew in advance it would be hollow and empty. I said nothing. She said nothing. There was just silence, but it was not an empty silence. I felt oddly calm but in a state of readiness. I was ready for something to surface from the silence, something that was unpredictable from our history together, something I could only hope would not lead to our drowning in negative affect. Breaking the silence, Dolores said in an angry voice,

> I had a dream last night where I was in the cafeteria of my company. I was eating ice cream, but I don't like the ice cream in the cafeteria. My mother was at the table and was saying "Eat it. There's nothing wrong with it." So I ate it and then I asked for another. Then I thought to myself, "Why am I eating this? I've been so good and lost so much weight. This is so fattening. I shouldn't be eating it. And I don't even like cafeteria ice

> cream." Then I had this thought, "Oh! It's okay. It's only a dream. As long as I'm really not eating it I won't get fat." But I saw my mother looking at me and I knew I was really eating it, and I began to get furious, and then I woke up.
>
> *It's freezing in here!* I don't know what I'm really annoyed with. Is it that I'm not getting what I want or that I don't understand why I'm not getting it? *It's so cold in here!* My mind's a blank. I'm the lowest weight I've ever been in my adult life. I'm controlling my impulses. But it doesn't get me what I want. If I stopped dieting I'd be fat. When my father is disappointed in me he turns to Joe—at least he used to before Joe got so crazy. He would hardly speak to me. When I spoke to him he would just grunt. *It's freezing in here. Why aren't you saying anything?*

What I said then was,

> Dolores, I can feel something in your tone of voice when you say, *"It's freezing in here?"* and *"Why aren't you saying anything?"* that for the first time makes me aware of another part of myself besides the one that wants to make it warmer in here and wants to say something so you won't feel so alone and cold inside. I wouldn't let that part of me come out before, because I think I was afraid if it did you would feel abandoned and criticized in the way you do with your mother. Even now, I can feel another part of me whispering, "Don't say it!" But I'm going to give it a try.
>
> What I was feeling, Dolores, is that nothing I do is good enough: Now it's too cold. What am I, a puppet on a string? I'll be damned if I'm going to talk just because you expect me to! And I'm not going to turn up the radiator either. I know you didn't ask me to, but I know you expect me to offer.

I was aware at that moment that it was very *hot* in the room. In fact, most of my patients complain that it is *always* too hot, a condition that I have long recognized as both accurate and attributable to my own idiosyncratic sense of temperature.

After a long silence, Dolores finally responded. What she said astonished me—not simply her words but her affect. She said that she, too, was in touch with different parts of herself reacting differently. One part of her wanted to quit analysis, stalk out of the room, and leave me in a puddle of guilt about the mess I had made. But she also could feel another part that was louder. That part could tell from how I was talking that I *did* care about her, and that that part was real also. She then revealed that she knew after the dream that her mother watching her also applied to me and that she could tell that I was now looking as much at *her* as at the things she was saying.

I replied that maybe when she was with me, in the room, it was just too difficult for her to think about any of that because her fear and her shame got in the way. Maybe she was afraid of feeling too needy and that I would "get off the line," as she was afraid Stanley would do in her other dream. There was some more give-and-take, during which she began to relax even more noticeably. She said that she felt more genuinely "with" me at that moment and that maybe we could come back to the dream later on because, "Maybe you do care about me and not simply about your analysis of me."

I view Dolores's "ice cream" dream as a transitional point, an important one, signaling a shift in mental structure from dissociative to conflictual. I think of the dream as representing her awareness of her dissociative processes and how she uses them—"Oh, it's only a dream. As long as I'm really not eating it, I won't get fat"—and a simultaneous awareness that her use of dissociation was no longer seamless. She saw her mother looking at her in a way that seemed real, and she knew that the same was true of me. She was unable automatically to withdraw her consciousness from what was taking place in our here-and-now relationship and was thus forced to be aware of her conflict among self-states, some holding her needs, desires, and wishes, and others holding her fear, shame, and rage. She, too, was now more conflicted than dissociated.

I think this shift contributed heavily to my being able to address a part of Dolores that formerly was "not-me" and was thus unable to participate in analytic self-reflection. I sensed that she could take in my otherness differently, and I became less afraid than I had been that our attachment would be ruptured irreparably. Looking back, I have come to see that my earlier sense that I dare not go there was responsive to a core of annihilation anxiety in Dolores that was later partially processed through the work we did together in response to her "payphone" dream. In other words, my eventual ability to gain access to my own "not-me" experience vis-à-vis hers, and tell her about it, was not simply a clinical judgment made unilaterally (see Bromberg, 1998a). It was part of a dyadic process that included a state shift in Dolores to which I had been responsive affectively but not yet cognitively, a shift in mental structure that communicated her greater capacity to stay in the moment with me and process, intersubjectively, what was taking place between us.

The following excerpt is from a session that took place about six months later, two days after Dolores had been rejected by yet another man, Peter, who at first seemed interested in her and toward whom Dolores's genuine regard had been palpable. The session attests to Dolores's growing ability to work in the transference–countertransference field and hold the experience of internal conflict more and more comfortably.

"Yesterday I went off my diet completely. What a waste! *I'm doing the same thing again!* Another guy who's ambivalent!"

"A waste of what?" I ask.

She replies, instantly and laconically, "Oh, all this time and effort."

"Time and effort?" I say.

With a contemptuous laugh, Dolores says, "Yeah, it's a lot of work making a guy think you like him more than you really do."

"Oh!" I reply. "I guess you fooled me too. I had the impression that a part of you was enjoying herself with Peter."

A long silence. "I feel so stupid now," she mutters. "You made me get back in touch with that part of myself that was happy being with him and wasn't thinking about my next date . . . and I hate that part of me. I feel like she's going to make me settle."

"Settle?" I ask.

"Yeah. The right man will still be out there and I won't have him. I'll have nothing."

I reply, "The man you *do* have will feel like nothing?"

She begins to cry. "Yeah. And *I* feel like nothing! Empty inside. I hate myself when I feel like this."

"So when you let yourself feel nourished by someone—*really* feel it—there's another part of you that makes you feel stupid."

"I think that's what happened when I was with Peter. Right near the end of the date. Maybe that's why he blew me off. I was feeling cooler and more distant and tried to cover it up by saying flattering things to him. It was so different than the way I was earlier. I could see that he knew it was fake and he looked confused. But I couldn't stop."

"Yes," I reply. "You liked being with him and didn't want to lose him, but you had to satisfy another part of you that was making you feel ashamed for *really* being involved, as if real involvement is stupidity because you are wasting the potentially better man who is still out there, somewhere. So you tried to find a way to satisfy both parts of you and could feel how impossible it is."

She responds angrily, "I *refuse* to believe that!! It's *not* impossible. You are making me feel like I'm asking for too much. Why *shouldn't* I have the best?"

"I can see that the way I put it made you feel ashamed. Does it seem that I am telling you that you are greedy?" I ask.

"Yeah! Exactly. Like I want everything! I don't have *anything!* What's the sense of being pretty and sexy! I'm furious." Silence.

Her voice changes here, and I can feel her struggling to deal with her conflict. "I was going to say that maybe that's why I stopped dieting, that I ate so much over the weekend because I was so angry. But I know that isn't so. The anger was there, but it made me feel better to be angry. It covered up the thing that really scares me. I feel like I'm going to disappear . . . like there's nothing inside and I start not to feel real. That's why I think I ate—not the anger. *Feeling hate makes me feel like a person again.*"

What follows, from a phase of my work with Dolores much further along in treatment, includes a series of dreams that led to her recalling some of her most painful memories. These dreams came at a point in her treatment when she was able to trust that I would not allow her to drown in shame while she was reliving early traumatic affect that felt as if it could get out of control. She felt that she could count on me to respond to her fear and shame and help her modulate them. I am including this material because I feel it is a uniquely interesting example of the relationship among dreams, enactment, dissociation, and trauma. But at the same time I am reluctant to include it because it seems too "neat," and I do not want to leave the impression that this is how most of my treatments turn out. Although Dolores and I did access and process some early traumatic memories, it has seldom been my experience that actual early events need be recovered if a treatment is to be successful with a trauma survivor. Here is Dolores's dream:

> I was in my apartment with another couple. We were preparing a dessert with a chocolate cream sauce. I left to get something I needed and saw a man watching me. I tried to hide because I was afraid he would take something I needed for the dessert. There were a lot of things I had, including some tequila. There were two bottles of tequila, and I took one of them to mix into the dessert. The reason I decided on the tequila was because there were two bottles, and I didn't want to use something I only had one of. Giving him the second bottle of

> tequila wouldn't matter because I wouldn't be left without any. I got very angry and felt that I now had nothing, even though I still had the other.

It was clear to both of us that this dream touched on the issue of choice, on her being unable to find the "right" man. If she picked one, she would leave herself without a way to have the other. Unless he was identical to the first, she would lose the other and feel as if she had nothing. But, unlike earlier dreams in which choice was impossible because it led to nothing but emptiness, the dreamer here seemed to be a part of her that could now actively struggle with the experience of choice and the experience of internal conflict between loss and satisfaction that accompanies it (see also chapter 6). In the next session, Dolores brought in another dream:

> I dreamed I was in the neighborhood where I grew up. I was on Third Street where there was a little stand that sold grilled sausages and grilled chicken sandwiches. Some guy bought a grilled sausage and left it there for a minute. When he came back it was gone, and where it was there was a grilled chicken sandwich instead. I don't like chicken sandwiches. but I love grilled sausages, and I especially used to love the ones from that stand when I was a kid. Joe used to binge on them.

I asked, "Do you think you might let yourself go back into the dream and feel what it is like to be in front of the stand—to look around and see what you notice as you stand there?" She had done this, with limited success, many times before, but this time her effort was clearly different. As she began to enter her dream space, I could feel how upset she was becoming and that she was trying to hide it. I told her that I could feel her upset and wondered aloud if she would like to come back or if she thought she could stay there a little longer and signal me, maybe by raising her hand, when it was beginning to feel like too much. She seemed much relieved and said she wanted to stay in it because she felt she was near something that was important but very scary.

I asked again what she saw when she looked around, and she replied that she saw a car parked near the stand. I asked if she could move closer to the car. She started to raise her hand but then put it down, saying she felt very small and scared:

> I can see a man in the car watching me. I think I can also see my brother and his friend playing around near the stand, and I'm trying to get their attention but they're ignoring me. The man in the car might be the same man who bought the sausage. I feel like my brother and his friend know him, but they're pretending they don't.

She suddenly began to sob hysterically and said she remembered something and wished she had not, something that happened when she was about 10 years old, with a man in a car—something sexual.

> I remember his exposing his penis to me but I don't remember what else happened. It's all a blank after that. But I remember running home and my mother was there and I was crying, the kind of crying where you can't breathe because of the heavy sobs. I don't remember what she said, but I don't think anyone really took me seriously. I also remember when I was about 13 there was a mouse in my room and I ran screaming to my mother but she wouldn't believe me. The same thing happened when my brother was watching me when my parents went out. I told them about something he did to me and she wouldn't believe me. I don't remember what it was. I felt like I had said something so bad that I could never be forgiven. I can see the expression on her face. It was like, for just a second, she was forced to believe me and I had ruined her image of me forever. I think it was the worst day in my life. I wished I had never said that.

We then began to talk about what it felt like to have revealed a secret that she knew her mother was forced to believe even though she then told herself it was not true. Gradually, more of the details of the secrets began to emerge, many of them connected to the details of her dreams, such as tequila, sausages, and "non-Kosher" men, and aspects of her relationship with Joe that almost tore her heart out to recall. As the analysis continued, still more secrets followed, including those about aspects of *our* relationship that she had been holding in a sequestered place—dissociated "truths" that now became thinkable, sayable, and relationally discussable, rather than new versions of something so unredeemably bad that our attachment would be smashed beyond repair if we let them out of the attic.

Coda

Thane Rosenbaum (2002) voices the bitter truth of trauma "survival" through irony:

> Shutting the door of your own home won't make it safe. But maybe you can shut the door on yourself. Hide in one of those rooms, maybe even in the attic. Crawl inside and take cover from the hurt. After a while, with any luck, no one will even notice that you've been gone. . . . All that's left to decide is when, if ever, to reemerge [p. 149].

Dolores did indeed finally reemerge, but I will let the story of her treatment end here. Let me say only that, yes, her bulimic symptoms did gradually stop; she did get married; and from what I have heard she is able to live life creatively and lovingly, with all the normal ups and downs of satisfaction, frustration, and hope. And, yes, she no longer seemed haunted.

The "truth" that is held by a dissociated state as an affective memory without a coherent autobiographical depiction of its traumatic origin haunts the rest of the self. It remains a ghostly horror, even in an otherwise successful analysis, unless a new perceptual reality is created between patient and analyst that can in some way alter the narrative structure that maintains the dissociation as though the past were still a present danger. I offer a view of psychoanalytic personality growth in which part of its therapeutic action depends on the freedom of the analyst to make optimal use of dissociation as an interpersonal process that includes the analyst's dissociative experience as well as the patient's, and in so doing maximizes the patient's capacity to self-regulate affect in those areas where trauma has left its mark.

The clinical implication is that the locus of therapeutic action is not in the material that is told to the analyst as if it were a buried fantasy uncovered by piecing together the links between a patient's associations. Rather, therapeutic action is organized *affectively,* through the process of enactment between patient and analyst, where it then has a chance to be symbolized by the verbal meaning attached to the affective perception of what is taking place in the here and now. Insight, from this view, is coconstructed through the interaction of the various and shifting self-states of both patient and analyst—through the interplay between the associative *content* and the dissociative *context* that organizes it.

One final note: The eruption of intense affect in therapy does not in itself signal the presence of trauma. Properly speaking, the "spontaneous overflow of powerful feelings," as William Wordsworth (1802) wrote, is what defines poetry, provided "it takes its origin from emotion recollected in tranquility" (p. 886).[2] To be sure, as therapists we know that the spontaneous overflow of powerful feelings often leads not to poetry but to its antithesis—a chaotic flooding of affect that has a life of its own, whose origin cannot be recollected in tranquility because it was not *experienced* in tranquility. One of our goals as analysts is to enable our patients to experience a spontaneous overflow of powerful feelings as safe rather than fearsome and shameful. If therapy is to provide a tranquil context for the relived emotion—if we are to help transmute traumatic affect into a potential for poetry—what is needed? My answer: a safe enough interpersonal environment, one that has room for both the analyst's affective authenticity and an enacted replaying and symbolization of early traumatic experience that does not blindly reproduce the original outcome. It is through this process that, I believe, the dissociated ghosts of "not-me" are best persuaded, little by little, to cease their haunting and participate more and more actively and openly as affectively regulatable, self-reflective aspects of "me."

---

[2]Interested readers are referred to Stuart Pizer's (2004) clinically moving and conceptually rich paper in which he draws centrally on Wordsworth's trope,"emotion recollected in tranquility," to explore the interface of impasse, dissociation, love, and discipline in the analytic process.

9

"Something Wicked This Way Comes":

Where Psychoanalysis, Cognitive Science, and Neuroscience Overlap[1]

In September 2001, while I was making some preliminary notes for this chapter on trauma, dissociation, and conflict, the attack on the World Trade Center took place. I put the writing aside for a while, and when I came back to it I realized I had to make a difficult choice. There was no way I could discuss the impact on my mind and my life of the September 11th attack, and the events that followed, without changing the focus of this chapter, which I did not want to do. And simply to allude to the events seemed a preposterous trivialization of the horror.

Even now, as I look back, I find I am not ready in a personal way to write about what happened to me and to people I know. And yet I feel that, as a psychoanalyst who writes about trauma and the manifold human responses to it, I should have something to say. This battle, in myself, goes on without resolution. I could say, by way of excusing myself for not going more fully into the events of 9/11 and its aftermath, that life must go on, that we must resume the endeavors that were so horrifyingly interrupted, in my case writing about trauma. I do not know if this reasoning will satisfy you—or even me. It would be closer to the truth to say that, as I have worked and reworked this chapter, my

[1]An earlier version of this chapter appeared in *Psychoanalytic Psychology,* 2003, 20:558–574. Adapted by permission.

memories and my felt indecision about what I should do kept returning and echoing along the tracks of my sentences as I reviewed them. The best I can hope for is that what I have to say here will cast some light on what I and many others felt that day and on our inability to come to any final feeling of resolution. Let me begin with a memory from my childhood that can perhaps be read as allegorical, a memory that emerged while I was in the throes of struggling with these feelings as I attempted to write.

When I was a kid, an endless source of fascination was looking out of my bedroom window at our backyard garden to observe silently the mysterious interactions among the animals, birds, trees, bushes, and flowers. But, like the Garden of Eden, our garden received periodic visits from an infamous inhabitant of our neighborhood, a cat that was referred to by everyone in the vicinity as Adolf (I was a World War II kid). Adolf was an aggressive, predatory, seemingly fearless animal, whose viciousness and mean-temperedness terrorized the other neighborhood cats and most of the dogs. I hated this animal totally, and I was afraid of him too. Adolf would suddenly appear in our garden as if by magic. It was a very well fenced in area, and we were never able to discover how he entered. What he seemed to enjoy most was climbing our fruit trees to see if he could find a nest containing a baby bird or two to feast on. He seemed totally indifferent to the parent birds wildly flapping their wings and shrieking hysterically overhead, far overhead I might add. In the animal world, he was like the neighborhood bully.

One morning, as I was watching the action in the garden, I spotted Adolf. He was climbing stealthily up the trunk of an apple tree, clearly on his way to a nest. As he neared the top branches, two adult birds materialized, seemingly out of nowhere, and began to put on a performance that was nothing short of awesome. They were blue jays, and those birds gave new meaning to the word tough. Screaming, they swooped down on Adolf, reversing course inches from his head, precisely at the point beyond which Adolf's claws could reach. I had not seen blue jays in full action before that moment, and, I suspect, neither had Adolf. Adolf and I were both in a state of shock, but for Adolf the shock was personal.

Over and over, the two jays repeated their dive-bombing until Adolf did what I had never before seen him do or believed he ever could do. Shinnying backward down the tree trunk, he fell the final eight to ten feet and began to run. But there was no escape. The two birds pursued him wherever he went although he was now far from their nest. Neither the ferocity nor the precision of their aerial attacks showed any sign of diminishing, and their abrasive bird-curses became, if anything, even louder.

To this day I can recognize a blue jay's call the instant I hear it, and I still love it. The sound has always reminded me of the strangely comforting rasp of a rusty clothesline pulley as the line was being yanked on by my mother. These guys were literally driving Adolf crazy, and I was cheering them on. He could not fight because they were not reachable. He could not flee because it was a fenced-in garden, and Adolf apparently had forgotten where his secret passageway was. And he could not hide because they could find him wherever he was. It was then that I observed (although I didn't know it then) what I now realize was a remarkable example of dissociation as a defense against trauma—what Putnam (1992) has called the "escape when there is no escape." Adolf suddenly lay down right where he was and remained motionless. His body took on a strange, almost flaccid shape, and I began to wonder if he had died of fright. The blue jays kept up their counterattack for a short while longer and then flew off. As I said, I hated this animal and was in no rush to help him if he was still alive. But I stayed at the window, somewhat numbed myself at seeing this feline predator reduced to mush. Was he dead?

No! Adolf, as if hit by an electric charge, suddenly sprang upright, fur standing on end, and took off to a far corner of the garden where he lay, shaking, behind a bush. As I look back on this now, I wonder what he was like after that incident. I have no recollection of him in the garden after that time. Did he develop a cat version of posttraumatic stress disorder? Was his apparent memory loss for the location of his hidden tunnel the first sign? I was too young to hope he was plagued by flashbacks of blue jays, but that is neither here nor there. After that fateful day, my backyard no longer existed as it once was—neither for Adolf nor for me, quite. Dissociation had served its evolutionary function in each of us differently, but for both of us the present and the future had been changed.

The point of this vignette is once again to make as vivid as I can the power of dissociation when used as a defense. It is a defense unlike any other defense. In human beings, it bypasses cognitive modulating systems and, as LeDoux's (1989, 1994, 1996) research powerfully demonstrates, is clearly anchored in an evolutionary response that is equivalent in survival terms to certain genetically coded response patterns of other animals to a life-threatening attack by a predator.

The difference between dissociative experience in human beings and dissociative responses in nonhuman animals (including Adolf) is that humans are blessed (sometimes it feels more like cursed) with a self and with self-awareness.[2] The similarity is that, in animals and humans alike, dissociative responses serve the Darwinian imperative for survival. For humans, however, the highest survival priority is survival as a self. For nonhuman animals survival means, primarily, surviving in the face of a potential threat to *biological* life. I think this difference accounts in large part for the fact that the emotion of *fear* is usually what is observed in traumatized animals and what is studied when they are used as subjects. (To be sure, evolution has endowed animals with three responses to threat–fight, flight, and hiding–and, when none of these are possible, "growing dead.")

But for humans threats to life are far more complex. For humans, selfhood (including its cohesiveness, coherence, and continuity) *is* life, and the need to sustain selfhood when it is in jeopardy overrides all else. The emotions we find when we look at human trauma certainly include fear, but they are far more complex because they are products not simply of biology but of self-awareness. In our day-to-day work, we are painfully familiar with stories of suicide attempts–sometimes successful–in the face of potential or actual situations that are taken in as unbearable assaults on the felt core of what defines "who I am to myself." We might also wonder if it is the perpetration of such assaults on selfhood that comes closest to the essence of what we are trying to capture when we speak of "evil." Certainly, it is a function of the self to anticipate evil and to avoid it. Indeed, if the self is unable to perform this function, all its other claims are moot. But what happens when this function miscarries? This is my central concern in this chapter.

Something Wicked This Way Comes

"By the pricking of my thumbs, Something wicked this way comes." This line, the last part of which I appropriated for my title, is cackled by one of the witches in act IV of Shakespeare's (1606) *Macbeth.* It alludes to the unnatural certainty with which she, being a witch, could sense the arrival of impending evil before it got there. In this lady's case, as we know, her tingling thumbs worked perfectly. Macbeth showed up right on cue. But with most people who attach the same

[2]Although it remains a controversial issue, some current research in the area of animal behavior suggests that there may exist in certain nonhuman animals a capacity for self-awareness that is greater than had been believed.

kind of importance to reading flawlessly the signs that "something wicked this way comes," the signs frequently speak to a history of past traumatization. The paramount importance of reading the signs may be an indication that this person has devoted a lifetime to waiting vigilantly for the proverbial other shoe to drop, so as to never be caught unprepared when it does hit. It is to these people that Emerson (1851) speaks in his short poem, "Borrowing":

> Some of the hurts you have cured,
> And the sharpest you still have survived,
> But what torments of grief you endured
> From evils which never arrived!
>
> [p. 321]

Emerson, to my way of reading him, was describing the ironic outcome of successful dissociation as a protection against the repetition of early trauma. Waiting for evils that never arrive is a serious problem for a traumatized adult, a problem that arises from the achievement of his own self-cure. The living present and the image of the future serve largely as warnings designed to protect him against trauma that has already occurred. The capacity for imagination is perverted into a way of making sure that the impersonally remembered original event cannot be repeated. By consistently mobilizing for disaster, the person is already prepared for it and his ego is set to master it. The terrifying experience yet to come is a retrospectively falsified temporal event. The nature of the fear is real enough, but the mind retains it as dread of what can happen or is happening rather than as a memory of what *has* happened. The result is that the person, by continually enacting the affective memory, creates a world of miniature versions of the original situation and lives in that world as a reality that is substantiated through his ongoing relationships. It is as though he is not to be allowed any peace. Around each corner is potential trauma. Peace is simply the calm before the storm, and nothing can convince him otherwise. The "fail-safe" security of his dissociative defense system makes certain of that.

In human beings, dissociation is fundamentally not a defense, but a normal hypnoid capacity of the mind that works in the service of creative adaptation. It is a normal *process* that can become a mental *structure*. As a process, it can be enlisted as a defense against trauma by disconnecting the mind from its capacity to perceive what is too much for selfhood and sometimes sanity to bear. It reduces what is in front of someone's eyes to a narrow band of perceptual reality so that the unbearable aspect of what is taking place is not happening to "me." The experience of actual trauma then creates, as a defense against any recurrence of trauma, a dissociative mental structure that serves as an early warning system. The key quality of this structure is its ability to retain the adaptational protection afforded by the hypnoid separateness of incompatible self-states, so that each can continue to play its own role, unimpeded by awareness of the others.

It is this early warning system that, regardless of diagnosis, I believe accounts for most of what makes us experience certain patients as difficult (see chapter 6), and it is also the cornerstone of all personality disorders (see Bromberg, 1995a, submitted; Chefetz and Bromberg, 2004; Howell, 2005). For instance, Yoram Yovell (2000) discusses his work with his patient Tara. "Like Freud's patients," Yovell writes,

> Tara did not want to talk about her history of abuse with me, and only reported it in response to a direct question during our initial consultation. Like Freud's patients, she was terribly ashamed of it, and her memories of it were patchy and disjointed. Whenever the subject would come up in therapy, Tara would feel "numb" and dissociate in my office. She would then often skip the next session. She is unwilling and probably unable to work overtly in the transference at this point in treatment [p. 179].

It is my belief that a patient's so-called inability or unwillingness to work in the transference, such as described by Yovell, is directly tied to the person's reliance on dissociation as a means of foreclosing potentially traumatic encounters with the mind of a needed other in the here and now. Such encounters could threaten to trigger affective hyperarousal, including shame, without hope of regulating the affect through the relationship itself. This vulnerability to affective triggering (something found in every patient in certain areas of the personality) requires that analytic treatment embody a process that facilitates the growth of the patient's confidence in his sense of affective competency as the work progresses. Further, I suggest, this process depends, optimally, not on *avoiding* such encounters but on enabling the patient's here-and-now experience of them to be felt as more and more relationally trustworthy, making it possible for him to rely less and less automatically on dissociation as a proactive early warning system. Thus, as a clinician, I try to be as attuned as possible (often unsuccessfully) to those moments when my patient is experiencing his self-structure as not stable enough and not sturdy enough to encounter the input from my subjectivity. Such an encounter threatens to destabilize his experience of selfhood and thus increase dissociation in order to block the potential flooding of both shame and fear. Why shame in addition to fear?

Shame and the Therapeutic Reliving of Trauma

The reliving with one's therapist of unprocessed traumatic affect from the past, such as fear, is almost always accompanied by a dissociated here-and-now shame experience. The dissociated shame is triggered by the analyst's inevitable unawareness that his therapeutic "success" in revivifying the trauma is also bringing about, in the relationship with him, a reliving of the hunger for relief and soothing without the patient's having a way to communicate this hunger directly. I contend that, just as the self is relational, the *destabilization* of the self is also experienced relationally. That is to say, it is experienced as shameful. But why can't the shame be directly communicated? Why can't a patient put it into words and get it on the table? The answer, I submit, is that the person whose behavior is creating the distress is also the person most necessary to alleviate it. The therapist is creating the distress by inquiring after the trauma and is thus making the threat of self-destabilization palpable for the patient. The net result is that the shame of being hungry for soothing triggers its own dissociation. The patient cannot directly communicate either his need or his shame about it. I say *directly* communicate because dissociated experience is indeed communicated, but through enactment, where its presence is first felt subsymbolically, to use Bucci's (1997a) term.

So the person (in this case the analyst) from whom the patient hungers for a soothing response is least likely to be the person to offer it on his own because he is also the person whose behavior, albeit inadvertently, is causing the pain. And in the act of trying to help his patient, the analyst inevitably relives with the patient a collision of realities that was unthinkable at the time it was lived. By trying to help, the analyst has placed his patient in a situation whereby their own relationship has become more affectively complex and dangerous than can be safely contained as internal conflict—that is, within a single state of consciousness. If the patient's dissociated shame caused by this unaddressed and unprocessed aspect of the enactment *continues* to be unrecognized in the here and now, his dissociative mental structure remains in place and his ability to experience and resolve internal conflict is impeded.

What I am saying is that we constantly find ourselves engaging self-states kept apart from one another by dissociation and that a patient's ongoing subjective experience is frequently limited to a very narrow range. But this constraint does not mean that what is excluded from conscious subjectivity ceases to function communicatively. The communication process between patient and analyst embodies what Bucci (2001) calls a "subsymbolic" component. She writes, "In normal functioning as in pathology, we are constantly sending out and receiving subsymbolic signals. . . . *[I]n pathology the subsymbolic representations are largely dissociated from the symbolic modes that would provide meaning for them*" (p. 68, italics added). It is this subsymbolic component that, from my perspective, is played out interpersonally through dissociated enactments—dissociated in both members of the dyad.

When an enactment remains unrecognized in the here and now, when the patient's unprocessed experience of shame remains operative, the patient's early warning system designed to prevent retraumatization also remains operative, making its presence felt through the subsymbolic channel of communication. In this context—I am thinking here of difficult patients—the capacity to experience intrapsychic conflict is not present and opportunities to develop it are, in the interest of safety, foreclosed by the patient or at least compromised. Such are the fruits of dissociation in the shadow of trauma.

Affect Regulation

I am proposing that dissociation and conflict are interpenetrating aspects of human mental functioning—a perspective on the mind to which relational analysts such as Aron (1996, 2001; Aron and Anderson, 1998), Davies (1996, 1998a, 2004), Ghent (1992, 1994, 1995), Harris (1996, 1998a, b, 2005), Mitchell (1988, 1991, 1993, 2000), Stuart Pizer (1998, 2004), Donnel Stern (1997, 2003, 2004), and others have contributed importantly, each in his or her own way.

In this context, let me say a few words about enactment. What interpersonal/relational analysts call the unconscious communication process of enactment is, from my vantage point, the patient's effort to negotiate unfinished business in those areas of selfhood where, because of one degree or another of traumatic experience, affect regulation was not successful enough to allow further self-development at the level of symbolic processing by thought and language. In this light, a core dimension of the therapeutic process is to increase competency in regulating affective states without triggering the dread of retraumatization. But why is this so difficult to accomplish in treatment? Why don't analysts do it better and more consistently?

Philip Roth (1997) in *American Pastoral* writes poignantly of treatment, "You go to someone and you think, 'I'll tell him this.' But why? The impulse is that the telling is going to relieve you. And that's why you feel awful—if it's truly tragic and awful, it's not better, it's worse" (p. 82). All too often, Roth is correct and we all know it. "If it's truly tragic and awful, it's not better, it's worse." I want to say to him, "Even though we still haven't completely gotten it right yet, Mr. Roth, we are definitely working on it, and I think we're making progress."

If it is truly tragic and awful, the telling is not relieving because what is truly tragic and awful almost always is traumatic. It has a component that has been too overwhelming to be processed cognitively and is held, unprocessed, as affective memory (what cognitive psychologists call "nondeclarative" memory or "procedural" memory). *The telling, therefore, is not relieving because the telling creates a reliving of the unprocessed affect.* When traumatic experience is retold, it is relived. And unless the shame generated by the telling is recognized and addressed, telling makes it worse not better, because the part of self holding the shame remains dissociated and the patient feels even more hopeless than before. And yet, if we understand this, why is it still so difficult to find a solution?

> What will it take [for a trauma survivor] . . . to be reassured that the world won't go away, that there are antidotes for emptiness, that the past doesn't always have to swallow the future, that faith and trust are not toxic, lethal impulses, that demons can be undone or even reformed into friends, that the way to fill a home is not with furniture alone? [Rosenbaum, 2002, p. 152].

The problem lies in the fact that the dissociated horror of the past fills the present with affective meaning so powerful that no matter how "obviously" safe a given situation may be to others, a patient's perceptual awareness that he himself is safe would require a moment of consciousness that could potentially increase self-reflective capacity and thereby decrease reliance on dissociative hypervigilance. This moment of self-reflectiveness would require that the patient not be overwhelmed by his sense that "something wicked this way comes." Relaxing one's dissociative hypervigilance entails a risk that is felt as too dangerous to the patient's felt stability of selfhood. Thus, those parts of the patient's self dedicated to safety remain dissociatively in control.

According to Kihlstrom (quoted in LeDoux, 1989), the "key to consciousness is *self-reference,*" and in order for what is dissociated to become symbolized in conscious awareness, a "link must be made between the mental representation of the event and a mental representation of the *self* as the agent or experiencer" (p. 281). As Kihlstrom makes clear, these episodic representations of trauma, the only kind of representation a traumatized person is likely to have, reside in short-term or working memory. Rephrased in these terms, our question is: What makes it so difficult to link, in working memory, the dissociated reliving of something "truly tragic and awful" with a mental representation of the self as the agent or experiencer?

There are many different vantage points from which answers might be offered, but an especially interesting one is suggested by neuroscience research, most notably the work of LeDoux (1989, 1994, 1995, 1996, 2002). When considered in conjunction with Bucci's (1997a, b, 2001, 2002, 2003) cognitive research, LeDoux's findings provide at the brain level an additional source of data that point to a remarkable convergence between cognitive and neuroscience research and an interpersonal/relational psychoanalytic approach that works at the interface of dissociation, conflict, and self-state communication.

LeDoux (2002), in neurobiological terms, shows that the enigma of brain processes is related to the enigma underlying multiplicity of self. Because the human self is a configuration of multiple states as well as being a functional unit (Bromberg, 1996a), the more intense the unsymbolized affect, the more powerful the dissociative forces that are preventing the linking of the isolated islands of selfhood, and the harder it is for episodic, or working, memory to represent the perceptual nature of the external stimulus or to access long-term memories. Consider in this light what LeDoux, a neuroscientist, has to say about the multiplicity of self:

> Though [the self] is a unit, it is not unitary. . . . The fact that all aspects of the self are not usually manifest simultaneously, and that their different aspects can even be contradictory, may seem to present a complex problem. However, this simply means that different components of the self reflect the operation of different brain systems, which can be but are not always in sync. While explicit memory is mediated by a single system, there are a variety of different brain systems that store memory

> implicitly, allowing for many aspects of the self to coexist. As William James (1890) said, "Neither threats nor pleadings can move a man unless they touch some one of his potential or actual selves." Or as the painter Paul Klee (1957) expressed it, the self is a "dramatic ensemble" [LeDoux, 2002, p. 31].

LeDoux's neurological research highlights that there are parallel but functionally dissimilar information-processing modes in the brain. The first, mediated by the brainstem and the limbic system, is responsible for nonverbal encoding of emotion; the second, mediated by the neocortex, is in charge of verbal and representational symbolization of experience. How to get the two systems to collaborate when they do not want to is the neuroscience version of the clinical question, Why is it so difficult to link the dissociated reliving of something "truly tragic and awful" with a mental representation of the self as the agent or experiencer?

Ledoux (1996) describes what takes place in the brain more or less as follows: The amygdala assesses the emotional significance of incoming information, which it passes on to areas in the brainstem that regulate the autonomic and hormonal systems. It then transmits this information to the hippocampus, whose function is to integrate it with previously existing information and with cortical input. Under ordinary conditions of amygdalic arousal, the event is then processed by the hippocampus, which transforms the experience into a thinkable event by "filing" it (van der Kolk, 1987b) within the cognitive schema to which it is most readily linked. If all goes well, increased cortical symbolization occurs, and a potentially traumatic situation can subsequently be more easily distinguished perceptually from one that may contain certain similarities but is otherwise relatively benign (such as a stressful moment in therapy). But, as we know, all does *not* always go well.

High levels of stimulation from the amygdala, such as those from emotional experiences that are truly tragic and awful, interfere with hippocampal functioning. When this happens, the person may consciously work at trying to fit the memory of the event into his day-to-day self and yet find himself unable to do so. The interference with hippocampal functioning is compounded by hemispheric specialization. Ordinarily, the cortical symbolization of experience is divided between a more sensory-based right-brain function, and a linguistically based left-brain function. To the degree this is accurate, then right-brain encoding, more mediated by the amygdala, tends to function most dramatically when the person is in an emotionally overwhelmed state (see Schore, 2003b, c).

When emotional life is calmer, the hippocampus is more able to get the information it needs, to associate it to a storehouse of knowledge in the left frontal lobes and other neocortical locations, and to assist in the creation of spoken narrative. Schore (2003a) proposes that "right brain attachment mechanisms are expressed within the regulating and dysregulating emotional communications of any dyad, including transference–countertransference interactions that lie at the core of the therapeutic alliance" (p. 43) and that "any successful treatment must optimally access not 'the trauma' but the immature biological systems that inefficiently regulate stress, *especially the right brain survival mechanism, dissociation, that is characterologically accessed to cope with dysregulating affective states*" (p. 42). Along with many other psychoanalytic clinicians, Schore sees the mechanism of projective identification (a core element in the process of enactment) as a major subsymbolic channel of communication that, neurobiologically, appears to mediate right-hemisphere to right-hemisphere communication between child and parent as well as between patient and therapist. He writes, more or less reflecting my own position, that this form of subsymbolic communication "may be the only way that infants or severely traumatized persons can communicate their stories of distress" (p. 43).

Traumatic experience, in other words, bypasses the hippocampus and is stored either somatically or as visual images that can return as physical symptoms or as flashbacks without cognitive meaning. This is why, in neurobiological terms, very high levels of affect in a therapy session may prevent a here-and-now cognitive evaluation of the ongoing experience and thus prevent the therapeutic process, especially the use of interpretation, from linking the dissociated reliving of something truly tragic and awful with a mental representation of the self as the agent or experiencer. In therapy, just as in real life, "feelings of fear come about when . . . working memory becomes occupied with the fact that the amygdala is active. Then we have some of the ingredients that turn an experience into a fearful experience" (LeDoux, 1999, p. 45) and, I might add, into a potentially shameful experience. When this occurs in treatment (as it inevitably does), the sensory imprints of experience that are stored in affective memory continue to remain isolated images and body sensations that feel cut off from the rest of self. Because the hippocampus is not playing its necessary role in helping to categorize information, these elements of affective and somatic experience continue to lead an unintegrated existence, and when the patient leaves the session "it's not better, it's worse."

It is on similar neurological ground that the warning system, the "twitching of thumbs," is erected. Van der Kolk (1995) puts it this way, "Physiological arousal in general can trigger trauma-related memories. Conversely, trauma-related memories precipitate generalized physiological arousal" (p. 45). This feedback loop creates a chronic readiness for trauma in which the "strength of the memories appear to be so deeply engraved that Pitman and Orr (1990) have called it the 'black hole'... [which] attracts all associations to it and saps current life of its significance" (p. 45). Van der Kolk goes on to say that "decreased inhibitory control may occur under a variety of circumstances: under the influence of drugs and alcohol, during sleep (as in nightmares), with aging, and after strong reminders of the traumatic past" (p. 49). Reminders of the traumatic past obviously surface when the therapist inquires about them, but they also do so when the therapist *does not* inquire about them. The reminders are just there. Both LeDoux and van der Kolk describe what is a likely physiological substrate for what I have portrayed as the patient's readiness to find disaster around every corner (Bromberg, 1994, p. 260). The patient operates under the burden of a backup system in the hippocampus that functions as what van der Kolk (1995) calls a "smoke detector." At the brain level, the readiness with which the smoke detector swings into action seems to account for the state of hypervigilant anticipation of trauma. It may help us to understand, biologically, why such hypervigilant persons so easily manifest autonomic hyperarousal of affect in response to anything that can remotely be associated with the original traumatic experiences, and why certain patients' negative affect is more readily triggered by a therapist's misattunement.

Neurochemical evidence seems to indicate that the hormonal neurotransmitter serotonin plays the largest role in regulating the sensitivity of what I call the early warning system (van der Kolk's smoke detector). Early trauma creates a decrease in the serotonin level, which then interferes with the subsequent ability to modulate arousal and produces hypersensitivity (exaggerated emotional reactivity) to seemingly mild stimuli. Patients with this hypersensitivity often react under pressure as if they were being traumatized all over again by the therapy, and dissociative activity increases within the therapeutic relationship itself. Neurochemically, if the serotonin level can be increased, a patient's threshold for affective hyperarousal will rise and the alarm will thus have a higher threshold for "smoke" and be less likely to be triggered when there is no fire. Homologously, if *through the therapeutic relationship* the threshold for affective triggering is increasingly elevated, and if the patient is better able "to achieve distance from the emotional impact of incoming stimuli and to use cognition" (van der Kolk, 1995, p. 51), one would expect that the serotonin level should also show corresponding elevation. Do I think this can be done through psychoanalytic psychotherapy? Yes, I do.

As LeDoux (1999) emphasizes, when the amygdala is providing working memory with the affective input of fear—the emotional component of what is truly tragic and awful—it does so implicitly, which is to say, unconsciously. However, the dissociative process that keeps the affect unconscious has a life of its own, a relational life that is interpersonal as well as intrapsychic, a life that is played out between patient and analyst in the dyadic dissociative phenomenon that we term enactment.

It is through his own subsymbolic awareness that an analyst first becomes cognizant that an enactment is taking place. While the analyst is working and absorbed cognitively, he begins to feel vaguely that something is a bit "off," something that Stern (2004) describes as an

> emotional "chafing" or tension, an unbidden "hint" or "sense" that something more than one has suspected is going on in the clinical interaction. Something feels inconsistent, countering an affective expectation we did not even know we had until that moment; it feels subtly "wrong" or contradictory, or just uncomfortable [p. 208].

Because this emotional "chafing" is not yet connected by the analyst to the clinical interaction, his mind will automatically attempt to preserve the stability of his ongoing self-experience by dissociating that part of himself that is experiencing it.

There is as yet no intersubjective room for the patient's dissociated affect and his own emotional chafing to coexist self-reflectively within the analyst's ongoing state of mind. He is drawn, at least for a time, into a dissociative process of his own that becomes part of a joint hypnoid cocoon that temporarily forecloses the potential for a symbolically mediated intersubjective connection in the moment. Eventually, if the analyst is sufficiently attuned to his own internal experience, he will emerge from the shared dissociative cocoon and consciously experience the "something else" that is going on without knowing what it is. Sometimes it is the patient who first calls it to the analyst's attention. As the analyst begins to find a way to address it in the moment, with his patient, what was a pattern of subsymbolic communication (the dissociative cocoon) is allowed to interface with language and thought. The analytic work is then drawn into a potentially productive dialectic between here-and-now experience and there-and-then memory. To be fully in the moment is, as Kihlstrom (1987, cited in LeDoux, 1989) stated, to fully allow new affective (as yet unprocessed) experience to interface perceptually and linguistically with episodic memory, thus optimizing its potential for symbolic integration into narrative memory and, ultimately, enriching self-narrative, the goal of any form of treatment. Bucci (2002), in a similar vein, conceptualizes this process of change as pivoting around what she terms "emotion schemas"—specific types of memory schemas dominated by subsymbolic sensory and somatic representations. She presents an argument much like my own, that

> emotion schemas can be changed only to the extent that experiences in the present and memories of the past are held in working memory simultaneously with the pulses of core consciousness that depend on activation of the bodily components of the schema. The activation of the dissociated painful experience in the session itself is central to the therapeutic process. This is a very different perspective from the metapsychological principle that structure depends on the inhibition of drive or desire [p. 787].

It is no easy task to do clinical work from this perspective because the relative absence of intersubjectivity during enactments increases the analyst's own potential for affective destabilization, not simply the patient's. It is therefore inevitable that any analyst, regardless of theoretical persuasion, will have a repertoire of dissociative reactions to his patient that he will not immediately be aware of as such. Ultimately, however, the therapeutic leverage depends on eventual negotiation between the patient's and the therapist's realities, which negotiation is mediated by the *shared* processing of their respective experiences. As the analyst becomes aware of his own dissociative reactions during enactments, both he and his patient increasingly derive their knowledge from verbal and nonverbal sources simultaneously; this shared knowledge, in turn, creates the needed context to link, in working memory, the dissociated reliving of something truly tragic and awful with a mental representation of the self as the agent or experiencer. One could say that the patient's reliance on dissociation is decreased because working in the transference–countertransference field feels affectively safer; there is less shame because there is less dread of reliving something truly tragic and awful that, in the reliving, becomes worse not better. It is my belief that what I have just described is the process through which the most enduring capacity for experiencing and resolving internal conflict is facilitated.

Safe but Not Too Safe

Thomas Scheff (1989), whose writing bridges communication theory, sociology, and psychotherapy, asks a critical question: How shall a therapy best make progress toward growth while simultaneously maintaining the patient's experience of safety? His answer supports Helen Block Lewis's (1971) finding that fully analyzed patients who later developed new problems were shown to have significant shame pathology. Scheff (1989) argues that, when shame is evoked but not acknowledged, an impasse occurs that can lead to either a treatment collapse or a pseudosuccess. Scheff believes, as do I, that working within the here-and-now affective experience between patient and analyst provides the most powerful context for growth and, further, that shame as part of the process cannot be avoided. The heart of the work, as I have already stated, is in watching for it so that, when it does occur, the shame evoked by the therapeutic process itself can begin to be addressed in a relational context, thereby allowing the traumatic affect held by a dissociated aspect of self to enter into the coconstruction of an intersubjective experience at the level of thought.

It is not necessary (or possible) to avoid encounters that might feel shamefully threatening to the patient. The goal is to provide sufficient safety so that the patient can make it back from the edge of the abyss and be aware of having done so. Anxiety and annihilation anxiety are not the same, and the optimal treatment context requires that the patient feel "safe but not too safe." That is to say, there is a difference between being scared and being scarred. As Sullivan (1953) put it, routine anxiety allows learning from experience because dissociation is not needed, but

> severe anxiety probably contributes no information. The effect of severe anxiety reminds one in some ways of a blow on the head, in that it simply wipes out what is immediately proximal to its occurrence. . . . Less severe anxiety does permit gradual realization of the situation in which it occurs [p. 152].

Sullivan used the term severe anxiety rather than the word trauma, but what he clearly had in mind were experiences that are, in current terms, distinguished as being traumatic in nature. When trauma makes its presence felt, what is affected is not simply mental contents but the coherence of self-states. The affect evoked is not merely unpleasant but a disorganizing hyperarousal that threatens to overwhelm the mind's ability to think, reflect, and process the experience cognitively. An experience of affective dysregulation so great that it threatens to carry the person to the edge of self-fragmentation and sometimes self-annihilation is no longer describable by the term anxiety. The continuity of selfhood is at stake; the emotional situation is far more complex than anything seen in the animal world; and shame, horrible unassimilable shame, contributes its own terrible coloring. It is the threat of shame, a threat equal to that of fear, that necessitates the early warning system designed to prevent a recurrence of the affective flooding originally created by trauma—a horrifyingly unanticipated sense of exposure of oneself to oneself. Shame, as Helen Lynd (1958) writes,

> is the outcome not only of exposing onself to another person but of the exposure to oneself of parts of the self that one has not recognized. . . . This comes about in part because one doesn't know how to fit shame into the network of other emotions with which it is interwoven. . . . It is as if a self of which we were not aware makes us unable to grasp the situation and to control what we do . . . when what is suddenly exposed is incongruous with, or glaringly inappropriate to, the situation, or to our previous images of ourselves [pp. 31–34].

Above all, shame is the signal that the self is or is about to be violated. It demands emergency action:

> What is exposed in shame is oneself. I am ashamed of what I *am*. Because of this over-all character, *an experience of shame can be altered or transcended only in so far as there is some change in the whole self*. . . . It is pervasive as anxiety is pervasive; its focus, [however], is not a separate act, but revelation of the whole self. The thing that has been exposed is what I am [p. 50, italics added].

The feeling that accompanies the activation of a patient's "smoke detector" is difficult to describe, if it can be captured at all. In the attempt to communicate the experience to another person (such as a therapist), the effort to find language that conveys one's experience as a humanly recognizable affect is painfully difficult, and the closest a patient can typically come to naming it is that one part of the feeling, at least in the telling *about* it, is shame. Lynd illuminates this situation:

> Because of the outwardly small occasion that has precipitated shame, the intense emotion seems inappropriate, incongruous, disproportionate to the incident that has aroused it. *Hence a double shame is involved;* we are ashamed because of the original episode and ashamed because we feel so deeply about something so slight that a sensible person would not pay any attention to it [p. 42, italics added].

Although it is possible, and even correct, to use the word shame as Lynd does and I do, to designate the affect that signals a loss of personal identity, in the context of a retelling the word fails to capture the full magnitude of the threatened traumatic loss of selfhood. With trauma, we must remember, retelling means reliving. Yet it is only through its reliving (the last thing that a patient wants to face) that it can be known by an other—this time, we hope, an other who will have the courage to participate in the reliving while simultaneously holding the patient's psychological safety as a matter of prime concern.

In the face of imminent depersonalization and collapse of selfhood, the mind falls back on its ultimate safety measure: its capacity for the emergency use of the otherwise normal process of fluidly and creatively withdrawing consciousness from certain aspects of immediate experience while enhancing other aspects. I am referring again to the process of dissociation—the hypnoidal unlinking of incompatible patterns of self-experience so that the domains of meaning that have been most adaptive to preserving sanity and survival are protected by insulating in uncompromised purity the self–other modes of interaction that define them.

What was formerly a flexible multiplicity of relatively harmonious self-states—a normal mind whose shifting configuration enabled the person to "feel like one self while being many"—becomes a rigid multiplicity of adversarial self-states. Each self-state is hypnoidally sequestered from the others and operates within its specific pattern of interpersonal engagement that gives it self-meaning, the most extreme form of this dissociative structure being dissociative identity disorder. The hypnoid isolation among self-states gives personal identity a subjective sense of consistency and coherence within each self-state regardless of which has access to consciousness and cognition at a given moment because the individual states are unlinked from one another so as to function independently. The security of the personality has now become totally linked to a trauma-based view of reality. Always, some dissociated part of the self is vigilantly "on call" because the person cannot afford to feel safe. Our work as analysts involves enabling restoration of the links among sequestered aspects of self to take place so that the conditions for intrapsychic conflict and its resolution can be present. The hermeneutic process of interpretation in psychoanalysis depends on these conditions' being there, because repression cannot always be assumed to exist as a dynamic. The process of interpretation, in other words, must contend always with the presence of a "smoke detector."

William

Consider, for instance, William, a man of superior intelligence who, as a young child, was humiliated as a sexual plaything by his older sister and survived the experience through major utilization of dissociation. As he grew up, he came to believe that the reason he did not have full use of his mind and could not think clearly was located in a genetic defect.

As we began to look more closely at the relationship between his use of dissociation and his continual feeling of cognitive haziness, the rigidity of his mental structure began to soften. Though still protesting that his mind was genetically impaired and hence "incurable," and that he had no feelings of any kind toward his sister, positive or negative, another part of William began to consider the possibility that what he called his "intellectual inadequacy" might indeed serve a self-protective function. He began to explore with me the idea that his strange absence of feeling toward his sister could relate to his having had to make certain that his mind would never again be flooded by more than it can bear and that the mental fog in which he had lived since childhood might be a result. But even as we worked, other parts of William were suspiciously observing what he and I were doing together on behalf of *change*. These other parts, self-states with agendas of their own, were, each in its own way, dedicated to safety and thus to *preserving* William's dissociative mental structure, his "early warning system," as his only trustworthy protection. One of these parts had the job of humoring me while not taking me seriously, making sure that I never realized the horrible truth that I was just another well-meaning but intellectually limited fool.

During one particular session, in the midst of protesting once again that not all intellectual inadequacy is due to psychological causes and that some people are simply stupider than others, William tried to underscore his point with what he believed to be humor. He abruptly ventured a one-liner that had just "come to him" about the "village idiot who didn't know the difference between incest and arson, and so, sadly, set fire to his sister." Oddly, neither of us laughed. We just sat there, looking at each other. A look of recognition crept into his eyes. And I am sure a similar look was also in mine. Unlike previous occasions when he would stay concretely wedded to the literal meaning of whatever he had said, this time William "got it." The part of him that had told the joke was joined by another part that understood its significance in another way. The look in his eyes announced that previously sequestered self-states were now in communication with one another. He knew, surprisingly, that the village idiot referred also to me, and he got this nuance. And he got it without dissociatively "setting fire" to the potentially traumatic confrontation between us, a risk that in subsequent sessions he acknowledged to be something he could feel as both exciting and dangerous. The session marks a point in time when William's capacity to experience intrapsychic conflict started to emerge for the first time; he was even becoming able to reflect on his shift away from rigid dissociation.

How did all this come about? Bucci (2002) once more provides an answer:

> In the session, the threatening dissociated affect must be activated to some degree, but in trace form, regulated sufficiently so as not to trigger new avoidance, and with some transformation of meaning. The questions of how much and when to activate or to permit this activation, so as to repair the dissociation rather than to reinforce it, must be addressed specifically for each patient [p. 787].

Bucci asks, "What permits dissociation to be repaired?" (pp. 767–768). I ask, what permitted William to make the shift from dissociation to a capacity for intrapsychic conflict? My answer may or may not surprise you, but I have little doubt that his increased self-reflective competence was facilitated by my "interpretive" interventions during the immediately preceding phase, although I am using the word interpretation in a way that goes far beyond its classical meaning.

I had for a while been verbally underscoring, in the here and now, those moments when I was most aware—sometimes even shocked—that William was *not* dissociating. I would comment openly at those times, and with considerable feeling, about the things I perceived and personally felt that suggested to me that in that moment he was feeling our relationship as more trustworthy and maybe even a bit safer than he had in the past. I would also comment on how remarkable it felt to me that, even though he was frightened, he was able to let himself stay in the moment even while he was moving into one or another dangerous area that seemingly could threaten the stability of our connection. This might not seem to be such a big deal, I would say, but it really was, because not so long ago the risk he felt of being emotionally overwhelmed and out of control was so great that being able to live with an experience of being frightened in my presence was not even possible. His "checking out" would automatically have been triggered to keep our connection intact, and I would make mention of this too.

Unlike his response to my words earlier in treatment, during this phase William did not experience them as hollow, devoid of meaning. Earlier in treatment, when my words were too much for William's mind to process, he would disconnect from me as a person. This disconnection did not occur at the level of consciousness; it would simply "happen" and we would be pulled into a dissociated enactment of some sort. Now I seemed to have in the room with me a partner who would listen to me and to my words, albeit with ambivalence, and who more often than not would think about how my perception of things compared with his. It is my belief that this part of him—this partner—was best able to share an overlapping space with me when my words matched my perceptual and affective experience of our relationship as it existed at that moment in time. When my words were mainly carriers of ideas unconnected to the relationship in the here and now, it was more difficult for William to find common ground that would allow him to be a partner in the process. When my spontaneous perception matched William's state of mind and was engaged by his perception of the same moment, then something new would happen, something not predictable from the past. Parenthetically, I might add that it was only from this shared affective/perceptual field that ideas were generated that began to link past and present in a way that *felt* right rather than being just persuasive.

One could say I try to *be* with a patient "out loud." Does what I do deserve to be called interpretation? In an article on narcissism and the treatment of narcissistic disorders, I (Bromberg, 1983) once made use of the term structuralizing interpretations, a concept I derived from Horner (1979), to refer to interpretations aimed at acquainting a patient with the functioning of his mind rather than its contents. In object relational terms, one might say that I was affirming William's valid need for his existing self and object structure, rather than responding to the content through which the need for that structure was being expressed at that moment. As a way of looking at the role of language in psychoanalytic growth, particularly in relation to the dialectic between conflict and dissociation, I find Horner's concept of structuralizing interpretation useful because it encourages the analyst to speak from a stance that is inherently experience near, rather than his struggling to hold a basically interpretive posture while *also* trying to be experience near. The analyst listens and speaks from a perspective that views what has been traditionally called an ego defense as an expression of a valid alternative reality coming from a different self-state—a different part of who the patient *is*. As a way of hearing and relating to a patient, this approach may fall short of what some call interpretation, but if one defines interpretation as an intervention that increases a patient's capacity to take his mental functioning as an object of self-reflection, then this way of working meets that criterion.

The clinical impact of this way of working is notable because it addresses each self-state as standing for something that, in its own terms, is necessary and perhaps even required for survival. Most important, the analyst is aware that a seemingly maladaptive way of being may for the patient be a self-organizing necessity involving an alternative part of the self that is not resisting insight but is refusing to be interpreted out of existence. As an analyst, I have found that this perspective makes me more aware of those moments when I am demonstrating favoritism to certain aspects of a patient's self (those I prefer) and neglecting other parts, some of which, for certain patients in particular, may be feeling what I am saying as equivalent to an invalidation of their reason for existing without any wish on my part to hear what that reason is.

This way of working helped William symbolize, in language, his growing capacity for affect regulation, making his surrender of dissociation something thinkable, without ignoring the feelings held by other parts of self that remained dedicated to preserving safety at any cost. Particularly during the difficult transition from dissociation to conflict, this way of relating helps a patient to reflect on his character structure as a functional part of his personality rather than as a shameful piece of "illness" for which he is being blamed under the pretense of being helped. One could say that the message I was trying to get across to William was, "I'm feeling you right now as more fully present in our relationship, and as starting to experience the difference between being frightened and being traumatized. Let me tell you, William, what that experience is like for me and what makes me notice it."

I expect you will have observed that in illustrating the kind of thing I would say to William—about moving into a dangerous area that not so long ago would have triggered the felt risk of being emotionally overwhelmed and out of control—I did not try to attribute a psychodynamic meaning to the emotion. I stayed with the structural implications of the experience, the effect on his mental functioning—not that psychodynamic possibilities did not suggest themselves, such as murderous rage or out-of-control lust—meanings that might well be heard in the "joke" about setting fire to one's sister. I have found that, as I work in the way I do, dynamic interpretations of content will inevitably invite themselves to be made by one party or the other when the patient's mind feels safe enough and, I might add, without the kind of intractable resistance one might otherwise encounter at such moments. So I seldom worry about neglecting content or fear "missing," for too long, an area of intrapsychic conflict that needs psychodynamic interpretation. Research support for this way of addressing clinical process is accumulating rapidly and speaks to a nonlinear relational theory of therapeutic action, as I have discussed more fully in chapter 7. The Boston Change Process Study Group has even come to the conclusion (Lyons-Ruth, 1998; Lyons-Ruth et al., 2001) that it is the process of communication (implicit relational knowing) rather than the content of the communication that is the foundation for the therapeutic action of psychoanalysis.

Transitional Space as the Gateway to Intersubjectivity

A patient's transition from a dissociative mental structure to increased affective tolerance for intrapsychic conflict is a complex process in which realities that have been kept apart by discontinuous states of consciousness are gradually able to be held within a single transitional state of mind. It is not unreasonable to look at the creation of transitional mental space as part and parcel of the development of intersubjectivity as the patient begins to play with and creatively struggle, internally, with an experience of otherness that formerly could be enacted only. This transitional mental space, which is often closer to a dream than to waking reality, serves as a playground for the intersubjective process to get going in a new way. Fonagy and Target (1995) describe this playground as encompassing a "third perspective, opening up a space for thinking between and about the patient and the analyst" (p. 499). It permits the coexistence of opposites, and its illogic must be not only accepted by the analyst, but also engaged as a valid relational context in its own right. The transitional state of mind must not be viewed as less real than any other, as if it were simply a way station to something healthier.

> A space for thinking between and about the patient and the analyst—a space uniquely relational and still uniquely individual; a space belonging to neither person alone, and yet, belonging to both and to each; a twilight space in which the "impossible" becomes possible; a space in which incompatible selves, each awake to its own "truth," can "dream" the reality of the other without risk to its own integrity. . . . How is this phenomenon possible? My answer is that the reciprocal process of active involvement with the states of mind of the "other" allows a patient's here-and-now perception of self to share consciousness with the experiences of incompatible self-narratives that were formerly dissociated [Bromberg, 1996a, p. 278].

Consider my comments in the context of Bion's (1962a) formulation of *reverie* as a state of mind in the mother

> which is open to the reception of any "objects" from the loved object and is therefore capable of reception of the infant's projective identifications whether they are felt by the infant to be good or bad. If the feeding mother cannot allow reverie . . . this fact will be communicated to the infant even though incomprehensible to the infant [p. 36].

Bion (1962b) further suggested that the "mother's capacity for reverie is the receptor organ for the infant's harvest of self-sensation gained by its conscious" (pp. 115–116).

Bucci's (1997a, b) writing on *referential processes* zeros in on this phenomenon from another angle and provides an important cognitive-research link between what I call "standing in the spaces" and Bion's (1962a, b) work on reverie (see also Ogden, 1997). Bucci writes,

> In addition to its function of linking subsymbolic systems to one another and to symbolic forms, the referential process has the further role of linking one individual's internal representations to another's, creating a new, shared referential space by this means. From its earliest development, the referential process, as applied to emotional experience, includes not only connections between one's own subjective state and overt expressions, but also *connection between one's inner experience and the expressions of others* [Bucci, 1997a, p. 220, italics added].

Safe Surprises

I would like to conclude by elaborating just a bit further a concept discussed earlier, which I believe holds the potential to link LeDoux's (1989, 1994, 1995, 1996, 1999) neurological research into fear and its memorialization in memory with my own thinking about clinical process. In chapter 5, I introduced my term safe surprises, a way of formulating the nature of therapeutic action that I feel merits a final, brief visit. Let me start by giving Philip Roth (1997) his say one more time, as he contemplates the vagaries of memory and its idiosyncratic disregard of objective reality:

> We don't just forget things because they don't matter but also forget things because they matter too much—because each of us remembers and forgets in a pattern whose labyrinthine windings are an identification mark no less distinctive than a fingerprint—it's no wonder that the shards of reality one person will cherish as a biography can seem to someone else who, say, happened to have eaten some ten thousand dinners at the very same kitchen table, to be a willful excursion into mythomania [p. 55].

As Roth says, things can matter *too* much. When they do, memory is particularly state dependent. The state that organizes self-experience during a particularly charged event also organizes its recall. A person will "remember" of the event only the details that are compatible with that self-state and are consistent with maintaining its integrity. One person may have been a passive witness to the same event in which another was an active participant. In other words, it may well be process rather than content—how the person was engaged with the scene at the time—that accounts for such astounding differences in memory between "witnesses" to the same event. What is remembered by each may also have fundamentally to do with the degree to which dissociation was operating and the function it served. What Roth calls the "shards of reality" are pieced together to form not a "snapshot" of the event but a state-dependent personal biography—an uncontextualized self-narrative, each part of which will "cherish" itself as truth.

As therapists, we are always encountering "cherished biographies"; the question is how to make them more amenable to self-reflection. LeDoux (1989) suggests that, "if we can work out how representations of stimuli and their affective significance come to coincide in working memory, we may be well on the way to understanding how these then interact with representations of the self to generate emotional experience" (p. 282). I contend that in clinical work emotional experience must be generated in a way that allows the self as agent to be present simultaneously with the self who experienced the event. It is the analyst's job to facilitate this process and thereby allow the patient to be fully present in all his particularity. During enactments, what LeDoux (1996) calls the fear system is activated under conditions that are safe but not *too* safe because the analytic relationship inevitably repeats the failures of the patient's past while, it is hoped, doing more than merely repeating them.

Obviously, the impact of life-threatening or sanity-threatening trauma shouts for our attention and, justifiably, receives it. But no less significant is our need to account for and understand the existence of dissociative pathology in the *absence* of the kind of gross invasion of mind and body associated with mental, physical, and sexual abuse or with the kind of sudden, unanticipated, and unspeakable horror to which we were subjected on September 11th. I am referring to the often undramatic but equally impactful "developmental trauma" of a child's living day in and day out in a family that systematically disavows the existence of the child's subjective experience and discredits the validity of her emotional states.

Whether trauma is massive or developmental, the relational construction of safe surprises in therapy depends on what the analyst and patient do together in the space between what is perceived as potentially traumatic and what is perceived as safe but "on the edge." And our job is to help rebuild faith in self–other experience regardless of how it came to be lost or compromised.

Epilogue

I began this chapter with my memory of an event from early childhood, a memory that entered consciousness while I was struggling with the impact of 9/11 as I was attempting to write. The event had to do with the traumatization of a frighteningly predatory cat named Adolf who, to my great pleasure, was receiving his "just desserts." The details, which came back to me a lifetime later, appeared with the kind of vividness and immediacy that is associated with flashbacks and, to my knowledge, had not been recalled at any prior time in my adult life. Why *that* memory, and why *then?* After all, the trauma had happened to Adolf the cat, not to me.

I asked myself if the memory perhaps represented the return of what we call vicarious traumatization? It is well known that such things happen frequently to therapists who work with severely traumatized patients, and the memory did indeed seem to appear in response to 9/11. But why should that event have been powerful enough to hold it so lucidly in place all those years? The idea of vicariousness didn't answer that question well enough to satisfy me; it might have been easier to accept it as an explanation if it weren't for the fact that I *hated* Adolf. I was a one-boy cheering section for the blue jays that had traumatized him. Furthermore, it was my hate that emerged most vividly in the memory, not fear, not empathy for the baby birds, and most certainly not empathy for Adolf. In other words, what was the key element that made the event traumatic to *me?*

I discovered that when I attended not to *Adolf's* affect, but to *my* dominant affect in the memory, hate, a potential answer started to take shape. In puzzling over the remarkably long time I had continued to hate this cat so intensely, I found myself considering the possibility that, perversely, it might be the very fact that my hatred of Adolf seemed to be so *cherished* by me, that shed most light on why the memory appeared in my mind as if it had a life of its own; a quasi-flashback without a genuine self-narrative context. I say perversely, not because I believe that hate itself is toxic, but because the cherished hate I felt toward Adolf may have been serving the function of preventing other feelings from reaching consciousness—feelings that might have included a genuinely traumatizing identification with the helpless baby birds. My cherished hate would allow no room for those other feelings to exist as long as it filled up all the space in my psyche. Other feelings would have to be dissociated and *remain* dissociated until future circumstances, such as my writing about and talking about trauma in the context of 9/11, allowed them slowly to reach consciousness and eventual symbolization in this epilogue.

My inability to empathize even slightly with Adolf's helplessness, though it protected me, in the moment, from the vicarious helplessness I would have had to face through my identification with the baby birds, prevented me from ever being able to process what was *truly* traumatic to me as a little kid. Clearly, if such a horrifying thing could happen to a supposedly unstoppable creature such as Adolf, the thought of what potentially could happen to *me* unexpectedly might indeed have been more than my mind could bear. This is all to say that my hate and the pleasure I took in Adolf's plight may well have remained unmodulated and in place for so long because it bolstered my dissociation, giving me the power, at least unconsciously, to be stronger than Adolf and thus less helpless than I felt in "real" reality.

Were I to live my childhood over, would I forgive Adolf? It is possible, but I am more confident that I at least would find within me a wish to help him. Forgiveness is often hard to achieve but it does seem to repay the effort when we accomplish it. Do you remember the metaphor of falling snow in chapter 3? There I described how two authors, C. S. Lewis (1961) and Conrad Aiken (1932), used the image of a blanketing snowfall to represent the mind's ability to protect itself, dissociatively, from potentially unbearable affect—in the first case, grief, and in the second, hate.

In ending both the chapter and the book, I ask you to again consider the metaphor of falling snow (Khaled Hosseini, 2003), but this time as it represents the ineffable quality of release that comes with forgiveness:

> I wondered if that was how forgiveness budded, not with the fanfare of epiphany, but with pain gathering its things, packing up, and slipping away unannounced in the middle of the night [pp. 357–359]. . . . The park shimmered with snow so fresh, so dazzling white, it burned my eyes. It sprinkled soundlessly from the branches of white-clad trees. . . . The muffled quiet, snow-quiet, was deafening. I looked down at Sohrab. One corner of his mouth had curled up just so.
>
> A smile.
> Lopsided.
> Hardly there.
> But there.

> It was only a smile, nothing more. It didn't make everything all right. It didn't make *anything* all right. Only a smile. A tiny thing. A leaf in the woods, shaking in the wake of a startled bird's flight. But I'll take it. With open arms. Because when spring comes, it melts the snow one flake at a time, and maybe I just witnessed the first flake melting [pp. 370–371].

Perhaps it is through the melting of hate one flake at a time, and the accumulation of unremarkable "tiny things" that come to be called forgiveness, that the dreamer most fully awakens.

References

Aiken, C. (1932), Silent snow, secret snow. In: *The World Within,* ed. M. L. Aswell. New York: McGraw-Hill, 1947, pp. 237–260.

Alvarez, A. (1992), *Live Company.* London: Routledge.

Aron, L. (1996), *A Meeting of Minds: Mutuality in Psychoanalysis.* Hillsdale, NJ: The Analytic Press.

_______ (1998), Clinical choices and the theory of psychoanalytic technique. *Psychoanal. Dial.,* 8:207–216.

_______ (2001), Intersubjectivity in the analytic situation. In: *Self-Relations in the Psychotherapy Process,* ed. J. C. Muran. Washington, DC: American Psychological Association.

_______ & Anderson, F. S., eds. (1998), *Relational Perspectives on the Body: Psychoanalytic Theory and Practice.* Hillsdale, NJ: The Analytic Press.

Bakhtin, M. M. (1929), *Problems of Dostoevsky's Poetics.* Ithaca, NY: Cornell University Press, 1984.

Balint, M. (1968), *The Basic Fault.* London: Tavistock.

Barach, P. M. (1991), Multiple personality disorder as an attachment disorder. *Dissociation,* 4:117–123.

Baring-Gould, W. S. (1967), Introduction. In: *The Annotated Sherlock Holmes: The Four Novels and the Fifty-Six Short Stories Complete by Sir Arthur Conan Doyle.* New York: Potter.

Barker, P. (1991), *Regeneration.* New York: Dutton/Plume, 1993.

Bataille, G. (1932), *Complete Works, Vol. 6.* Paris: Gallimard, 1970.

_______ (1962), *Death and Sensuality.* New York: Walker.

Benjamin, J. (1995), *Like Subjects, Love Objects: Essays on Recognition and Sexual Difference.* New Haven, CT: Yale University Press.

Bernstein, J. W. (1999), Countertransference: Our new royal road to the unconscious? *Psychoanal. Dial.,* 9:275–297.

Bion, W. R. (1962a), Learning from experience. In: *Seven Servants.* New York: Aronson, 1977.

_______ (1962b), A theory of thinking. In: *Second Thoughts.* London: Maresfield Library, 1967, pp. 110–119.

_______ (1970), *Attention and Interpretation.* London: Maresfield Library, 1984.

_______ (1978), *Four Discussions with W. R. Bion.* Strathclyde, Scotland: Clunie.
Boris, H. N. (1984), The problem of anorexia nervosa. *Internat. J. Psycho-Anal.,* 65:315–322.
_______ (1986), The "other" breast: Greed, envy, spite and revenge. *Contemp. Psychoanal.,* 22:45–59.
Bosnak, R. (1989), *Dreamwork with an AIDS Patient.* Boston: Shambhala.
_______ (1996), *Tracks in the Wilderness of Dreaming.* New York: Delacorte Press.
_______ (2003), Embodied imagination. *Contemp. Psychoanal.,* 39:683–695.
Bowlby, J. (1969), *Attachment.* New York: Basic Books.
Breger, L. (1989), *Dostoevsky: The Author as Psychoanalyst.* New York: New York University Press.
_______ (2000), *Freud: Darkness in the Midst of Vision.* New York: Wiley.
Breuer, J. & Freud, S. (1893–1895), Studies on hysteria. *Standard Edition,* 2. London: Hogarth Press, 1955.
Bromberg, P. M. (1983), The mirror and the mask: On narcissism and psychoanalytic growth. In: *Standing in the Spaces: Essays on Clinical Process, Trauma, and Dissociation.* Hillsdale, NJ: The Analytic Press, 1998, pp. 73–96.
_______ (1986), Discussion of dialogue between Lawrence Epstein and Mildred Schwartz, on "Love and Hate in Psychoanalysis." *Contemp. Psychother. Rev.,* 3:54–68.
_______ (1989), Interpersonal psychoanalysis and self psychology: A clinical comparison. In: *Standing in the Spaces: Essays on Clinical Process, Trauma, and Dissociation.* Hillsdale, NJ: The Analytic Press, 1998, pp. 147–162.
_______ (1993), Shadow and substance: A relational perspective on clinical process. In: *Standing in the Spaces: Essays on Clinical Process, Trauma, and Dissociation.* Hillsdale, NJ: The Analytic Press, 1998, pp. 165–187.
_______ (1994), "Speak!, that I may see you": Some reflections on dissociation, reality, and psychoanalytic listening. In: *Standing in the Spaces: Essays on Clinical Process, Trauma, and Dissociation.* Hillsdale, NJ: The Analytic Press, 1998, pp. 241–266.
_______ (1995a), Psychoanalysis, dissociation, and personality organization. In: *Standing in the Spaces: Essays on Clinical Process, Trauma, and Dissociation.* Hillsdale, NJ: The Analytic Press, 1998, pp. 189–204.
_______ (1995b), Treating patients with symptoms—and symptoms with patience. Presented to New York University Postdoctoral Program in Psychotherapy and Psychoanalysis, New York City, May 6.
_______ (1996a), Standing in the spaces: The multiplicity of self and the psychoanalytic relationship. In: *Standing in the Spaces: Essays on Clinical Process, Trauma, and Dissociation.* Hillsdale, NJ: The Analytic Press, 1998, pp. 267–290.
_______ (1996b), Hysteria, dissociation, and cure. In: *Standing in the Spaces: Essays on Clinical Process, Trauma, and Dissociation.* Hillsdale, NJ: The Analytic Press, 1998, pp. 223–237.
_______ (1997), The analyst's right to privacy. *Psychologist/Psychoanalyst,* 17: 31–33.

_______ (1998a), Staying the same while changing: Reflections on clinical judgment. In: *Standing in the Spaces: Essays on Clinical Process, Trauma, and Dissociation.* Hillsdale, NJ: The Analytic Press, pp. 291–307.

_______ (1998b), "Help! I'm going out of your mind." In: *Standing in the Spaces: Essays on Clinical Process, Trauma, and Dissociation.* Hillsdale, NJ: The Analytic Press, pp. 309–328.

_______ (1998c), *Standing in the Spaces: Essays on Clinical Process, Trauma, and Dissociation.* Hillsdale, NJ: The Analytic Press.

_______ (2000), Reply to reviews by Cavell, Sorenson, and Smith. *Psychoanal. Dial.,* 10:551–568.

_______ (2002), Speak to me as to thy thinkings: Some reflections on "Interpersonal psychoanalysis' radical façade" by Irwin Hirsch. *J. Amer. Acad. Psychoanal.,* 30:605–620.

_______ (2003), On being one's dream: Some reflections on Robert Bosnak's "Embodied imagination." *Contemp. Psychoanal.,* 39:697–710.

_______ (in press), "Ev'ry time we say goodbye, I die a little . . .": Commentary on Holly Levenkron's "Love (and hate) with the proper stranger." *Psychoanal. Inq.*

_______ (submitted), Multiple self-states, the relational mind, and dissociation: A psychoanalytic perspective. In: *Dissociation and the Dissociative Disorders: DSM-V and Beyond,* ed. P. F. Dell, J. O'Neil & E. Somer.

Broughton, R. J. (1968), Sleep disorders: Disorders of arousal? *Science,* 159: 1070–1078.

Bucci, W. (1997a), *Psychoanalysis and Cognitive Science: A Multiple Code Theory.* New York: Guilford Press.

_______ (1997b), Patterns of discourse in "good" and troubled hours: A multiple code interpretation. *J. Amer. Psychoanal. Assn.,* 45:155–187.

_______ (2001), Pathways of emotional communication. *Psychoanal. Inq.,* 21:40–70.

_______ (2002), The referential process, consciousness, and sense of self. *Psychoanal. Inq.,* 22:766–793.

_______ (2003), Varieties of dissociative experience: A multiple code account and a discussion of Bromberg's case of "William." *Psychoanal. Psychol.,* 20:542–557.

Burke, E. (1757), *A Philosophical Enquiry into the Origin of Our Ideas of the Sublime and the Beautiful.* London: Penguin, 1998.

Caligor, L. (1996), The clinical use of the dream in interpersonal psychoanalysis. *Psychoanal. Dial.,* 6:793–811.

Carson, A. (1999), *Autobiography of Red.* New York: Knopf.

Cavell, M. (2000), Review essay: Self-reflections. *Psychoanal. Dial.,* 10:513–529.

Chefetz, R. A. & Bromberg, P. M. (2004), Talking with "me and not-me": A dialogue. *Contemp. Psychoanal.,* 40:409–464.

Ciocca, A. (1998), Psychosomatic dissociation and eating disorders. In: *Psychotherapeutic Issues on Eating Disorders,* ed. P. Bria, A. Ciocca & S. de Risio. Rome: Società Editrice Universo, pp. 49–55.

Clemente, F. (1999), Guggenheim Museum Audioguide No. 20, Fall.

Cooper, S. H. (2000), *Objects of Hope: Exploring Possibility and Limit in Psychoanalysis.* Hillsdale, NJ: The Analytic Press.

Davies, J. M. (1994), Love in the afternoon: A relational consideration of desire and dread in the countertransference. *Psychoanal. Dial.,* 4:153–170.

_______ (1996), Dissociation, repression, and reality testing in the countertransference: The controversy over memory and false memory in the psychoanalytic treatment of adult survivors of sexual abuse. *Psychoanal. Dial.,* 6:189–218.

_______ (1998a), Multiple perspectives on multiplicity. *Psychoanal. Dial.,* 8:195–206.

_______ (1998b), Between the disclosure and foreclosure of erotic transference–countertransference: Can psychoanalysis find a place for adult sexuality? *Psychoanal. Dial.,* 8:747–766.

_______ (1999), Getting cold feet, defining "safe-enough" borders: Dissociation, multiplicity, and integration in the analyst's experience. *Psychoanal. Quart.,* 68:184–208.

_______ (2004), Whose bad object are we anyway? Repetition and our elusive love affair with evil. *Psychoanal. Dial.,* 14:711–732.

de Monchaux, C. (1978), Dreaming and the organizing function of the ego. *Internat. J. Psycho-Anal.,* 59:443–453.

Dickinson, E. (1863), Poem 670. *The Complete Poems of Emily Dickinson,* ed. T. H. Johnson. Boston: Little Brown, 1960.

Edelman, G. M. (1989), *The Remembered Present: A Biological Theory of Consciousness.* New York: Basic Books.

_______ (1992), *Bright Air, Brilliant Fire.* New York: Basic Books.

_______ (2004), *Wider Than the Sky: The Phenomenal Gift of Consciousness.* New Haven, CT: Yale University Press.

Edmundson, M. (1997), *Nightmare on Main Street: Angels, Sadomasochism, and the Culture of Gothic.* Cambridge, MA: Harvard University Press.

Ehrenberg, D. B. (1992), *The Intimate Edge.* New York: Norton.

Emerson, R. W. (1851), Borrowing. In: *What Cheer,* ed. D. McCord. New York: Coward-McCann, 1945.

Erikson, E. (1968), *Identity: Youth and Crisis.* Austen Riggs Monogr. No. 7. New York: Norton.

Everill, J. T., Waller, G. & Macdonald, W. (1995), Reported sexual abuse and bulimic symptoms: The mediating role of dissociation. *Dissociation,* 8: 155–159.

Fisher, C., Byrne, J. V., Edwards, A. & Kahn, E. (1970), A psychophysiological study of nightmares. *J. Amer. Psychoanal. Assn.,* 18:747–782.

_______ Kahn, E., Edwards, A. & Davis, D. (1974), A psychophysiological study of nightmares and night terrors. In: *Psychoanalysis and Contemporary Science, Vol. 3,* ed. L. Goldberger & V. Rosen. New York: International Universities Press, pp. 317–398.

Fonagy, P. (1991), Thinking about thinking: Some clinical and theoretical considerations in the treatment of a borderline patient. *Internat. J. Psycho-Anal.,* 72:639–656.

_______ & Target, M. (1995), Understanding the violent patient: The use of the body and the role of the father. *Internat. J. Psycho-Anal.,* 76:487–501.

_______ & _______ (1996), Playing with reality: I. Theory of mind and the normal development of psychic reality. *Internat. J. Psycho-Anal.,* 77:217–233.

_______ Gergely, G., Jurist, E. L. & Target, M. (2002), *Affect Regulation, Mentalization, and the Development of the Self.* New York: Other Press.

Frank, K. (1997), The role of the analyst's inadvertent self-revelations. *Psychoanal. Dial.,* 7:281–314.

Freud, S. (1893), Charcot. *Standard Edition,* 3:9–23. London: Hogarth Press, 1962.

_______ (1900), The interpretation of dreams. *Standard Edition,* 4 & 5. London: Hogarth Press, 1953.

_______ (1907), Delusions and dreams in Jensen's *Gradiva. Standard Edition,* 9:7–93. London: Hogarth Press, 1959.

_______ (1908), Creative writers and daydreaming. *Standard Edition,* 9:141–153. London: Hogarth Press, 1959.

_______ (1913), On beginning the treatment (Further recommendations on the technique of psycho-analysis, I). *Standard Edition,* 12:121–144. London: Hogarth Press, 1955.

_______ (1923), The ego and the id. *Standard Edition,* 19:3–66. London: Hogarth Press, 1961.

Fridley, D. (2001), Critical Issues: Attachment and dissociative disorders. *Internat. Soc. Study Dissoc. News,* 19:4–5.

Friedman, L. (1988), *The Anatomy of Psychotherapy.* Hillsdale, NJ: The Analytic Press.

Fromm, E. (1951), *The Forgotten Language.* New York: Grove Press.

Gallese, V. & Goldman, A. (1998), Mirror neurons and the simulation theory of mind-reading. *Trends Cogn. Sci.,* 2:493–501.

Gerson, S. (1996), Neutrality, resistance, and self-disclosure in an intersubjective psychoanalysis. *Psychoanal. Dial.,* 6:623–645.

Ghent, E. (1990), Masochism, submission, surrender. *Contemp. Psychoanal.,* 26:108–136.

_______ (1992), Paradox and process. *Psychoanal. Dial.,* 2:135–159.

_______ (1994), Empathy: Whence and whither? *Psychoanal. Dial.,* 4:473–486.

_______ (1995), Interaction in the psychoanalytic situation. *Psychoanal. Dial.,* 5:479–491.

Gilbert, W. S. & Sullivan, A. (1885), *The Mikado.* In: *The Complete Plays of Gilbert and Sullivan.* New York: Modern Library, 1948, pp. 343–400.

Ginot, E. (1997), The analyst's use of self, self-disclosure, and enhanced integration. *Psychoanal. Psychol.,* 14:365–381.

Gladwell, M. (2005), *Blink: The Power of Thinking Without Thinking.* New York: Little, Brown.

Gleaves, D. H., May, M. C. & Eberenz, K. P. (1996), Measuring and discriminating dissociative and borderline symptomatology among women with eating disorders. *Dissociation,* 9:110–117.

Goldbarth, A. (2003), *Pieces of Payne.* Saint Paul, MN: Graywolf Press.

Goldberg, S., Muir, R. & Kerr, J. (1995), *Attachment Theory: Social, Developmental, and Clinical Perspectives.* Hillsdale, NJ: The Analytic Press.

Goldberger, M. (2000), Daydreams: Another royal road. Presented to PEP–CD ROM Conference, New York City, February.

Greenberg, J. R. (1995), Editorial. *Contemp. Psychoanal.,* 31:5–8.

_______ (2001), The analyst's participation: A new look. *J. Amer. Psychoanal. Assn.,* 49:359–381.

Greene, M. (1954), *Bataille's Wound.* Barrytown, NY: Station Hill Arts, 1995.

Haley, J. (1993), *Jay Haley on Milton H. Erickson.* New York: Brunner/Mazel.

Hammer, L. (2005), Overheard speech. *The New York Times Book Review,* October 16, p. 8.

Harris, A. (1996), The conceptual power of multiplicity. *Contemp. Psychoanal.,* 32:537–552.

_______ (1998a), Psychic envelopes and sonorous baths: Siting the body in relational theory and clinical practice. In: *Relational Perspectives on the Body: Psychoanalytic Theory and Practice,* ed. L. Aron & F. S. Anderson. Hillsdale, NJ: The Analytic Press, pp. 39–64.

_______ (1998b), The relational unconscious: Commentary on papers by Michael Eigen and James Grotstein. *Psychoanal. Dial.,* 14:131–137.

_______ (2005), *Gender as Soft Assembly.* Hillsdale, NJ: The Analytic Press.

Harrison, K. (1997), *The Kiss.* New York: Random House.

Havens, L. L. (1973), *Approaches to the Mind.* Boston: Little, Brown.

Hazen, B. S. (1974), *The Gorilla Did It.* Hartford, CT: Atheneum.

Heimann, P. (1950), On countertransference. *Internat. J. Psycho-Anal.,* 31: 81–84.

Hirsch, I. (2002), Interpersonal psychoanalysis' radical façade. *J. Amer. Acad. Psychoanal.,* 30:595–603.

Hoffman, E. (1989), *Lost in Translation.* New York: Dutton.

Hoffman, I. Z. (1994), Dialectical thinking and therapeutic action in the psychoanalytic process. *Psychoanal. Quart.,* 63:187–218.

_______ (2000), At death's door: Therapists and patients as agents. *Psychoanal. Dial.,* 10:823–846.

Horner, A. (1979), *Object Relations and the Developing Ego in Therapy.* New York: Aronson.

Hosseini, K. (2003), *Kite Runner.* New York: Riverhead Books.

Howell, E. F. (2005), *The Dissociative Mind.* Hillsdale, NJ: The Analytic Press.

James, W. (1890), *Principles of Psychology.* New York: Holt.

Janet, P. (1907), *The Major Symptoms of Hysteria.* New York: Macmillan.

Jefferson, M. (1999), On having the grace to grow old, gracefully or not. *The New York Times,* August 23.

Johnson, S. (2004), *Mind Wide Open: Your Brain and the Neuroscience of Everyday Life.* New York: Scribner.

Katz, B. E. & Gleaves, D. H. (1996), Dissociative symptoms among patients with eating disorders; Associated feature or artifact of a comorbid dissociative disorder? *Dissociation,* 9:28–36.

Kihlstrom, J. (1987), The cognitive unconscious. *Science,* 237:1445–1452.

Kimmelman, M. (2000), Making the simple riveting. *The New York Times,* June 30, pp. E33, E35.

Klauber, J. (1980), Formulating interpretations in clinical psychoanalysis. *Internat. J. Psycho-Anal.,* 61:195–201.

Klee, P. (1957), *The Diaries of Paul Klee 1898–1918.* Berkeley: University of California Press.

Knoblauch, S. H. (2000), *The Musical Edge of Therapeutic Dialogue.* Hillsdale, NJ: The Analytic Press.

Korzybski, A. (1954), *Time-Binding: The General Theory.* Lakeville, CT: Institute of General Semantics.

LaBerge, S. (1985), *Lucid Dreaming.* New York: Ballantine Books.

Laing, R. D. (1962), *The Self and Others.* Chicago: Quadrangle.

LeDoux, J. E. (1989), Cognitive-emotional interactions in the brain. *Cognition & Emotion,* 3:267–289.

_______ (1994), Emotion, memory, and the brain. *Sci. Amer.,* 270:32–39.

_______ (1995), Emotion: Clues from the brain. *Annu. Rev. Psychol.,* 46:209–235.

_______ (1996), *The Emotional Brain.* New York: Touchstone.

_______ (1999), Psychoanalytic theory: Clues from the brain [Commentary on "Emotions as viewed by psychoanalysis and neuroscience: An exercise in conciliance" by J. Panksepp]. *Neuro-Psychoanalysis,* 1:44–49.

_______ (2002), *The Synaptic Self.* New York: Viking.

Levenkron, H. (in press), Love (and hate) with the proper stranger. *Psychoanal. Inq.*

Levenson, E. A. (1972), *The Fallacy of Understanding.* New York: Basic Books.

_______ (1983), *The Ambiguity of Change.* New York: Basic Books.

_______ (1988), The pursuit of the particular. *Contemp. Psychoanal.,* 24:1–16.

_______ (1991), *The Purloined Self.* New York: Contemporary Psychoanalytic Books.

Lewis, C. S. (1961), *A Grief Observed.* New York: HarperCollins, 1989.

Lewis, H. B. (1971), *Shame and Guilt in Neurosis.* New York: International Universities Press.

_______ (1987), Shame and the narcissistic personality. In: *The Many Faces of Shame,* ed. D. L. Nathanson. New York: Guilford Press, pp. 93–132.

Lewis, M. (1992), *Shame: The Exposed Self.* New York: Free Press, 1995.

Liotti, G. (1992), Disorganized/disoriented attachment in the etiology of the dissociative disorders. *Dissociation,* 5:196–204.

_______ (1995), Disorganized/disoriented attachment in the psychotherapy of dissociative disorders. In: *Attachment Theory: Social, Developmental, and Clinical Perspectives,* ed. S. Goldberg, R. Muir & J. Kerr. Hillsdale, NJ: The Analytic Press, pp. 343–363.

_______ Intreccialagli, B. & Cecere, F. (1991), Unresolved mourning in mothers and development of dissociative disorders in children: A case–control study. *Riv. di Psichiatria,* 26:283–291.

Little, M. (1951), Countertransference and the patient's response to it. *Internat. J. Psycho-Anal.,* 32:32–40.

Lynd, H. M. (1958), *On Shame and the Search for Identity.* New York: Harcourt Brace.

Lyons-Ruth, K. (1998), Implicit relational knowing: Its role in development and psychoanalytic treatment. *Infant Ment. Health J.,* 19:282–289.

_______ & Boston Change Process Study Group (2001), The emergence of new experiences: Relational improvisation, recognition process, and nonlinear change in psychoanalytic therapy. *Psychologist/Psychoanalyst,* 21: 13–17.

MacDonald, G. (1858), *Phantastes.* Grand Rapids, MI: Eerdmans, 1981.

Main, M. (1995), Recent studies in attachment: Overview, with selected implications for clinical work. In: *Attachment Theory: Social, Developmental, and Clinical Perspectives,* ed. S. Goldberg, R. Muir & J. Kerr. Hillsdale, NJ: The Analytic Press, pp. 407–474.

_______ & Morgan, H. (1996), Disorganization and disorientation in infant strange situation behavior: Phenotypic resemblance to dissociative states. In: *Handbook of Dissociation: Theoretical, Empirical, and Clinical Perspectives,* ed. L. Michelson & W. Ray. New York: Plenum Press.

Maroda, K. (2000), Reflections on Benjamin Wolstein, personal analysis and co-participation. *Contemp. Psychoanal.,* 36:241–249.

Marshall, K. (1996), Termination of an "infinite conversation": Post-structuralist literary figures, Greene, Blanchot and Bataille aid reflections on the last day of an analysis. Presented to Northwest Center for Psychoanalysis, Seattle, WA, December.

_______ (1998), Desire and/or self: Reflections on "*The Many Faces of Eros*" by Joyce McDougall. Presented to International Federation for Psychoanalytic Education, New York City, November.

McCallum, K. E., Lock, J., Kulla, M., Rorty, M. & Wetzel, R. D. (1992), Dissociative symptoms and disorders in patients with eating disorders. *Dissociation,* 5:227–235.

Mitchell, S. A. (1988), *Relational Concepts in Psychoanalysis.* Cambridge, MA: Harvard University Press.

_______ (1991), Contemporary perspectives on self: Toward an integration. *Psychoanal. Dial.,* 1:121–147.

_______ (1993), *Hope and Dread in Psychoanalysis.* New York: Basic Books.

_______ (1995), Response to Charles Brenner. Presented to Columbia Association for Psychoanalytic Medicine, New York City, November.

_______ (1998), The emergence of features of the analyst's life. *Psychoanal. Dial.,* 8:187–194.

_______ (2000), *Relationality: From Attachment to Intersubjectivity.* Hillsdale, NJ: The Analytic Press.

Morrison, A. P. (1987), The eye turned inward. In: *The Many Faces of Shame,* ed. D. L. Nathanson. New York: Guilford Press, pp. 271–291.

_______ (1989), *Shame: The Underside of Narcissism.* Hillsdale, NJ: The Analytic Press.

Muller, J. P. (1996), *Beyond the Psychoanalytic Dyad.* New York: Routledge.

Nathanson, D. L. (1992), *Shame and Pride: Affect, Sex, and the Birth of the Self.* New York: Norton.

_______ (1996), Interview with Donald Nathanson. *Nathanson Biosketch | Behavior OnLine Home Page | Behavior Online Forums,* www.behavior.net/column/nathanson.

Ogden, T. H. (1997), *Reverie and Interpretation.* Northvale, NJ: Aronson.

Pessoa, F. (1913–1934), *The Book of Disquietude,* ed. & trans. R. Zenith. Riverdale-on-Hudson, NY: Sheep Meadow Press, 1996.

Pitman, R. K. & Orr, S. P. (1990), The black hole of trauma. *Biolog. Psychiat.,* 26:221–223.

Pizer, S. A. (1992), The negotiation of paradox in the analytic process. *Psychoanal. Dial.,* 2:215–240.

_______ (1998), *Building Bridges: The Negotiation of Paradox in Psychoanalysis.* Hillsdale, NJ: The Analytic Press.

_______ (2004), Impasse recollected in tranquility: Love, dissociation, and discipline in the analytic process. *Psychoanal. Dial.,* 14:289–311.

Putnam, F. (1988), The switch process in multiple personality disorder and other state-change disorders. *Dissociation,* 1:24–32.

_______ (1992), Discussion: Are alter personalities fragments or figments? *Psychoanal. Inq.,* 12:95–111.

Ratliff, B. (2005), Monk as he's seldom heard. *The New York Times,* February 12, p. B17.

Racker, H. (1953), The countertransference neurosis. *Internat. J. Psycho-Anal.,* 34:313–324.

_______ (1957), The meanings and uses of countertransference. *Psychoanal. Quart.,* 26:303–357.

Reik, T. (1936), *Surprise and the Psycho-Analyst.* London: Kegan Paul, Trench, Trubner.

Renik, O. (1996), The perils of neutrality. *Psychoanal. Quart.,* 65:495–517.

_______ (1999), Playing one's cards face up in analysis: An approach to the problem of self-disclosure. *Psychoanal. Quart.,* 68:521–539.

Rogers, R. & Hammerstein II, O. (1984), "I whistle a happy tune" from the show *The King and I.*

Rosenbaum, T. (2002), *The Golems of Gotham.* New York: HarperCollins.

Roth, P. (1997), *American Pastoral.* New York: Vintage, 1998.

Ruff, M. (2003), *Set This House in Order.* New York: HarperCollins.

Russell, P. L. (1975), The theory of the crunch. Presented to Paul L. Russell Psychotherapy Symposium on Crisis and Repetition, Chestnut Hill, MA, November 6, 1998.

Rycroft, C. (1962), Beyond the reality principle. In: *Imagination and Reality.* London: Maresfield Library, 1968, pp. 102–113.

_______ (1979), *The Innocence of Dreams.* New York: Pantheon.

Safran, J. D. & Muran, J. C. (2000), *Negotiating the Therapeutic Alliance: A Relational Treatment Guide.* New York: Guilford Press.

Sands, S. H. (1994), What is dissociated? *Dissociation,* 7:145–152.

Schecter, D. E. (1973), On the emergence of human relatedness. In: *Interpersonal Explorations in Psychoanalysis,* ed. E. G. Witenberg. New York: Basic Books, pp. 17–39.

Scheff, T. J. (1989), Cognitive and emotional conflict in anorexia: Reanalysis of a classic case. *Psychiatry,* 52:148–160.

Schore, A. N. (1994), *Affect Regulation and the Origin of the Self.* Hillsdale, NJ: Lawrence Erlbaum Associates.

_______ (2003a), Summary of panel on "Trauma and neuroscience: Bringing the body more deeply into psychoanalysis." *Psychologist/Psychoanalyst,* 23: 42–43.

_______ (2003b), *Affect Regulation and the Repair of the Self.* New York: Norton.

_______ (2003c), *Affect Dysregulation and Disorders of the Self.* New York: Norton.

Shakespeare, W. (1604), Othello. In: *The Complete Plays and Poems of William Shakespeare,* ed. W. A. Neilson & C. J. Hill. Cambridge, MA: Riverside, 1942, pp. 1096–1135.

_______ (1606), Macbeth. In: *The Complete Plays and Poems of William Shakespeare,* ed. W. A. Neilson & C. J. Hill. Cambridge, MA: Riverside, 1942, pp. 1184–1212.

Slavin, M. O. & Kriegman, D. (1998), Why the analyst needs to change: Toward a theory of conflict, negotiation, and mutual influence in the therapeutic process. *Psychoanal. Dial.,* 8:247–284.

Smith, H. F. (1995), Analytic listening and the experience of surprise. *Internat. J. Psycho-Anal.,* 76:67–78.

Sonenberg, J. (2003), *Dreamwork for Actors.* New York: Routledge.

Stechler, G. (2003), Affect: The heart of the matter. *Psychoanal. Dial.,* 13: 711–726.

Stern, D. B. (1997), *Unformulated Experience: From Dissociation to Imagination in Psychoanalysis.* Hillsdale, NJ: The Analytic Press.

_______ (2003), The fusion of horizons: Dissociation, enactment, and understanding. *Psychoanal. Dial.,* 13:843–873.

_______ (2004), The eye sees itself: Dissociation, enactment, and the achievement of conflict. *Contemp. Psychoanal.,* 40:197–237.

Stern, D. N., Sander, L., Nahum, J. P., Harrison, A. M., Lyons-Ruth, K., Morgan, A. C., Bruschweiler-Stern, N. & Tronick, E. Z. (1998), Non-interpretive mechanisms in psychoanalytic therapy: The "something more" than interpretation. *Internat. J. Psycho-Anal.,* 79:903–921.

Stern, M. M. (1988), *Repetition and Trauma: Toward a Teleonomic Theory of Psychoanalysis*. Hillsdale, NJ: The Analytic Press.

Sullivan, H. S. (1953), *The Interpersonal Theory of Psychiatry*. New York: Norton.

_______ (1954), *The Psychiatric Interview*. New York: Norton.

Szymborska, W. (1983), Autotomy. In: *Postwar Polish Poetry,* 3rd ed., ed. & trans. C. Milosz. Berkeley: University of California Press, pp. 115–116.

Target, M. & Fonagy, P. (1996), Playing with reality: II. The development of psychic reality from a theoretical perspective. *Internat. J. Psycho-Anal.,* 77:459–479.

Tart, C. (1969), *Altered States of Consciousness*. New York: Wiley

Tauber, E. S. (1954), Exploring the therapeutic use of countertransference data. *Psychiatry,* 17:331–336.

_______ & Green, M. R. (1959), *Prelogical Experience*. Hillsdale, NJ: The Analytic Press, 2005.

Terr, L. C. (1984), Time and trauma. *The Psychoanalytic Study of the Child,* 39:633–665. New Haven, CT: Yale University Press.

Tronick, E. Z. & Weinberg, M. K. (1997), Depressed mothers and infants: Failure to form dyadic states of consciousness. In: *Postpartum Depression and Child Development,* ed. L. Murray & P. Cooper. New York: Guilford Press, pp. 54–81.

van der Kolk, B. (1987a), The separation cry and the trauma response: Developmental issues in the psychobiology of attachment and separation. In: *Psychological Trauma,* ed. B. A. van der Kolk. Washington, DC: American Psychiatric Press, pp. 31–62.

_______ (1987b), The psychobiology of the trauma response: Hyperarousal, constriction, and addiction to traumatic reexposure. In: *Psychological Trauma,* ed. B. A. van der Kolk. Washington, DC: American Psychiatric Press, pp. 63–87.

_______ (1995), The body, memory, and the psychobiology of trauma. In: *Sexual Abuse Recalled,* ed. J. A. Alpert. Northvale, NJ: Aronson, pp. 29–60.

Whyte, L. L. (1960), *The Unconscious Before Freud*. Garden City, NY: Anchor Books, 1962.

Winnicott, D. W. (1949a), Mind and its relation to the psyche–soma. In: *Collected Papers: Through Paediatrics to Psycho-Analysis*. London: Tavistock, 1958, pp. 243–254.

_______ (1949b), Hate in the countertransference. *Internat. J. Psycho-Anal.,* 30:69–74.

_______ (1951), Transitional objects and transitional phenomena. In: *Playing and Reality*. New York: Basic Books, 1971, pp. 1–25.

_______ (1958), The capacity to be alone. In: *The Maturational Processes and the Facilitating Environment*. New York: International Universities Press, 1965, pp. 29–36.

_______ (1963), Communicating and not communicating leading to a study of certain opposites. In: *The Maturational Processes and the Facilitating Environment*. New York: International Universities Press, 1965, pp. 179–192.

_______ (1967), The location of cultural experience. In: *Playing and Reality.* New York: Basic Books, 1971, pp. 95–103.

_______ (1969), The use of an object and relating through identifications. In: *Playing and Reality.* New York: Basic Books, 1971, pp. 86–94.

_______ (1971), Dreaming, fantasying, and living: A case-history describing a primary dissociation. In: *Playing and Reality.* New York: Basic Books, pp. 26–37.

Woolf, V. (1928), *Orlando.* New York: Harcourt Brace.

Wordsworth, W. (1802), *William Wordsworth: The Poems, Vol. I,* ed. J. O. Hayden. New Haven, CT: Yale University Press, 1981.

Yovell, Y. (2000), From hysteria to posttraumatic stress disorder: Psychoanalysis and the neurobiology of traumatic memories. *Neuro-Psychoanalysis,* 2:171–181.

Zerbe, K. J. (1993), Selves that starve and suffocate: The continuum of eating disorders and dissociative phenomena. *Bull. Menn. Clin.,* 57:319–327.

Index

A

E